Judy Cain

THINKING
and
PROBLEM SOLVING:
An Introduction to Human Cognition and Learning

Richard E. Mayer

University of California at Santa Barbara

SCOTT, FORESMAN and COMPANY

Glenview, Illinois

Dallas, Texas
Oakland, New Jersey
Palo Alto, California
Tucker, Georgia
Abingdon, England

Dedicated to
Beverly and Kenny,
my parents,
and my brothers.

Library of Congress Cataloging in Publication Data

Mayer, Richard E   1947–
   Thinking and problem solving.

   Bibliography: p. 195
   Includes index.
   1. Thought and thinking.   2. Problem solving.
I. Title.
BF455.M346   153.4'2   76-28752
ISBN 0-673-15055-0

   2 3 4 5 6 7 8 –RRC– 82 81 80 79 78 77

Acknowledgments for Boxes and Quotations

(O–1) Humphrey, G. *Thinking: An Introduction to Its Experimental Psychology,* pp.
134, 137, and 138. London: Methuen & Co., Ltd. Reprinted by permission.   (1–1)
Thorndike, E. L. "Animal intelligence: An experimental study of the associative processes in animals." *Psychological Monographs,* Vol. 2, 1898. Washington: American Psychological Association.   (2–3) Hull, C. L. Illustration in "Quantitative aspects of
evolution of concepts." *Psychological Monographs,* Vol. 28, 1920. Washington:
American Psychological Association.   (2–4) Kendler, H. H., and Kendler, T. S. "Vertical
and horizontal processes in problem solving." *Psychological Review,* Vol. 69, p. 5. Copy-

Foreword

The study of thinking and problem solving is once again popular in psychology. In a sense, these topics, having to do with the processes, events, and actions a person can "do in one's head," were the raison d'être for the formal discipline of psychology. It was clear to our nineteenth-century forebears that armchair philosophizing and nonempirical speculation could not settle the important issues of the human mind. But, for a variety of reasons, the formal discipline of psychology turned its back on mental processes in the early part of this century and the study of thinking and problem solving became largely dormant. The last twenty years have seen a resurgence. For an experimental psychologist to speak in mental terms has become legitimate once again. The importance of psychology's fundamental problem has risen past the constraints of more trivial pursuits. In recent years, psychology has developed both empirical and theoretical methods which afford rather remarkable insights into the mentality of human beings.

Human thought is a complicated subject matter, probably the most complex psychology has to deal with. What has happened in this area during the last twenty years is not easy to describe. Despite the progress that has been made, there are still few truly definitive answers to the questions one would like to ask. Vast gaps in the fabric of our knowledge remain as a challenge to future researchers. It is no mean trick to organize and to communicate what we presently know about thinking. It requires a broad perspective, an ability to integrate sometimes disparate facts, and a tolerance for the ambiguity created by all those matters which remain to be settled. Instructors of cognitive psychology and those who have attempted to write in textbook style about the field understand better than most of us what the real difficulties are. But, at the same time, this subject matter needs a textbook. Courses in thinking and problem solving are now standard in college curricula, if not required as an element of a psychology major.

In my view, this book by Richard Mayer, *Thinking and Problem Solving: An Introduction to Human Cognition and Learning,* fills that need. The book is organized around the major theoretical-empirical trends in the psychology of thinking as they have evolved, first subtly and then more visibly, in recent years. Professor Mayer's description of these trends gives both a historical and a contemporary perspective on the field. The treatment is broad in the sense that no important development is overlooked. At the same time, Professor Mayer does not overwhelm the reader with excessive detail. The text is written at an introductory level and makes no assumptions about prior training or instruction in psychology. Thus, the book might be used either as outside resource material in the introductory course or as a designated textbook with a second-level offering.

The text is highly readable. Primarily this is due to Professor Mayer's intimate knowledge of the subject matter. In addition, however, the consistency of style from chapter to chapter helps establish a certain framework and set of expectations into which the reader can assimilate the new material each chapter provides and evaluate that material against related ideas presented earlier. I think it is also important to note the many pertinent examples used by Professor Mayer. Not only are they interesting and challenging to the reader, they help to get the presentation off to a good start within each chapter.

Having read thus far, you cannot help but realize that I have been deeply impressed by this textbook. I've looked at it, in an editorial capacity, from initial manuscript to final copy. Professor Mayer has made the work of this reviewer simple indeed. I trust that students and teachers who use this text will find it a pleasant way to be introduced to the difficult field of human thinking and problem solving. I sincerely hope that you will enjoy the final product just as much as I did watching it evolve.

L. E. Bourne, Jr.
Boulder, Colorado

Preface

This book is written for anyone who is interested in how human beings think, reason, and solve problems. It presents the major concepts, methods, and research findings which have been produced by the psychology of thinking during its short seventy-five-year span of existence. My goal has been to present in an organized and systematic way the basics of what we now know about human thinking and to do so by presenting a survey of approaches and tasks rather than limiting the book to one single point of view. Modern advances such as computer simulation of thinking, models of semantic memory and human information processing, and cognitive development are presented as well as the basic findings concerning deductive reasoning, concept learning, stages in problem solving, learning to solve problems, and other issues.

The text is intended as an introduction to the psychology of thinking and assumes no prior formal experience on the part of the reader. It is designed for use in courses on learning, memory, and cognitive psychology as well as in fields where problem solving is important, such as education, business, or mathematics. Finally, it is also written for the general reader (or the avid problem solver) who would like to find out what psychologists know about thinking.

Many colleagues and many of my own students have expressed the need for a book to teach the "higher" end of learning and cognitive psychology. Books in this field have tended to be summaries of research on one particular problem, such as Bruner, Goodnow, and Austin's classic, *A Study of Thinking* (1956); or they have tended to integrate a number of tasks around one single, specific theory, such as Newell and Simon's impressive book, *Human Problem Solving* (1972). Books aimed at educators and others interested in providing instruction for "how to solve problems," such as Polya's little classic, *How to Solve It* (1957), often lack any reference to the psychological literature. The present book attempts to overcome these problems by providing a basic, systematic, and current (well over two-thirds of the references were published after 1960) introduction to the psychology of thinking. My only hope is that you will enjoy reading this book as much as I have enjoyed writing it.

Now, where do we begin our study of the psychology of thinking? Let's start with a little-known problem we could call the "Flour Predicament": Suppose a baker was kneading dough in front of and facing the center pole of his tent. He needed more flour but the bag containing it was behind the pole. To get the flour he bent down, encircling the pole with his arms, cupped his hands, and scooped some from the bag. However, now the baker had a problem. When he tried to get the flour to the dough he had been kneading, he found that the tent pole obstructed his cupped hands. He did not want to drop the flour back into the bag for fear of wasting it. What should our baker do? Think about this for a minute or two.

This example comes from a seminar held by the famous Gestalt psychologist Max Wertheimer during the late 1930s (we'll talk more about the Gestalt approach in Chapter 3); it is based on a published version of the class notes of Wertheimer's students as compiled by Luchins and Luchins (1970, p. 11). The Luchins' class notes reveal that Wertheimer never really explained how anyone goes about solving such a problem; however, it is just this kind of problem that has stimulated psychologists to try to discover what solution processes a person goes through and why some people solve it while others do not. The solution to the flour predicament, by the way, is simply for the baker to walk around the tent pole until his cupped hands are directly over the dough he has been kneading and drop the flour onto the dough.

We can begin *our* inquiry into human problem solving in the same way that Wertheimer did forty years ago, for although he may not have had the answers, he certainly asked interesting questions: "Wertheimer started the seminar with these questions: 'Why is it that some people, when they are faced with problems, get clever ideas, make inventions and discoveries? What happens, what are the processes that lead to such solutions? What can be done to help people to be creative when they are faced with problems?' After a pause during which no one spoke, he continued, saying that throughout the centuries such questions had been asked and a variety of conjectures, proposals and counter proposals had been made in response to them. He urged the students to respond by saying that it was necessary to try to answer these questions for both theoretical and practical reasons. Perhaps because the seminar members regarded the questions as rhetorical, or perhaps because the ice of the first meeting had not yet been broken, no one responded. He tried to elicit responses by asking other questions. He asked, 'How should we proceed in this seminar? How would you go about studying productive thinking?' " (Luchins & Luchins, 1970, p. 1).

The remainder of this book is really a summary of the methods that psychologists have used in response to Wertheimer's questions; and although we now can begin to answer Wertheimer, you will soon see that the job is far from finished.

Acknowledgments

My students, teachers, and colleagues have been instrumental in helping me write this book. In particular, I am indebted to James Greeno for his kindly and "productively" teaching me most of what I know about human problem solving. In addition, my years at the University of Michigan provided me with many stimulating encounters which helped shape and produce this book, including discussions with: Bill McKeachie, Robert Bjork, Art Melton, Ed Martin, Steve Kaplan, Joe Payne, Dennis Egan, Dave Kieras, Tim Salthouse, Jane Malin, John Thomas and others. The book has also been influenced by many useful discussions with colleagues while I was at Indiana University, including: Frank Restle, Rich Shiffrin, Lloyd Peterson, George Potts and other members of the Cognitive Institute. Finally, my colleagues and students at the University of California, Santa Barbara, have provided many more interesting ideas: Russ Revlis, Bobby Klatzky, Howard Kendler, Tracy Kendler, Jack Loomis and others.

Lyle E. Bourne, Jr., has been particularly helpful and encouraging with respect to improving the original manuscript, and I appreciate that he has gone far beyond his duties as a consulting editor for the publishers. In addition, I have enjoyed working with Jim Romig and Isobel Hoffman at Scott, Foresman and Company and I appreciate the fact that their efforts have greatly improved the manuscript.

Many authors and publishers have kindly granted permission to reproduce quotes and tables; to them, and to others who have labored to advance our understanding of human thinking, I am grateful.

And finally, I wish to thank my parents, James S. Mayer and Bernis L. Mayer, my brothers, Robert Mayer and Bernie Mayer, and, of course, my wife, Beverly Mayer, and our son, Kenny, all of whom have encouraged both this book and my interest in human behavior. I dedicate this book to them, with love.

Richard E. Mayer
Santa Barbara, California

Contents

Overview

introspection task

Introduction

Introspection Task

In a moment you will be given a word and a question about the word. Your job is to say the first answer that comes to your mind and then to describe all the details of the thought process that led to it.

Your test word is BITE, and your question is, What is the CAUSE? Now describe the thinking process that led you to whatever word you answered.

If the word "dog" came to your mind, your response corresponds to that obtained by the German psychologist Otto Selz in the early 1900s (Humphrey, 1963). Check the top of Box O-1 to see how Selz's subject described his chain of thought. Note that an image of a wounded leg came first followed by the conscious words, "dogs bite." Did you also experience an image while you were thinking?

Now try the word—and question:

POEM. In what LARGER CATEGORY does it belong? A typical response from Selz's experiment is "work of art" and the introspections of one subject about how the answer was derived are given in the middle of Box O-1. Note that no images were involved in the subject's thinking about this problem. Did you experience an image?

Finally, try to describe your thought process for:

PARSON. What is an EQUIVALENT OCCUPATION? The introspections of a typical subject are given at the bottom of Box O-1. The answer this

BOX 0-1   METHOD OF INTROSPECTION

Problem 1
BITE. CAUSE?
"As soon as I had read the [words] the search was on. I had also a picture of a leg
with a wound on it, and saw nothing else. Then 'dog' came to me in the form of an
idea, with the consciousness: dogs bite."

Problem 2
POEM. In what LARGER CATEGORY does it belong?
"Once again, immediately a full understanding of the [question]. Then again an in-
tensive glance, the symbolic fixation of that which is sought; then at once the flit-
ting memory of Art, Poetry, etc., appeared. The word 'art,' I think, in auditory-
motor terms. Then the thought that I cannot subsume poetry under art but only
under artistic production. With this, I am certain, no words and images; then I said,
'work of art.' "

Problem 3
PARSON. What is an EQUIVALENT OCCUPATION?
"I read the words successively and with understanding. Immediately came the
consciousness that something [equivalent] was very familiar. Then came the word
'Chaplain,' internally spoken. It is certain that the consciousness of the familiarity
of a solution preceded the, as yet, uneffected appearance of the word 'Chaplain.' "

From Humphrey (1963)

subject made was "chaplain" (remember these introspections are trans-
lations from German) and again no imagery was involved.

These tasks are examples of the first type of experimental studies on
human thought processes ever carried out. The method is called *introspection* because the thinker must inspect his or her own mental events
and report them to the experimenter. Long before the birth of psychology
human beings undoubtedly introspected, perhaps trying to understand
themselves, but it was not until the beginning of this century that the
method of introspection was taken into the experimental laboratory and
systematically applied to the study of human thought. We shall talk more
about introspection later in this overview.

Definition of Basic Terms

In order to study human cognitive processes effectively, it is useful to
define the basic terms such as "problem" and "thinking."

Problem

Although they express the terms differently, most psychologists
agree that a problem has certain characteristics:

Givens—The problem begins in a certain state with certain conditions, objects, pieces of information, and so forth being present at the onset of work on the problem.

Goals—The desired or terminal state of the problem is the goal state, and thinking is required to transform the problem from the given to the goal state.

Obstacles—The thinker has at his or her disposal certain ways to change the given state or the goal state of the problem. The thinker, however, does not already know the correct answer; that is, the correct sequence of behaviors that will solve the problem is not immediately obvious.

In short, any definition of "problem" should consist of the three ideas that (a) the problem is presently in some state, but (b) it is desired that it be in another state, and (c) there is no direct, obvious way to accomplish the change. This definition is broad enough to include problems ranging from geometry (Polya, 1957), to chess (Newell & Simon, 1972), to riddles (Reitman, 1965).

Reitman (1965) has further analyzed four categories of problems according to how well the given and goal states are specified.

Well-defined given state and well-defined goal state: "How can you turn a sow's ear into a silk purse?" Note, however, that although the given state (sow's ear) and the goal state (silk purse) are clearly specified in this problem, there is a serious lack of possible ways to solve it.

Well-defined given state and poorly defined goal state: "How can you redesign a Cadillac El Dorado to get better gas mileage?" The given state, the automobile, is clearly designated, but what does "better gas mileage" mean exactly?

Poorly defined given state and well-defined goal state: "Explain the mechanisms responsible for sun spots." The goal, "sun spots," is clear but the initial state that causes this goal is not.

Poorly defined given state and poorly defined goal state: "What is red and goes put-put?" The answer is "an outboard apple," and you can blame Reitman for this one.

Thinking and Problem Solving

There are many definitions of *thinking, problem solving,* and *cognition,* but this book will use these three terms interchangeably based on a single, general definition common to them all. Unfortunately, we begin with a serious lack of agreement among psychologists as to whether thinking should be generally defined as an external, behavioral process or an internal, cognitive process. The behavioral argument is that the science of psychology must deal only with empirical, observable behaviors as its primary data; internal states or processes cannot be directly observed and therefore cannot be part of psychology. Behaviorists consider a view of thinking as an internal process with no relationship to behavior to be useless; for example, a famous critique by Guthrie of an early cognitive theory of rat maze learning was that the rat was "left buried in thought at the choice point"—there was no relationship between internal mechanisms and external observable events. In this view, psychological definitions must be tied firmly to behavior. The cognitive argument, on the other hand, is that behavior is merely the manifestation or result of thinking and therefore psychological definitions must be tied firmly to the mechanisms that underlie behavior.

A compromise that most, but not all, psychologists who study thinking might accept is that concepts such as internal, cognitive processes have a place in psychology if and only if they generate clearly testable predictions, that is, if they suggest observable predictions concerning human behavior.

In short, a general definition of thinking includes three basic ideas:

Thinking is *cognitive,* but is inferred from behavior. It occurs internally, in the mind or cognitive system, and must be inferred indirectly.

Thinking is a *process* which involves some manipulation of, or set of operations on, knowledge in the cognitive system.

Thinking is *directed* and results in behavior which "solves" a problem or is directed towards solution.*

In other words, thinking is what happens when a person solves a problem, i.e., produces behavior which moves the individual from the given state to the goal state—or at least tries to achieve this change. Thus, Johnson (1972) defined thinking as "problem solving" and similarly Polya (1968, p. ix) suggested that problem solving is based on cognitive processing that results in "finding a way out of a difficulty, a way around an obstacle, attaining an aim that was not immediately attainable." The remainder of this book aims at making the general definition of thinking more specific although, as you will see, at this time in the history of psychology, there is agreement neither on a definition of thinking nor on exactly what mechanisms underlie thinking.

---

*Some types of thinking may not be directed, such as autistic thinking, daydreaming, or the fragmented thinking of schizophrenics; however, this book will deal mainly with normal, directed thinking.

There are other terms used in the study of thinking such as induction, deduction, and reasoning. These terms have more restricted meanings than those we have discussed above, and can be considered as subsets of thinking. *Induction,* which we shall examine in Chapter 2, refers to a situation in which a thinker is given a series of examples and must "leap" to the creation of a general rule; *deduction* refers to a situation in which a thinker is given a set of general rules and must draw a logical conclusion, as we shall see in Chapter 6. Induction and deduction are both types of *reasoning.*

Place of the Study of Thinking in Psychology

Human beings are endowed with a number of basic cognitive processes which, although closely related, have been separated and studied individually by psychologists. These cognitive processes include: sensation and perception (the reception and recognition of input stimuli), learning (the encoding of input information), memory (the retrieval of input information), and thinking (the manipulation of perceived, learned, and remembered information). These topics form the core of what has been called *cognitive psychology,* and to the extent that each involves active manipulation of information, each involves thinking. Bruner (1973) emphasized the role of problem solving in perception by suggesting that perception involves "going beyond the information given," and Bartlett (1932) emphasized the role of problem solving in memory and learning by suggesting that learning and recall require an "effort after meaning." Thinking has also been investigated in many other contexts in psychology including social psychology (attitude formation and change), developmental psychology (cognitive development), personality (cognitive style), and testing and measurement (intelligence tests).

Thinking is thus a component of experimental psychology; while the main focus is on a high level cognitive process, thinking depends on and is part of "lower" processes. Because thinking is so complex and because it may be based on lower cognitive processes, many psychologists have argued that we should understand the lower or simpler cognitive processes before trying to study the higher processes. However, there have always been some psychologists who ignored these warnings and who were challenged by the prospect of studying one of the supreme achievements of the human species, the ability to think and deal with complex learning:

> . . . the topic has fascinated psychologists in and out of the laboratory. They have worried it as a dog worries a bone. It was always there, sometimes buried, sometimes dug up again and brought to a high sheen, never quite cracked or digested, and never forgotten. Even the Wundts and the Hulls

promised themselves to get back to the problem sooner or later while they counseled patience and attention to simpler problems that seemed to contain the principles needed to unlock the complexities of human thought. But for every Wundt psychology had a Buhler, for every Hull a Wertheimer—psychologists impatient with the programmatic building-block approach, unwilling to wait for the solution of the simple, and eager to plunge into the complexities and wonders of full-blown human thought (Mandler & Mandler, 1964, p. 1).

Main Topic Areas in the Psychology of Thinking

The psychology of thinking and complex learning has held a regular, albeit modest, position in the mainstream of psychology ever since William James (1890) included a chapter on "reasoning" in his famous textbook. Yet the subject has never been completely unified or well-understood, and the basic knowledge has remained hard to define. There are now, however, encouraging signs that some progress has been made since Humphrey's (1963, p. 308) assessment of the first fifty years of work by experimental psychologists on thinking: "Fifty years' experiments on the psychology of thinking or reasoning have not brought us very far, but they have at least shown the road which must be traversed."

New roads which have been traversed since Humphrey's critique include: exciting developments in an information processing approach to cognition such as computer simulation of human thinking (Chapters 6 and 7 of this book), new theories of semantic memory representation (see Chapter 5), and the new interest of American psychologists in cognitive development motivated largely by Piaget's work (Chapter 8). Older roads which have continued to stimulate further travel include the Gestalt approach to problem solving based on the idea that thinking involves "restructuring" a problem (see Chapters 3 and 4), the study of concept learning which suggests that the testing of "hypotheses" may be a part of thinking (Chapter 2), and the associationist approach to thinking which is based on the principle of learning by reinforcement (Chapter 1).

This book then, is organized into eight chapters, each covering a main road or subroad of the study of thinking:

Chapter 1 (Associationism) investigates the idea that thinking is based on the principle of learning by reinforcement; it includes classic research like Thorndike's work on cats in a puzzle box as well as more recent research such as the analysis of anagram solving and the physiological correlates of thinking.

Chapter 2 (Rule Learning) examines the idea that thinking involves forming and testing hypotheses; it describes the original research on concept learning by Hull and by Heidbreder as well as up-to-date work on strategies in concept learning, mathematical models of concept learning, serial pattern learning, and analysis of the structure of rules used by subjects in experiments on learning.

Chapter 3 (Gestalt) investigates the idea that thinking involves "restructuring" the elements of the problem in a new way; the famous Gestalt experiments on insight and rigidity in problem solving, as well as current work on the analysis of stages in problem solving are covered in this chapter.

Chapter 4 (Meaning) investigates a refinement of the Gestalt approach that describes thinking as relating the new problem to ideas or experiences already familiar to the solver; included are the classic studies of meaningful learning of mathematics and solution of mathematical puzzles, as well as recent work on instructional methods for teaching "productive" thinking.

Chapter 5 (Semantic Memory) explores the problem of how people answer verbal questions; topics covered include the exciting developments in psycholinguistics stimulated by Chomsky, studies of meaningful learning from text, and recent work on models of semantic memory.

Chapter 6 (Computer Simulation) presents the information processing approach to thinking and describes the ongoing work on computer simulation of human thinking.

Chapter 7 (Deductive Reasoning) investigates how the information processing approach may be applied to deductive and syllogistic inferences and presents the classic work on deduction as well as emphasizing the ongoing work on models of reasoning, inference from text, and memory representation of propositions.

Chapter 8 (Cognitive Development) presents the currently popular theories of cognitive development based on Piaget's work and includes relevant research on development of the concept of number, development of memory representations, and the development of adult logic.

Historical Foundations of the Psychology of Thinking

Associationist Philosophy

Before psychology began as an experimental science in the late nineteenth century, the issues of psychology were already well established within the domain of "mental philosophy." The dominant philosophy of human mental processes then was *associationism,* the belief that mental life can be explained in terms of two basic components: "ideas" (or elements) and "associations" (or links) between them. Associationism is usually traced back to three laws of learning and memory expressed by the Greek philosopher Aristotle:

> *Doctrine of association by contiguity*—events or objects that occur in the same time or space are associated in memory, so that thinking of one will "cause" thinking of the other.

> *Doctrine of association by similarity*—events or objects which are similar tend to be associated in memory.

> *Doctrine of association by contrast*—events or objects which are opposites tend to be associated in memory.

In addition, Aristotle claimed that thinking involves moving from one element or idea to another via a chain of associations, and that such thought was impossible without images: "We cannot think without imagery" (Humphrey, 1963, p. 31). Aristotle's dogma about imagery later became a key issue when the psychology of thinking was first subjected to empirical rather than philosophical study.

The British Associationists, led by Hobbes and Locke in the seventeenth and eighteenth centuries, reformulated the concepts and principles of associationism including the three laws of Aristotle. Their theory of mental life can be summarized as containing four main characteristics:

> *Atomism*—the unit of thinking is the "association" between two specific "ideas." All mental life can be analyzed into specific ideas and associations.

> *Mechanization*—the process of "thinking" or of moving from one idea to another is automatic and based solely on strength of associations.

> *Empiricism*—all knowledge, that is, all ideas and associations, come from sensory experience. The mind begins as a "blank slate" and is filled by reproducing the world exactly as it is received through the senses.

> *Imagery*—thus, thinking is merely the automatic movement from point to point along mental paths established through learning, and since each point is a sensory experience, thinking must involve imagery (or some other sensory experience).

Wundt: Founder of Psychology

By the late nineteenth century, people were increasingly applying the methods of empirical science to the study of the physical world all around them—to the planets and space (astronomy), to moving objects and weights (physics), to the makeup of earth, water, and fire (chemistry), to the world of plants and animals (biology), and even to their own bodies (physiology and medicine). Interestingly, one of the last areas to be subjected to scientific study was what Wilhelm Wundt called the "new domain of science": the human mind and behavior.

Wundt is often identified as the "father" of psychology and his opening of a psychology laboratory at the University of Leipzig is generally considered the beginning of psychology as a science. Wundt subjected some of the old issues of "mental philosophy" to the rigors of empirical science and experimental study, and created the new science on the principle that "all observation implies . . . that the observed object is independent of the observer" (Mandler & Mandler, 1964, p. 132).

Wundt also did something that had a major influence on the course of the study of thinking. He divided the subject matter of psychology into two classes: "simple psychical processes" such as physiological reflexes and sensation/perception which could be studied by direct experimental methods; and "higher psychical processes" which "are of too variable a character to be subjects of objective observation." Thus Wundt decreed that the higher level mental processes *could not* be studied in the scientific laboratory; instead they could be studied by looking at the "mental products" of an entire society such as its art, stories, and so on. Although Wundt had shown that science could be directed at ourselves, our own mental processes and behaviors, he drew the line at studying thinking and complex learning. The nineteenth century ended with no major experimental work having yet begun on the psychology of human thinking.*

The Wurzburg Group

Working against Wundt's dogma forbidding the study of thinking, a group of German psychologists known as the Wurzburg group, after the name of the city in which they worked, did finally in the early part of this century attempt to study human cognitive processes experimentally. They set out to refine the old associationist theory of the philosophers by using the new experimental method of "introspection."

A typical early experiment was to present a word to a subject, ask the subject to give a free association to the word, and then ask the person to describe the thought process that led to the response; or to ask a subject

---

*A notable exception was Ebbinghaus' (1885) exciting monograph, *Memory*, which provided a solid study of learning and memory of verbal material.

to describe the thought process of answering some question (Mayer & Orth, 1901; Marbe, 1901; Messer, 1906; Buhler, 1907). A major finding of these studies was a sort of negative result—many of the subjects reported that they were not consciously aware of any images in their associations (see Box O-1). This finding was called "imageless thought."

A second type of experiment was to use different questions for the same stimulus words. For example, Watt (1905) found a different pattern of response for a word if he presented flash cards that said "name a whole of" rather than "name an example of." In a more elaborate experiment, Ach (1905) hypnotized subjects and while they were under hypnosis, instructed them to "add," "subtract," "multiply," or "divide" numbers; then he brought them out of the hypnotic state and gave them cards with number pairs, such as 4/2, and asked the subjects to respond. Answers such as 2 or 8 came instantly, depending on the hypnotic suggestion, in this case to divide or to multiply. A major conclusion of this line of research was that thought is directed by some "determining tendency" that is relevant for a particular problem (Kulpe, 1912).

The work of the Wurzburg group has been justly criticized: their method of introspection was challenged as being based on subjective experience rather than observable data; their results were largely negative; they had no theory. However, they did show it was possible to study human thinking, and their work began to cast doubts on the foundations of the associationist philosophy as their results showed:

Anti-atomism—preliminary reports indicated that the elements of thought changed as they were combined.

Anti-mechanization—evidence showed that thought is directed and guided by some human motive or purpose.

Anti-empiricism—evidence began to mount that experience is not reproduced or copied in the mind exactly as it occurs in the world.

Anti-imagery—images are particular, but the Wurzburgers found examples of general and abstract thought, and also of "imageless thought."

Selz

Although the early research of the Wurzburg group began to challenge the philosophy of associationism, alternative theories did not develop until the work of Otto Selz (1913). Selz used the method of introspection and examples like those shown in Box O-1, but unlike his predecessors, he developed a theory independent of images and associations. The main concepts in Selz's theory were that the unit of thought is a structural complex of relations among thoughts rather than a string of particular responses, and that the process of thinking is filling in or completing a gap in the structural complex rather than following a chain of associations.

For example, in Benjamin Franklin's problem of how to bring electricity from the lightning to the ground, Selz claimed the solution involved the development of a "complex" of ideas, e.g., a kite as a means of producing contact between the earth and the storm clouds. The solution involved filling in the complex with "kite" to build an organized structure in which objects had certain relationships to each other. Thus, thinking is simply the tendency of a "complex toward completion." Selz's contributions can be summarized in three points: he confirmed that thinking can occur independently of images; he produced the first nonassociationist theory of thinking; and he developed the idea that thinking involves organized complexes or "wholes."

Two events have heavily influenced the course of the study of thinking since Selz's time. The rise of Nazism in Germany put an end to the work of many Gestalt psychologists who were attempting to take Selz's theory one step further (Chapter 3), although many did continue their work elsewhere, mostly in the United States. The rise of behaviorism in America, partly brought on as a reaction against the abuses of the introspection method, emphasized the study of observable stimuli and observable responses only; to some psychologists this meant that internal mental events such as thinking could not be observed and therefore should not be studied. This view helped stifle research on thinking until the current rebirth of "cognitive psychology." These events are summarized in Box O-2.

Evaluation

One major criticism of the early work in thinking is methodological. The method of introspection is a very difficult one since the experimenter must rely on the subject's self-reports. It fits the requirements of science only if we assume that the data are the subjects' reports rather than the subjects' experiences: the reports are observable for all to see and hear, but the experiences are not. The real problem is that these reports may not have much to do with the actual mental processes involved; that is, subjects may not be able to report on their own cognitive experiences accurately. Since the days of the early twentieth century, many clever methods have been developed to study thinking. In addition, the method of introspection has been ingeniously used and refined in recent work on computer simulation in an attempt to program computers to behave the way humans do during problem solving (Chapter 6).

400 B.C.	Aristotle's doctrine of association by contiguity, similarity, and contrast.
300 B.C.	
1700 A.D.	British Associationists reformulate associationism.
1800 A.D.	
	1879. Wundt opens the first psychology laboratory, but thinking is not studied.
1900	The Wurzburg group brings thinking to the laboratory, discovers imageless thought and determining tendencies.
1910	
	1913. Selz proposes first nonassociationist theory of thinking.
1920	Rise of Gestalt psychology in Germany.
1930	Behaviorism stifles American research into thinking. Nazism destroys Gestalt psychology in Germany; some Gestaltists move to the United States.
1940	
1950	
1960	Rebirth of interest in cognitive psychology.
1970	
1980	

A second criticism of the early work in thinking is theoretical. The associationist theory of the philosophers was inconsistent with some of the findings of the Wurzburg group, but the early psychologists proposed no real alternative and Selz's theory was vague. The clash between the associationist theory and the pre-Gestalt work of Selz is still far from resolved, although many current theories such as "information processing" (Chapters 6 and 7) may be seen as compromises.

Finally, we are left with the question of legitimacy. Although there is currently a strong rebirth of interest in cognitive psychology, there is still some question of the place of thinking and complex learning in psychology. Ultimately, the question of "can we find out how the human mind works" will be answered in the laboratory.

Suggested Readings

Humphrey, G. *Thinking: An introduction to its experimental psychology.* New York: Wiley, 1963. An excellent introduction to the historical ideas and findings underlying modern cognitive psychology.

Mandler, J. M., & Mandler, G. *Thinking: From association to Gestalt.* New York: Wiley, 1964. A set of condensed readings from the early studies in the psychology of thinking.

1

Associationism: Thinking as Learning by Reinforcement

anagrams

Preview of Chapter 1

Introduction

Anagram Task

Suppose someone gave you the following letters and asked you to rearrange them to form a word: GANRE. Get a piece of paper and work on this one.

There are two solutions to this anagram (that we know of). Most college students give the answer RANGE, and their median response time is about eight seconds. A less frequent answer is ANGER, which takes about one hundred fourteen seconds (median solution time).

OK. If you cheated on GANRE, here's another to try before you read on: TARIL.

This anagram also has two solutions, so try to find both. Don't read on until you have found both words or until you give up.

The easiest answer seems to be TRAIL, which takes about seven seconds, and the more difficult is TRIAL, which takes about two hundred forty seconds.

For more anagrams and median solution times to amuse yourself and your friends, see Tresselt and Mayzner (1966). Anagrams like these have long been enjoyed as mental puzzles, but recently their solutions have been analyzed in psychological experiments. Since each five-letter anagram has 120 possible letter arrangements,* solving anagrams may be viewed as trying arrangements until one works.

Puzzle Box Task

Another favorite task that has been studied closely involves problem solving in a puzzle box—a closed box with an escape hatch like the one shown in Box 1-1—in which an animal must perform a certain response to "solve" the problem. In 1898, Edward Thorndike published his famous monograph, *Animal Intelligence,* in which he described the process of thinking and problem solving. Thorndike placed a cat into what he called a puzzle box and if the cat performed a certain response, such as clawing down a loop of string or pushing a lever, a trap door opened and allowed it to escape and eat food set out nearby. Thorndike supposed (correctly) that cats do not like being cooped up in a box and do like the chance to get out and have a snack.

From his observations of cats in the puzzle box, Thorndike developed a theory of thinking and problem solving that formed the basis for further ideas which we call in this book the *associationist* theories of thinking. One of Thorndike's most famous observations was that his cats solved the puzzle box problem by *trial and error*—that is, they responded in an almost random fashion without much evidence at all of any "thinking." The cat might meow, or squeeze a bar, or claw at a loose object, or jump onto things in the box until it would hit accidentally upon the required solution of, for example, pulling the string to open the escape hatch. Thorndike observed that the next time the cat was put in the box, it still performed by trial and error—by trying various responses at random until one worked—but as practice increased the animal had a tendency to perform the responses that didn't work less often and to perform the responses that did work sooner. Eventually, after being placed in the box many times, the cat would go to the string and pull it almost immediately. According to Thorndike, the cat was learning "by trial, and error, and accidental success."

---

*If you are baffled trying to figure out how there can be 120 possible arrangements for a five-letter anagram, then read this footnote; otherwise you can skip it. Suppose you have five letters, *a, b, c, d, e,* and five blank spaces to fit one letter each: — — — — —. Pick one letter and place it in any one of the five spaces; you have five choices as to where to put it. Let's say you pick the second blank: — *a* — — —. Now there are four spaces left for the next letter so you have only four choices. Let's say you decide to put *b* in space five: —*a*— —*b*. No matter where you put *a,* you have four places to put *b;* and no matter where you put *b,* you have three places to put the next letter. You may pick the following arrangement: *ca*— —*b;* there are now two choices for the next letter. When you pick one, say *cad*—*b,* there is one blank left for the last letter: *cadeb.* Therefore, there are always 5 first choices, 4 second choices, 3 third choices, 2 fourth choices, and 1 last choice; this yields 5 x 4 x 3 x 2 x 1, or 120 ways to arrange five letters in five spaces. The number of ways to arrange X things in X spaces is called the number of permutations, and the general formula for calculating it is: Number of Permutations =X! The "!" is read "factorial" and simply means to multiply the number times one less than the number, times two less than the number, times three less, and so on down to one. In this example: 5! = 5 x 4 x 3 x 2 x 1 = 120.

BOX 1–1   THORNDIKE'S PUZZLE BOX

"When put into the box the cat would show evident signs of discomfort and of impulse to escape from confinement. It tries to squeeze through any opening; it claws and bites at the wire; it thrusts its paws out through any opening and claws at everything it reaches . . . It does not pay very much attention to the food outside but seems simply to strive instinctively to escape from confinement . . . The cat that is clawing all over the box in her impulsive struggle will probably claw the string or loop or button so as to open the door. And gradually all the other unsuccessful impulses will be stamped out and the particular impulse leading to the successful act will be stamped in by the resulting pleasure, until, after many trials, the cat will, when put in the box, immediately claw the button or loop in a definite way."

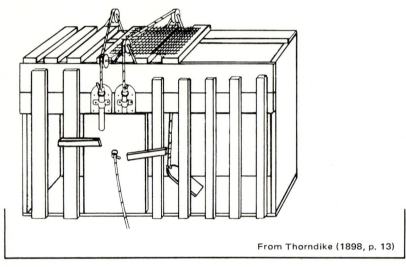

From Thorndike (1898, p. 13)

Both solving anagrams and the puzzle box task may require a subject to try many responses until one solves the problem, and the thinking process may, among other things, be conceived of as *response learning.*

Associationist Definition of Thinking

Trial and Error Application of Habit Family Hierarchy

According to the associationist view, thinking can be described as the trial and error application of the preexisting response tendencies we call "habits." This view is called associationist because it assumes that for any problem situation, S, there are associations or links to many possible responses, R_1, R_2, R_3 and so on. Thus the three elements in an associationist theory of thinking are: the stimulus (a particular problem solving situation), the responses (particular problem solving behaviors), and the associations between a particular stimulus and a particular response. The links are assumed to be in the problem solver's head, where they form a "family" of possible responses associated with any given problem situation. In addition, the responses may vary in strength with some associations being very strong and some being very weak. Thus the responses for any given situation may be put into a hierarchy in order of their strength.

A typical habit family hierarchy for Thorndike's puzzle box is shown in Box 1-2. A similar hierarchy could be constructed for behavior in the anagram problem since there are 120 possible responses for a five-letter anagram, some of which are initially stronger than others. In the problem solving situation, the problem solver (either overtly or covertly) tries the most dominant response, R_1, in the habit family hierarchy for that situation and if that fails, tries R_2 and so on until one works.

BOX 1-2   HABIT FAMILY HIERARCHY FOR PUZZLE BOX

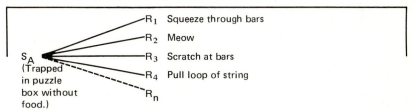

R_1 Squeeze through bars

R_2 Meow

R_3 Scratch at bars

R_4 Pull loop of string

R_n

S_A
(Trapped in puzzle box without food.)

At the start, the cat may have a habit family hierarchy as above. The dominant responses for being in a confined situation are squeezing, meowing, scratching. However, after the cat has been put into the box a few times, the successful responses for this situation become stronger and the unsuccessful ones become weaker, as suggested below.

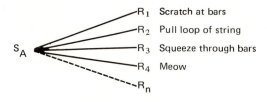

R_1 Scratch at bars

R_2 Pull loop of string

R_3 Squeeze through bars

R_4 Meow

R_n

S_A

Finally, after much experience, the cat has completely rearranged its hierarchy, as suggested below.

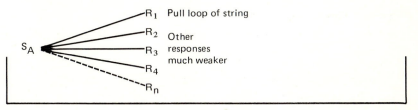

R_1 Pull loop of string

R_2 Other

R_3 responses

much weaker

R_4

R_n

S_A

Laws of Exercise and Effect

Two additional laws of learning, which Thorndike termed the *law of exercise* and the *law of effect,* are required to describe the solution process.

The law of exercise states that responses which have been previously practiced many times with a given situation are more likely to be performed when that situation is presented again; or, to state it another way, practice tends to increase the specific S-R link.

The law of effect states that responses to a problem situation which do not help solve the problem lose strength and are "demoted" on the hierarchy while the responses which do solve the problem increase in strength and go up on the hierarchy until after many trials they reach the top.

Thus the associationists describe problem solving as the trial and error application of a thinker's existing "habit family hierarchy." In a new situation, such as the puzzle box or anagrams, subjects try their most dominant response first (scratch head?), then their second strongest, and so on. Maltzman (1955) summarizes this view as follows: "thinking is not a response" but thinking results in a change in "a new combination of habit strengths" within a habit family hierarchy.

Covert and Overt Responding

Thorndike observed cats in his puzzle box and saw trial and error learning of solution responses. When the Gestalt psychologist Kohler (1925) presented similar problems to apes, he did not observe trial and error performance or activity at all but rather was sure that his animals solved by a flash of *insight*—that they thought about the problem and the solution suddenly fell into place. We shall talk more about the Gestalt interpretation of problem solving in Chapter 3, but it is a bit puzzling that two psychologists observing a similar kind of problem solving task in animals saw such different things and were inspired to develop such different theories.

Let's assume for a moment that both Thorndike and Kohler were correct, at least in their observations of trial and error and of insight. How would an associationist explain the phenomenon of "apparent" insight? That question was solved by the associationists in an ingenious way. Sometimes, and this seems to be especially true of humans, trial and error may be *covert* as well as *overt*. In other words, people tend to try out various solutions *in their minds* (or sometimes even in their muscles). According to this view, thinking is simply covert doing: thinking involves trying all the likely responses mentally until the one that will work is found. Since this form of the trial and error process cannot be seen, the solution therefore appears to be achieved suddenly, as by a *flash of insight.*

Thinking as Covert Behavior

Mediation

The idea that thinking involves a chain of covert responses has led to changes in the traditional associationist idea that a stimulus (S) goes in, a response (R) comes out, and everything that goes on in between can be summarized by a hyphen (S-R). How then does the habit family hierarchy change? Or, to put it another way, what comes between or *mediates* between the overt problem solving situation (S) and the solution response (R)? A mediational theory suggests that the S evokes a miniature internal response called mediational response or r_m; the r_m creates a new internal state or s_m, this new s_m may evoke another different r_m followed by a new s_m and so on until an s_m finally evokes an overt solution response, R. For example, Berlyne (1965) presents a comprehensive mediational theory based on the principle that thinking is a chain of symbolic responses; thus, the "train of thought" may be represented as a series of internal responses and stimuli mediating an S and R:

$$S - r_{m1} - s_{m1} - r_{m2} - s_{m2} - r_{m3} - s_{m3} - \ldots - r_{mn} - s_{mn} - R$$

The capital S is the overt problem situation, the capital R is the overt response, and the lower case s's and r's represent internal covert responses and stimulus situations.

Mediational theories such as Berlyne's are generally extensions of Hull's (1943) claim that animals make tiny responses in anticipation of the goal as they learn to solve a maze; he called these responses "fractional goal responses." For example, rats made miniature licking movements as they ran down a maze towards a liquid reward. These fractional goal responses helped the animal mediate between being put in the maze and performing the needed solution behavior. More recently, Kendler and Kendler (1962) used the idea of mediating responses to describe developmental changes in discrimination learning; Osgood (1957, 1966) has used the idea of "mediating reaction" to explain the human use of language meanings; and Underwood (1966) has used the idea of "implicit associative responses" to explain the course of human verbal learning. These theories are examples of mediational theory because they are based on the idea that tiny, covert responses mediate between a stimulus and a response.

Two Views of Covert Thinking

There are various ways to interpret how covert or mediational responses relate to the habit family hierarchy approach to thinking. A relatively liberal interpretation, such as that cited by Maltzman (1955), is that the habit family hierarchy represents a set of dispositions, and that thinking can be conceived of as changes in the state of the hierarchy. According to this view, thinking is not a chain of responses but "responses may be taken as a criterion or manifestation of thinking" (p. 282). In other words, covert responses may occur as a result of thinking but they are not equivalent to thinking.

A more strict and literal interpretation which is probably less popular today than the one given above is that thinking *is* covert responding, especially covert verbal responding. This view received very serious attention during the 1920s and 1930s because it was consistent with the behaviorist revolution in psychology—the idea that psychologists must study only what can be directly observed (behavior) and should not hypothesize about unseen phenomena (thoughts). One focus of this interest was to determine where in the human body the covert responses occur: the "peripheralists" tended to study muscle changes during thinking because they claimed that responses occurred in the muscles; the "centralists" tended to study electrical brain activity during thinking because they claimed that responses occurred in the brain.

Peripheral Theory: Muscle Activity

The behaviorist psychologist Watson (1930) claimed that since human problem solving involves language, silent thinking is simply subvocal speech. In other words, thinking is simply "talking to oneself," and the locus of thinking behavior should be in the muscles related to talking. For example, Jacobson (1932) measured electrical activity in the muscles of human subjects during various periods of intellectual activity. When the subjects were relaxed and not concentrating on anything, their muscles showed little electrical activity. However, when he asked them to *think* about picking up a heavy object with their left hands, changes occurred in readings for muscles in their left arms. Similarly, when Jacobson asked a subject to imagine a certain object, he noted increased electrical activity from the muscles around the eyes.

Max (1935, 1937) investigated the muscle activity of deaf mutes when they were thinking. Since his subjects normally used sign language to communicate, he thought that perhaps "subvocal speech" could be detected by changes in electrical activity in the arm muscles even if no overt signs were made. As Max expected, he did find increased electrical activity in the arm muscles of these deaf mute subjects when they were thinking about how to solve a problem or about a past conversation, and even when they were asleep and apparently dreaming.

Although the peripheral theory of thinking has not received much attention since Max's interesting study, there has been some further work in this area (McGuigan, 1966; McGuigan & Schoonover, 1973). For example, McGuigan, Keller, and Stanton (1964) measured the muscle activity of students while they read silently. As these researchers predicted, changes occurred in chin and lip muscle activity and in the breathing rates of the students during the reading period but not during rest. Unfortunately, a major problem with this study, as with earlier studies by the peripheralists, is that muscle changes may be due to the awareness of the subject of that part of the body being studied or to factors other than "thinking." McGuigan (1966) has suggested that a more convincing test of the peripheralist theory might be to inject subjects with a chemical (curare) which numbs both the smooth and the skeletal muscles and then ask them to solve problems. If injected subjects were still able to solve problems, it would follow that something must be wrong with the theory that thinking occurs in the muscles.

Centralist Theory: Brain Activity

Although there are now more sophisticated techniques for measuring physiological correlates of mental activity, including some which focus on the electrical activity of brain neurons (see Penfield, 1958, 1969; Delgado, 1969), little work has been done as yet to relate physiological changes in the body to thinking. In a typical study, Chapman (1973) implanted electrodes in the brains of human subjects and recorded general electrical activity while the subjects solved problems. The pattern of electrical activity showed sharp changes during critical phases of problem solving.

McGuigan (1966) has suggested that since the centralist theory predicts that electrical stimulation of specific brain neurons should "cause" spontaneous thinking, further research using these new techniques is needed. McGuigan (1966, p. 294-95) concluded: ". . . if the peripheralist theory that thinking is a behavioral phenomena is confirmed, thinking can be studied directly by recording responses . . . if the centralist theory is confirmed . . . brain events can often be indirectly studied by recording their consequent responses . . . in either case we should get on with the measurement of covert responses."

At this time, most psychologists are willing to concede that electrical and other physiological changes in the body are probably correlated with thinking, but very few people are willing to accept the extreme position that body muscle activity *is* thinking. In addition, the work on the psychophysiology of thinking has not yet stimulated useful theories of thinking nor has it been well integrated with other approaches. Thus, while we hope that some day we shall be able to describe thinking in physiological terms, the remainder of this chapter will focus on thinking defined as a change in the habit family hierarchy.

Habit Family Hierarchy: Stereotyped Responses

As a follow-up to Thorndike's famous observations, a more thorough study was conducted by Guthrie and Horton (1946) half a century later. These researchers took motion pictures of cats in a puzzle box and analyzed the behaviors of a given cat on each successive trial. Each specific behavior was carefully defined in detail and the order of behaviors was tallied for each trial. The results showed that the movements of a given cat were almost identical for a particular response from trial to trial, e.g., it pulled the string and so on in the same way. Since the behaviors were stereotyped, Guthrie and Horton concluded that the cats had specific response tendencies that changed in strength during problem solving rather than general plans.

The habit family hierarchy or trial and error description that Thorndike, and Guthrie and Horton proposed for cats in the puzzle box has also been observed in human beings. For example, Ruger (1910) provid-

BOX 1-3   THE HEART AND BOW PROBLEM

The heart and bow problem is a typical mechanical puzzle used to study trial and error problem-solving in humans. The problem is to disentangle the two pieces. Usually time to solution decreases for each successive trial since unsuccessful responses are weakened and the successful "twist" response becomes dominant.

Based on Ruger (1910)

ed subjects with mechanical puzzles like the heart and bow problem shown in Box 1-3. At first the subjects tended to exhibit a series of apparently random behaviors, often not realizing what brought about the solution. Solution times fell from trial to trial but the subjects in this experiment also tended to persist in using certain specific behaviors on several trials until finally only the successful twist response remained.

Habit Family Hierarchy: Response Dominance

A few cats locked into puzzle boxes may not seem like much on which to build a theory of human problem solving. However, there is further evidence in support of the associationist theory, some of which has come from studying how people solve anagrams. One reason there has not been more research may be that the associationists have concentrated their efforts on the psychology of learning; you probably have sensed that Thorndike's theory is also the basis of a theory of learning and memory. On the other hand, the Gestaltists—the main competitors of the associationists—have focused on the psychology of thinking and perception and their chapter will be a bit longer than this one.

Familiarity of Goal Word

One nice thing about the S-R association representation of thinking is that it makes precise predictions that can be tested. For example, suppose you presented a subject with one of the five-letter anagrams shown in Box 1-4. There are 120 different ways of arranging the letters, each of which can be considered a response in the habit family hierarchy. Of course, for any given subject some potential responses should be stronger than others and thus higher on the hierarchy and more likely to be tried. If the solution for an anagram is a common word that subjects often use in ordinary conversation, for instance, it should come faster than if the solution word is an uncommon one.

To test this prediction, Mayzner and Tresselt (1958, 1966) constructed anagrams based on rearranging either common five-letter words or uncommon five-letter words in the same way. To measure how common a word was, they used the lists compiled by Thorndike and Lorge (1944) which contained a tally of how many times each of thirty thousand words appeared in books, magazines, newspapers, and other randomly selected printed sources. Mayzner and Tresselt found that anagrams were generally solved more than twice as fast if the solution word occurred frequently in print—more than one hundred times per million words—than if it occurred infrequently. Examples are given in Box 1-4. For example,

Familiar Words	Time	Unfamiliar Words	Time
beahc to beach	3.0	hroac to roach	9.5
odelm to model	4.5	ypeon to peony	12.0
ntrai to train	5.0	patoi to patio	22.0
chari to chair	10.0	tanog to tango	45.0
ugars to sugar	10.5	obrac to cobra	50.5

Low LTP Anagrams	Time	High LTP Anagrams	Time
rhtae to heart	28.5	ahter to heart	168.5
oeshr to shore	8.5	osher to shore	39.0
ietdr to tried	18.0	dteri to tried	71.0
aephs to phase	11.0	hesap to phase	115.5
aecrt to crate	18.0	atcer to crate	48.5

Familiar words occur one hundred times per million or more and unfamiliar words occur one or less per million. Both familiar and unfamiliar word solutions require moving only one letter, yet familiar words are generally easier, presumably because they are higher on the habit family hierarchy. Solving anagrams made of pairs of letters that seldom occur together (low letter transition probability) is generally easier than high LTP anagrams for the same solution words, presumably due to the difficulty in breaking up dominant letter pairs.

Based on Tresselt & Mayzner (1966)

TANGO, PEONY, or COBRA, which occurred less than one time per million words, took much more time to solve than CHAIR, SUGAR, or TRAIN, which occurred more than one hundred times per million. In addition, with anagrams which have two solutions, such as TABLE (more than one hundred per million) and BLEAT (seven per million), the more common word was usually found first. These results are consistent with the idea of habit family hierarchy since the most dominant response—assuming past experience with word frequencies influences dominance—occurred before the weaker response in problem solving.

Letter Transition Probability of Goal Word

The associationist theory also predicts that past experience with the way one letter usually follows another letter should influence the response hierarchy. Certain letter pairs have high "transition probabilities" because the second letter often follows the first in normal English words, such as ch, th, es, and others. Since each five-letter word has four successive pairs of letters, word transition probabilities can be generated for them based on how common each of the four two-letter pairs are in ordinary English (Mayzner & Tresselt, 1959, 1962, 1966). For example,

RANCH, TRAIN, and BEACH contain letters in a more common order (higher transition probability) than ENJOY, KNIFE, TRIBE. In general, solution words with high letter transition probabilities are solved faster than those with low. Again, these results are consistent with the idea that problem solving involves trial and error rearrangement of the letters based on 120 responses, but beginning with the *most dominant responses first.*

Number of Moves

An additional finding consistent with the dominant-response-first view of problem solving is that anagram letter order influences problem solving (Mayzner & Tresselt, 1958, 1963, 1966). In general, the fewer the number of letters which must be moved, the faster the solution. If two solution words are possible, such as TABLE and BLEAT, or ANGER and RANGE, the order in which the anagram letters are presented can influence which word is discovered. Again, subjects tend to make dominant responses such as moving just one or two letters first, and if that doesn't work they try weaker responses such as moving around all five letters.

Letter Transition Probability of Presented Word

Finally, a fourth typical result with anagram problem solving is that if the anagram is already in the form of a word or if it has a high transition probability, it is more difficult to solve than if it is in the form of a nonsense syllable or if it has a low transition probability (Mayzner & Tresselt, 1959; Devnich, 1937; Beilin & Horn, 1962; Beilin, 1967). Typical results are given in Box 1-4. For example, discovery of KANGAROO is generally easier if the subject is given OAG KRNOA than if given AGO KORAN. Beilin and Horn's (1962) subjects required about seventeen seconds to solve word anagrams like CAUSE to SAUCE but only nine seconds for nonsense anagrams matched for frequency and other variables such as ERTEN to ENTER. Mayzner and Tresselt (1966) also found that going from low transition probability words as anagrams (BOARD, TRIAL, ANGER, EARTH) to high transition probability solution words (BROAD, TRAIL, RANGE, HEART) was much easier than the other way around. However, Dominowski and Duncan (1964) found that anagrams with high transition probabilities (such as NILEN, GSEAT, HECAB) were more difficult than low transition probabilities (such as LNNIE, TSGAE, AEBHC) only when the solution words had high transition probabilities (LINEN, STAGE, BEACH). In general, these results seem to indicate that subjects have trouble "breaking up" letter combinations that occur frequently together. This kind of inflexibility can be compared to what the Gestaltists call rigidity of mental set, and we shall talk more about that in Chapter 3. In the anagram experiments, it seems that subjects try the dominant response of rearranging loose letters first before they begin on the more complex responses which involve breaking up frequent letter combinations.

In summary, the experiments with anagrams offer four different lines of support for the idea that problem solving involves trial and error application of a subject's habit family hierarchy. With 120 possible ways to arrange a five-letter anagram, it is clear that subjects do not try solutions at random but rather begin with the most dominant responses and go on to the weaker ones if those don't work. Thus, frequently used words, high transition probability solution words, words which require only minor rearrangement, or words which do not require breaking up a high transition probability letter combination are solved more quickly than others.

Problem Solving Set

In solving problems, not only is the general past experience of a subject important in determining the "response hierarchy," but so are his or her experiences just prior to and during the problem solving situation. These experiences form the subject's *problem solving set*.

For example, Rees and Israel (1935) gave subjects ambiguous anagrams that could be solved by either one or two words. When the subjects were instructed to look for a certain type of word, such as "nature words," they found more words in this category than the subjects in a control group found. Subjects who found a high number of "nature words" in one block of anagrams were also more likely to find more nature words in the next block than were the controls. Maltzman and Morrisett (1952, 1953) also found that giving instructions to look for a certain class of words to subjects who had previous experience with anagrams soluble by that set strongly influenced the solutions of the ambiguous anagrams in the direction of the set.

Safren (1962) used two methods of dividing thirty-six anagrams into six sets of six anagrams each. In one grouping, solution words often associated with one another (like MILK, CREAM, SUGAR, COFFEE, SWEET, and DRINK) appeared on the same list. The other grouping of anagrams was in unorganized lists, with the associated words appearing on each of the six different lists. Overall, the median solution time for the organized lists was about seven seconds compared with twelve seconds when the same anagrams were presented in separate lists.

In terms of the response hierarchy framework, these results indicate that several different habit family hierarchies (or response hierarchies) may exist for a given problem situation. According to Maltzman (1955), problem solving "may involve the selection of habit family hierarchies as well as the selection of specific response sequences within a hierarchy." Thus the response hierarchy shown in Box 1-2 must now be changed into a "compound habit family hierarchy" in order to account for the effects of set. Thinking about nature words may lead to response hierarchy A, thinking about beverage words may lead to hierarchy B, thinking about no particular category of words may lead to hierarchy C, and so on.

Evaluation

The associationist approach offers a means of representing thinking and problem solving that allows for clear predictions. Perhaps for this reason, associationist concepts are reappearing in some contemporary theories of human thinking, learning, and memory. For example, Anderson and Bower's (1973) book, *Human Associative Memory*, offers clearly testable "neo-associationist" theories of human memory; and Berlyne's (1965) *Structure and Direction in Thinking* offers an associationist theory of thinking.

However, the associationist approach may fail to capture the full-blown powers of human thought: is all thinking simply the trial and error application of past habits? Apparently, some kinds of thinking can be explained by the response hierarchy model, but there seems to be much more to human thinking than trial and error, and the following chapters will explore some other theories and possibilities.

Suggested Readings

Berlyne, D. E. *Structure and direction in thinking.* New York: Wiley, 1965. A modern extension of the associationist theory of thinking.

Duncan, C. P. (Ed.) *Thinking: Current experimental studies.* Philadelphia: Lippincott, 1967. Articles by Maltzman; Maltzman & Morrisett; Mayzner & Tresselt provide associationist theory and research in problem solving.

McGuigan, F. J., & Schoonover, R. A. *The psychophysiology of thinking.* New York: Academic Press, 1973. A book of readings on the psychophysiology of thinking. The papers by Jacobson, by McGuigan, and by Osgood & McGuigan are particularly interesting.

Thorndike, E. L. *Animal intelligence.* New York: Macmillan, 1911. Describes Thorndike's work with cats in the puzzle box.

2

Rule Learning: Thinking as Hypothesis Testing

concept learning

DOG!

Introduction

Concept Formation Task

Suppose you have in front of you a pile of cards with pictures of different colors, shapes, sizes, and number of objects. The colors are RED or GREEN, the shapes are CIRCLE or SQUARE, the sizes are SMALL or LARGE, and the number of objects is ONE or TWO. The experimenter picks out one card and places it in one of two boxes—Box Yes or Box No. Each time the experimenter picks out a card you must "guess" which box it belongs in. The cards and their group, Yes or No, are shown in Box 2-1. Cover the column marked Correct Group with a piece of paper and try to "guess" the group membership for each card, then check the correct answer and go on. See how long it takes you to predict group membership without error.

In another example of this kind of task, an experimenter enters the room, points down to the metal legs of a table, and says, "Oogle." Then he goes to a wooden chair, lifts it for all to see, points up to it and says, "Aagle." Having accomplished these two "scientific" tasks, he moves toward a door, points down to the metal doorknob and again utters, "Oogle." Next he points up to the top half of the wooden door and says, "Aagle." Suppose you were in a classroom experiencing all this; by now you might be sitting a little higher in your seat with your eyes brightening up a bit. When the experimenter points to the spout of a water fountain, what response do you suppose fills the room?

BOX 2-1 A CONCEPT LEARNING TASK

You will be given a series of stimuli, individually, with each item varying in shape (circle or square), size (large or small), color (red or green), and number (one or two). Cover the column labeled "Correct Group" with a folded piece of paper. For each item listed on the left, guess its group (either Group Yes or Group No), then slide the folded paper down one notch to check the correct answer and so on.

Instance	Your Prediction	Correct Group
1 red large square	_____	No
1 green large square	_____	No
2 red small squares	_____	Yes
2 red large circles	_____	No
1 green large circle	_____	No
1 red small circle	_____	Yes
1 green small square	_____	Yes
1 red small square	_____	Yes
2 green large squares	_____	No
1 red large circle	_____	No
2 green small circles	_____	Yes
2 red small circles	_____	Yes
2 green large circles	_____	No
2 green small squares	_____	Yes
2 red large squares	_____	No
1 green small circle	_____	Yes

A chorus of "Oogle" you say? To this the experimenter smiles and replies, "No, it's an aagle." This process of pointing to things and telling to which category they belong continues until the people in the room are getting long runs of correct anticipations. The rule, the subjects later report, is based on which way the experimenter's finger points: if it points up, the object is an "oogle," if it points down, the object is an "aagle."

Consider another example. Young Billy is looking out the window and sees a poodle. His mother points to the poodle and says, "Dog." Then a German shepherd walks by and again mom points and says, "Dog." Next, a terrier wanders down the street and again mom points and says, "Dog." By now Billy is beginning to catch on, so when a new creature strolls into view he jumps up and down wildly, pointing to the little animal and shouting, "Dog!" However, this time mom says, "No, Billy, that's a cat."

All these tasks are examples of *concept learning* because the subject must learn a rule for classifying objects into mutually exclusive categories. In general, each particular presentation of a to-be-classified stimulus is called a *trial* or *instance* (e.g., one-red-large-circle is the first instance of a No category), each instance may have several *dimensions* (e.g., number, color, size, and so on), and each dimension may have several possible *values* or *features* (e.g., red or green color, large or small size, and so on).

These examples illustrate two main types of concept learning tasks. When all the basic stimulus dimensions are described in advance to the subject who must then identify the relevant rule, this type of concept learning is called *concept identification;* in the first example, for instance, you were told all the dimensions such as red *vs.* green color, large *vs.* small shape, and so on. When the subject does not know the basic set of potentially important stimulus dimensions and must develop or produce it in addition to identifying the relevant rule, the task is called *concept formation;* the oogle-aagle problem, in which you were not told that the dimensions included wood *vs.* metal, up *vs.* down finger, etc., is an example of that kind of concept learning. Note that when people try to solve problems like any of these, they sometimes begin by forming rules or hypotheses that are based on the wrong or too few dimensions—for example, Small = Yes; Metal = Oogle; Animal = Dog—but as more experience is acquired, correct performance increases. The remainder of this chapter will investigate the thinking process that underlies this improvement.

Rule Learning Definition of Thinking

The concept learning example provides a basis for a theory of thinking that can go beyond the simple response hierarchy model. The thinking process required in concept learning has been characterized in a number of ways, including two basic classes of theories:

> The *continuity theory* views concept learning as a direct extension of the S-R associationist model. Each feature of an instance serves as a stimulus, and the particular response is strengthened for all presented features on each trial; thus, after many instances are presented, only the relevant features will have consistent (and therefore strong) responses associated with them. Thinking, then, is simply building response hierarchies.

> The *noncontinuity theory* views concept learning as *inducing rules* (or hypotheses) and *testing* them. If the rule can predict class membership for any instance, it is retained, but if it cannot predict class membership, a new hypothesis is generated. Thinking, then, is hypothesis testing.

The continuity or S-R associationist view and the noncontinuity or hypothesis testing view yield different predictions about subject behavior which the next two sections of this chapter will investigate in more detail.

Continuity Theory

The most obvious and straightforward theory of thinking is that the concept learning task is a simple extension of the response (or habit) hierarchy model described in Chapter 1. During concept learning, the subject forms a response hierarchy for each attribute in the problem by tallying the number of times each category response has been or has not been associated with a given attribute. When a new example is given, the sub-

---

BOX 2-2 CONTINUITY THEORY OF CONCEPT LEARNING

Using the example given in Box 2-1, the continuity theory suggests that subjects keep a tally of the number of times each attribute (e.g., red, circle, etc.) has been associated or not associated with a Yes or a No. For the first few instances the tally could be as follows:*

		Number		Color		Size		Shape	
Instance	*Group*	*1*	*2*	*R*	*G*	*L*	*S*	*C*	*S*
1 red large square	No	–	+	–	+	–	+	+	–
1 green large square	No	–	+	+	–	–	+	+	–
2 red small squares	Yes	–	+	+	–	–	+	–	+
2 red large circles	No	+	–	–	+	–	+	–	+
1 green large circle	No	–	+	+	–	–	+	–	+
1 red small circle	Yes	+	–	+	–	–	+	+	–

*Minus means the attribute was part of an object put into Group No or not part of an object put into Group Yes; plus means that the attribute was part of an object put into Group Yes or not part of an object put into Group No.

To determine the response hierarchy for each new instance, the tendency to say Yes or No for each attribute must be added up for all previous instances. For example, after the first three instances, the response tendencies for the fourth instance are:

Two—3 Yes and 0 No
Red—2 Yes and 1 No
Large—0 Yes and 3 No
Circle—2 Yes and 1 No

To determine the response for 2 red large circles, the total is 7 Yes and 5 No, so there may be a weak tendency to say Yes, the wrong answer. However, after more experience the irrelevant dimensions become neutral. If the seventh instance is 1 green small square, the tallies are:

One—2 Yes and 4 No
Green—2 Yes and 4 No
Small—6 Yes and 0 No
Square—3 Yes and 3 No

The totals are 13 Yes and 11 No, so the response may be a mild Yes.

---

ject simply "adds" the response strengths for all the attributes present in the new example.

For example, consider the situation in Box 2-1 in which subjects are shown cards with drawings that are either red or green in color, large or small in size, round or square in shape, and one or two in number. The continuity theory assumes that each type of color, size, number, and shape builds its own response hierarchy (with the associated responses either Yes or No) based on past experience, as shown in Box 2-2. For example, suppose that the subject has just been shown the first six objects described in Box 2-1 and now must determine whether one-green-small-square is a Yes or a No. In Box 2-2, the response hierarchy for green favors a No response since it has been associated with No many times and few times with Yes; similarly the hierarchy for one favors No; the hierarchy for small is strongly Yes, and there is equal preference for Yes and No for square. The individual tendencies for one, green, small, and square add (or subtract) to yield a weak Yes response as shown in Box 2-2. If one-green-small-square turns out to be a Yes, the response strength for yes for each attribute would be modified and so on. As practice continues, the difference between Yes and No response strengths will become closer to zero for all nonsize attributes and the differences for large vs. small size will continue to grow.

Hull (1920) was the first to investigate this abstraction process in concept learning experimentally. Subjects learned to give one of twelve responses to twelve Chinese characters like those in Box 2-3. First the character was shown, the subject made a response such as "oo," "li," "ta," and the correct response was then given to the subject. Once a subject had correctly responded to all twelve characters, a second pack of twelve was shown but the same twelve responses were associated with each character as with the first group. This process continued with several different packs. Chinese characters contain certain basic features called "radicals" and in the experiment the same radical was always associated with the same response. Subjects showed much improvement with later packs of characters and were often able to "guess" the correct response for characters they had never seen before. Hull concluded that they had abstracted the basic radicals and had developed strong tendencies to respond to them as described by the continuity theory. The relevant attributes, in this case the radicals, strongly evoked different responses while the irrelevant features around the radicals tended to become neutral. The abstraction process could be speeded up by coloring the radicals red, thus drawing the subject's attention to the relevant dimension. This speed-up is an example of "cue salience" discussed in a later section of this chapter.

BOX 2-3   HULL'S CONCEPT LEARNING EXPERIMENT

Six of the Chinese radicals that Hull used are shown here. First, the subject was shown a Chinese character and guessed its "name" (e.g., oo); then the experimenter gave the correct name and so on. Characters with the same radicals always were given the same name so that after going through several packs of characters, the subjects improved their performances and were eventually able to correctly name characters they had never seen before.

Word	Concept	Pack I	Pack II	Pack III	Pack IV	Pack V	Pack VI
oo							
yer							
li							
ta							
deg							
ling							

From Hull (1920)

Noncontinuity Theory

Can concept learning be explained by this straightforward view of the thinker as passively and gradually tallying past experience into multiple response hierarchies? An alternative view is that concept learning is not a process of gradually strengthening associations at all, but rather a noncontinuous or discontinuous process of constructing and testing hypotheses until one works. According to the hypotheses testing view, individuals actively try to formulate rules and they stick with their rule until it fails to work—this has been called the "win stay, lose switch" strategy.

For example, in the task shown in Box 2-1, a subject who is first told that one-red-large-circle is No might hypothesize that "Red is No, Green is Yes," and when shown one-green-large-square, will guess Yes. Since that is a wrong guess, the subject will make up a new hypothesis such as "One is No, Two is Yes" which works for two-red-small-squares, but when this fails on two-red-large-circles may change the hypothesis to "Small is Yes, Large is No" and from then on make no more errors. In this noncontinuity view, thinking involves making a hypothesis and keeping it until it is disconfirmed rather than being a gradual learning of associations. Finding the correct solution is an "all-or-none" process.

The Kendlers (Kendler & D'Amato, 1955; Kendler & Kendler, 1959; Kendler & Kendler, 1962; Kendler & Kendler, 1975) attempted to investigate the two theories of concept learning in a series of experiments involving "shifts" in the rules. Stimuli were presented in pairs, the subject picked one and the experimenter then gave the correct answer. For example, suppose a subject learns the set of responses given in Box 2-4: Yes for black-large and white-large and No for black-small and white-small. The rule can then be switched in two ways: a *reversal shift,* in which the two larges become No and the two smalls become Yes, or a *nonreversal shift,* in which a new dimension is used such as labeling black as Yes and white as No. If concept learning involves strengthening single S-R associations (continuity theory) then the reversal shift should be more difficult to learn since it requires changing *four* associations while the nonreversal shift requires changing only two links. However, if concept learning involves forming a rule which *mediates* between the stimulus and the response (noncontinuity theory), then in a reversal shift the same dimension mediates and only new labels need be added while in the nonreversal shift a new dimension must be found as well as new labels. A long series of studies showed that the reversal shift was easier to learn than the nonreversal shift for college students and verbal children (children over five years), but that the nonreversal shift was easier for preverbal children (children under five years) and for laboratory animals.

In another set of experiments, subjects were taught that the appropriate responses for figures such as black-large and white-large were Yes and for black-small and white-small were No. Then there was an ambiguous switch—for example, subjects learned black-small was now Yes and white-large was now No. What was black-large or white-small? If the subject responded that black-large was Yes and white-small was No, that was a nonreversal shift—two of the original associations were retained and the classification rule was based on a new dimension, color. If the subject said Yes for the black-large or white-small object, that was a reversal shift—all four of the original associations were changed but the original dimension, size, was retained. Since a nonreversal shift re-

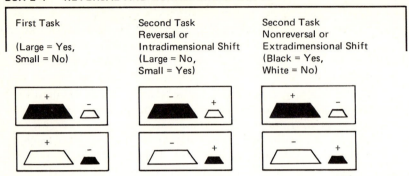
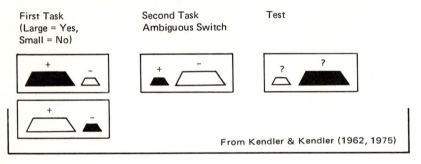
quired changing fewer new associations, it could be predicted by the con-
tinuity view; the noncontinuity theory would predict that since thinking
is based on rules instead of individual associations, a reversal shift was
more likely. Typical results were that younger children preferred nonreversal but older children and adults tended to prefer reversal shifts. This
is illustrated by the percentages of reversal shifts: 37 percent for three-
year-olds, 50 percent for five-year-olds, and 62 percent for ten-year olds.
Kendler and Kendler concluded that as age increases thinking in the concept learning situation is more likely to be mediated by a general rule
rather than by individual associations.

Another test of the continuity-noncontinuity argument was conducted by Bower and Trabasso (1963; Trabasso & Bower, 1964, 1968).

They gave college student subjects a concept learning task similar to the one shown in Box 2-1 made up of six dimensions each with two attributes: color (red or blue), size (large or small), shape (square or hexagonal), number (three or four), position (right or left), shaded area (upper right and lower left or upper left and lower right). The stimuli were presented one at a time, with the subject asked to anticipate which of two classes each stimulus belonged to, the experimenter then giving the correct answer, and so on. In observing the performance of their subjects, Bower and Trabasso noted that the pattern of performance remained at chance level for a long time, then jumped suddenly to 100 percent correct. This observation seemed consistent with the noncontinuity theory but in order to test the theory more closely, Bower and Trabasso performed a further experiment in which the solution rule was changed while the subjects were still responding at chance level, that is, before they had learned the original Red = 1, Blue = 2. The continuity theory predicts that such a switch would seriously hurt learning since associative strengths have been slowly getting stronger for the relevant cues; the noncontinuity theory predicts that the switch will not make any difference since the problem solver has not yet induced the classification rule. The results clearly supported the noncontinuity view: changing the solution rule prior to learning did not slow learning in a group of subjects as compared with another group that retained the same rule throughout the experiment. Apparently these subjects formed a hypothesis, tested it on new stimuli, and changed it on the basis of negative feedback without the need to tally past experiences with particular attributes. In fact, the Bower and Trabasso results seemed to indicate that when these subjects picked a new hypothesis they did not benefit at all from a long chain of past experience; each new selection of a hypothesis may have been made independently of previous hypotheses. Mathematical models based on this idea were discussed by Restle and Greeno (1970).

On the basis of these findings, the noncontinuity theory seems to be the better description of the thinking of college students and some verbal children. Osler and Fivel (1961) investigated the pattern of performance before solution on a concept identification task with high-school students. They observed that the students with IQs over 110 showed the same "sudden" learning noted by Bower and Trabasso—a period of chance performance, presumably while incorrect hypotheses were being selected, followed by 100 percent performance when the correct hypothesis was finally chosen. However, students of average and below average intelligence displayed a pattern in which the rate of correct response for each individual rose gradually. One interpretation of these findings is that the strategy of the bright students was to make successive hypotheses while the strategy of the other students was that of learning by association.

Dominance of Cues

Dominance Hierarchy

When people form hypotheses for rule classification, they may not be choosing the features they notice entirely at random; certain elements of the stimuli may attract their attention more readily than others. In a classic series of concept learning experiments, Heidbreder (1946, 1947) investigated this question. These experiments were like Hull's in that Heidbreder showed her subjects a series of pictures like those in Box 2-5 one at a time and asked them to guess the nonsense word associated with each picture. She then gave the correct response. After going through one set of pictures, Heidbreder repeated this procedure with a second set, and so on. The subjects did not see the same picture-name pair more than once but the response words were always associated with a certain kind of picture: for example, *leth* for building; *fard* for circle; *relk* for face; *mulp* for tree; *ling* for two; *dilt* for five. The subjects could only guess on the first trial, of course, but as they continued through more trials they began to identify the names of the pictures correctly. Thus, like Hull's subjects, the subjects in Heidbreder's studies were able to abstract the appropriate feature of the picture and base their responses on it. Heidbreder was particularly interested in the fact that certain pictures were easier to learn than others. Pictures with concrete characteristics, like the buildings, faces, and trees were generally easier to identify than were shapes like circles or crosses, and pictures of very abstract concepts, like the numbers two and five, were the hardest of all to identify.

Although other researchers have observed different patterns in their subjects (Dattman & Israel 1951; Baum, 1954), such work as Heidbreder's seems to indicate that subjects may enter the experimental situation with a set of preferences for which features of the situation they will attend to. Heidbreder referred to these preferences as a "hierarchy of dominance"; that is, subjects may have a tendency to attend to concrete objects first, and when these have been learned, to shapes, and then to abstract concepts like numbers. Dattman and Israel, and Baum found that a factor influencing this hierarchy of attention was the number of interfering, similar concepts in the problem. For example, subjects often made errors with the number concepts by giving the word that stood for sixness when the picture called for the word for twoness; if only a single number concept was used it was learned much faster. In other words, when several number concepts were used, they may have been first interpreted as "number," and only later classified as particular numbers two or six, etc., whereas trees, faces, and buildings were initially classified as such by the subjects.

BOX 2-5   HEIDBREDER'S CONCEPT LEARNING EXPERIMENT

Subjects were shown drawings like these, one at a time, and asked to name them. Then the correct name was given. After Set 1, the drawings in Set 2 were given but the same name was given to the same kind of picture. After several trials, the subjects began to "guess" the names of new objects correctly.

Trial 1	Trial 2	Trial 3	Trial 4
LING	RELK	LETH	(tree)
FARD	DILT	LING	(face)
RELK	MULP	FARD	(house)
LETH	LING	DILT	(clock)
DILT	FARD	MULP	(boots)
MULP	LETH	RELK	(stars)

Adapted from Heidbreder (1947)

Dominance Level

Underwood and Richardson (1956) developed the concept of *dominance level* to indicate the probability that a certain stimulus will elicit a certain sense impression as a response. For example, the concept of *white* has a high dominance level for words like milk, chalk, and snow, because people generally identify them as white, but a low dominance level for words like baseball, fang, and sugar because they rarely elicit the idea of white as a first response. In concept learning experiments like Heidbreder's, words which shared the same high dominance level for a sense impression were much easier to learn than words which shared low dominance level. Thus, modifying Heidbreder's idea that certain attributes are attended to before others, the dominance level theory supposes that when a stimulus is presented it elicits a response based on one of its characteristics, and that characteristic is attended to unless it fails to help predict the concept. In that case, the second most dominant feature of the stimulus is attended to and so on.

Cue Salience

Trabasso (1963) investigated concept learning using flower designs that varied in the number and shape of the leaves, the angles of the branches, the colors, and so on. Trabasso found that certain cues were more meaningful or *salient* than others. For example, in one experiment in which the classfication rule was based on color (angle fixed), the errors averaged 4.05, but when the relevant dimension was angle (color fixed), errors averaged 19.50. Using these results, Bower was able to assign salience weights to the factors in his flower designs that indicated the tendency of subjects to base their hypotheses on each cue. One interesting finding was that the weightings of cue saliences were cumulative; for example, if angle was the relevant dimension but color was always correlated with angle size, learning was much faster than when angle was relevant but the color varied.

These studies seem to indicate that in a given concept learning situation, hypotheses are likely to be formed on the basis of certain "dominant" or "salient" dimensions, and that only if those hypotheses fail is the subject likely to develop new hypotheses on the basis of less salient dimensions. As you may remember, these ideas are closely related to the idea of "habit family hierarchy" discussed in Chapter 1.

Strategies

Probably the best known and most often-cited concept learning experiment was conducted by Bruner, Goodnow, and Austin (1956) and published in their classic monograph, *A Study of Thinking*. Bruner et al. used a set of eighty-one stimuli, shown in Box 2-6, which consisted of four *dimensions* with three *values* (or attributes) per dimension: *shape*—circle, square, cross; *color*—red, green, black; *number of borders*—1, 2, or 3; *number of objects*—1, 2, or 3.

BOX 2-6   STIMULI USED BY BRUNER, GOODNOW, AND AUSTIN

Subjects either selected or were given one card at a time. Then they "guessed" whether it was a positive or negative instance and were told the correct answer. The cards varied in shape, color, number of borders, and number of objects.

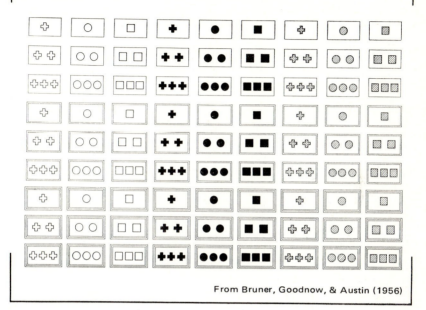

From Bruner, Goodnow, & Austin (1956)

Classification rules could be made in several ways but the three main classes of rules used by Bruner et al. were:

single-value concepts, in which the concept was defined as having one particular value on one particular dimension, ignoring all other dimensions (e.g., red);

conjunctive concepts, in which the concept was defined as having one value on one dimension *and* another value on another dimension (e.g., red crosses);

disjunctive concepts, in which the concept was defined as having one value on one dimension *or* a different value on another dimension (e.g., red or cross).

Once a classification rule had been selected by Bruner et al., a method of presenting the desired positive *instances* (or exemplars) of the concept and the negative instances (or nonexemplars) to the subject was needed. The two most important methods used were:

the *reception method,* in which the experimenter picked the stimulus cards one at a time, the subject said whether he thought each card was a negative or positive instance, and the experimenter told him whether or not he was correct; and

the *selection method,* in which the subject looked at the entire board of eighty-one stimuli, picked the cards one at a time and said for each whether he thought it was a positive or negative instance of the rule, and the experimenter indicated whether or not the answer was correct.

In observing the solution process of concept learning problems under these conditions, Bruner et al. noted that their subjects seemed to use certain strategies. With the reception method, for example, two distinct *reception strategies* were noted:

wholist strategy, in which the subject had to remember all the attributes common to those instances where the response was correct and ignore everything else, thus eliminating attributes that were not part of a positive instance; and

partist strategy, in which the subject focused on one hypothesis at a time (for example, color green = Yes), kept the hypothesis if it correctly predicted the membership of a stimulus card and formed a new one based on all past experience if it did not.

These strategies are specified in Box 2-7.

In general, Bruner et al. found that wholist strategy resulted in better learning performance, especially when the subjects were under time pressure. The partist strategy requires the subject to retain all prior information and select a hypothesis consistent with this information while wholist strategy incorporates a record of all past instances within the current hypothesis. This is because the subject using a wholist strategy remembers all the values of the first correct response or positive instance, and gradually eliminates those that fail to reappear on subsequent positive instances. Although negative instances have not been an important part of our discussion of Bruner's theory, other researchers have found that subjects can learn equally well with negative instances as with positive (Freibergs & Tulving, 1961).

With the selection method of presentation, Bruner et al. noted several similar selection strategies:

simultaneous scanning, in which the subject began with all possible hypotheses and eliminated the untenable ones after each instance;

BOX 2-7   STRATEGIES IN CONCEPT LEARNING

When subjects are presented with a series of instances selected from those shown in Box 2-6 and told whether each is a positive or negative instance, they may adopt one of the following strategies or a mixed combination.

Wholist Strategy
Take the first positive instance and retain all the positive attributes as the initial hypothesis. Then, as more instances are presented, eliminate any attribute in this set which does not occur with a positive instance.

	Positive Instance	Negative Instance
Confirming	Maintain the hypothesis now in force	Maintain the hypothesis now in force
Infirming	Take as the next hypothesis what the old hypothesis and the present instance have in common	Impossible unless one has misreckoned. If one has misreckoned, correct from memory of past instances and present hypothesis

Partist Strategy
Begin with part of the first positive instance as an hypothesis (e.g., choose just one attribute). Then retain or change it in the following way.

	Positive Instance	Negative Instance
Confirming	Maintain hypothesis now in force	Maintain hypothesis now in force
Infirming	Change hypothesis to make it consistent with past instances: i.e., choose an hypothesis not previously infirmed	Change hypothesis to make it consistent with past instances; i.e., choose hypothesis not previously infirmed

From Bruner, Goodnow, & Austin (1956)

successive scanning, in which the subject began with one hypothesis, kept it if it correctly predicted class membership, and changed it to another based on all past experience if it did not;

conservative focusing, in which the subject picked one positive instance and selected subsequent cards which changed one attribute value at a time;

focus gambling, in which the subject picked one positive instance and selected subsequent cards which changed several attribute values at a time.

The scanning strategies are similar to the partist strategies and the focusing strategies are similar to the wholist. Again, focusing is usually far more efficient because it does not require as much memory load.

Models of Hypothesis Testing

The strategies by Bruner et al. suggest that subjects create and test hypotheses based on all relevant past instances. However, Restle (1962) and Bower and Trabasso (1964; Trabasso & Bower, 1968) have proposed a basic model to account for the hypothesis testing process consisting of:

the *sampling idea* that the subject samples one hypothesis (or a set of hypotheses) from a pool of all possible hypotheses which may be correct, incorrect, or irrelevant;

the *no-memory idea* that if the hypothesis results in correct classification of an instance it is retained, otherwise it is replaced in the pool and a new hypothesis (or set of hypotheses) is selected.

This model is represented in Box 2-8.

To test this kind of model, Levine (1966) used a new approach to determine what strategy a subject was using in concept learning. In Levine's

BOX 2-8   HYPOTHESIS SAMPLING MODELS

On the first instance, a subject selects one hypothesis (or a set) from the pool of all possible hypotheses. If the selection is in C, the subject makes a correct response and retains the hypothesis; if it is in W, the response is incorrect and the hypothesis is returned to the pool to be resampled on the next trial; if it is in I, then it may lead to either a correct response (retain the hypothesis) or an incorrect response (replace the hypothesis and resample). If "red" is the defining characteristic of positive instances, then the hypothesis "red" would be in C, "green" would be in W, and "large" would be in I, and so on.

Adapted from Restle & Greeno (1970)

BOX 2-9   STIMULI USED IN LEVINE'S CONCEPT LEARNING TASK

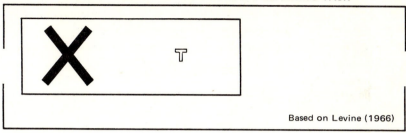

Based on Levine (1966)

experiments subjects had to choose between two letters on a stimulus card like those shown in Box 2-9. The letters differed in color (black or white), position (left or right), size (large or small), and form (X or T). The subjects were told that they could choose from only eight possible hypotheses—right, left, large, small, black, white, T, or X—and were given four trials without being told if they were correct, followed by a fifth trial in which the experimenter randomly said either "Correct" or "Wrong." Levine noted it was clear that the subjects used hypotheses since their responses on any set of four nonfeedback trials were consistent with one of the eight hypotheses over 92 percent of the time, and based on the prior four responses, their choices on the fifth trial could be correctly predicted 97 percent of the time. Furthermore, the subjects tended to retain the same hypothesis if they were given positive feedback (95 percent of the time) and to change to another hypothesis if given negative feedback on the fifth trial (98 percent of the time). Levine's experiment is consistent with the idea that subjects use strategies, that they sample hypotheses one at a time, and that they use the win-stay, lose-switch policy, but it does not support the no-memory assumption of the model. For example, if the subjects sampled with replacement, they had a 12.5 percent (1 in 8) chance of picking the same hypothesis after an "error"; yet the retention rate was only 2 percent. Levine's results indicate that subjects used some of their past experience, but certainly not all of it.

In a further experiment, Wickens and Millward (1971) gave their subjects large amounts of practice on a concept learning task and tried to describe performance in terms of a hypothesis sampling model. The results were consistent with the idea that subjects tend to consider a small number of dimensions simultaneously, that a dimension paired inconsistently with the correct response is eliminated, and that when all the dimensions in a set are eliminated the subject samples a new set. These subjects apparently retained some information about previous dimensions which had been tested but there were large individual differences in how many prior hypotheses could be remembered. It was always more than zero—indicating some memory load—but it was definitely limited.

Factors That Influence Difficulty

There have been many studies investigating what factors make concept problems more or less difficult. One question concerns the role of positive and negative instances. In general, a subject who has developed a hypothesis tends to pick test cards which confirm it—that is, subjects tend to rely on positive instances to test their hypotheses, and may be less able to use the information from a negative instance they have correctly predicted. In a typical experiment, Freibergs and Tulving (1961) gave twenty different concept learning problems to a group of subjects. With each problem the subjects were given either all positive or all negative instances of the to-be-learned concept. For the first few problems, the subjects solved much faster with all positive instances (the median solution times were fifty to one hundred forty seconds) than with all negative (no solutions within two hundred ten seconds). However, after about fifteen problems there was no difference between the groups. Apparently these subjects had a preference for using information in positive instances but could learn, in a relatively short time, to effectively use the information in negative instances as well.

Another important factor that influences the difficulty of concept learning problems is the complexity of the concept rule that must be induced. For example, several experiments have shown that increasing the number of relevant dimensions tends to decrease solution time since a subject can use any dimension to solve the problem, while increasing the number of irrelevant dimensions makes the problem more difficult because it allows the subject more chances to pick a useless hypothesis (Bourne, 1966; Bourne, Ekstrand & Dominowski, 1971; Bourne & Haygood, 1959, 1960; Walker & Bourne, 1961). In addition, solution performance was made more difficult under some conditions* by increasing the number of values per dimension (Battig & Bourne, 1961) and by using disjunctive rather than conjunctive classification rules (Bourne, 1966; Haygood & Stevenson, 1967).

Hunt, Marin, and Stone (1966) have represented classification rules as sequential decision trees such as the one shown in Box 2-10. Since decisions about new instances are based on a series of tests going down the tree, more complex trees should be harder to learn. Evidence to support this idea came from a study by Trabasso, Rollins, and Shaughnessy (1971) in which the subjects read statements like, "Large triangle and red

---

*Haygood, Harbert, & Omlor (1970) have defined the limited conditions under which increasing the number of values per dimension increases problem difficulty.

BOX 2-10   A SEQUENTIAL DECISION TREE

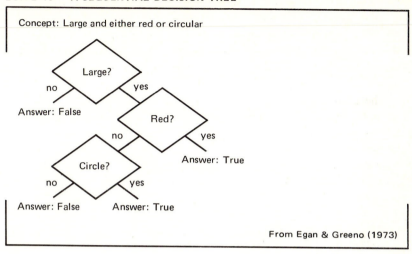

Concept: Large and either red or circular

Large?
no   yes
Answer: False
Red?
no   yes
Answer: True
Circle?
no   yes
Answer: False   Answer: True

From Egan & Greeno (1973)

circle" and were shown a triangle and circle on a slide. The task was to verify the statement by responding Yes or No to the slide. Reading times were longer for complex trees than for simple ones, and decision times were also longer. Apparently, the classification can be represented as a sequential decision tree, and as more decisions are needed the problem becomes more difficult.

Bourne (1970) obtained similar results in a concept learning task in which subjects were presented with objects that varied in size (square, circle, triangle) and color (red, green, blue) and were asked to classify them as Yes or No. The experimenter provided feedback based on either very complex or on shorter rules which were not stated to the subject. For example, a complex rule which defined red triangle and red circle as No and all others as Yes took an average of forty-five trials to learn: "If an object is red and is also a square, answer yes; if an object is red and is not a square, answer no; if an object is not red, answer yes." A simpler rule that defined red triangle as Yes and all others as No took an average of eighteen trials to learn: "If an object is red and is also a triangle, answer yes; otherwise answer no." Bourne (1970) suggested that concept learning may require learning a hierarchy of rules and subrules with complex problems incorporating several lower-level rules.

Serial Pattern Learning

Consider the problem shown in Box 2-11. Here the subject is given a series of letters and must figure out by induction what the next letter

BOX 2-11   LETTER SERIES COMPLETION TASK

1. atbataatbat___

2. aaabbbcccdd___

3. wxaxybyzczadab___

4. urtustuttu___

From Simon & Kotovsky (1963)

should be. Simon and Kotovsky (1963) found that the rule the subject must learn consists of four main ingredients:

cycle—the subject must determine how many letters make up one cycle; for example, in each of the problems cited the cycle is three (atb/ata/atb/at-)   (aaa/bbb/ccc/dd-)   (wxa/xyb/yzc/zad/ab-) (urt/ust/utt/u-);

initialization—the subject must note each of the letters in the first cycle; for example, in the first problem, letter 1 is a, 2 is t, and 3 is b;

alphabet—the subject must determine what are the possible letters that could occur for each letter space in the cycle; for example, in the first problem the first two spaces of each cycle are fixed and the third is either a or b; however, in the fourth problem the first and third positions are fixed but the second position can be any letter in the alphabet;

sequence interaction—the subject must determine what operation is performed on each letter when a new cycle occurs; for example, in the first problem, letter 1 is the same, letter 2 is the same, and letter 3 is changed to the next letter in the alphabet (only a and b appear in the cycles so this sequence goes from a to b to a, etc.).

The rules for each sequence can be represented as a program of things to do. For example, the sequence can be listed for the fourth problem as:

Write the letter L1.
Write the letter L2.
Add one letter to L2.
Write L3.
Go back to first step.

All the subject needs to know is that the system begins with L1 = u, L2 = r, and L3 = t.

Simon and Kotovsky found that rules which required long descriptions (such as long computer programs) were more difficult both for humans and computers, and rules which placed large demands on immediate memory, like the one in the third problem, were especially difficult.

How do subjects select rules to try in such complex situations? There is some evidence that when people are confronted with a serial pattern problem, they tend to rely on the most obvious or simplest rule based on their past experience and will not change that rule to a more complex one unless it fails. For example, Pollio and Reinhart (1970) presented number cards one at a time and asked their subjects to anticipate what numbers would be on each card. The cards were ordered by base 2, base 3, or base 4 such as 0, 1, 10, 11, 100, 101, 111, 1000, etc. (base 2).* The results indicated that the subjects had the hardest time with base 2 (301 errors to learning), then with base 3 (143 errors to learning), and the least with base 4 (91 errors). Most errors occurred at the point of shift to a higher base unit (for example, with base 2, the subject would say 3 instead of 10, or 12 instead of 100). At first, there was generally a long pause *after* each base change (e.g., 1 to 10, 11 to 100, 111 to 1000) but following a little practice there was a long pause *before* the change, suggesting that the subject was aware that something "different" happened at base changes. Pollio and Reinhart concluded that these subjects initially assumed that base 10 was being used (based on their successful past experience) but after they had made several errors discovered the correct solution rule. That the subjects learned a *rule* rather than a set of independent responses was suggested by the fact that they could add and subtract in base 2, base 3, and base 4 and could learn new base systems with relative ease.

When subjects are given a series of symbols, such as a sequence of numbers, more than one simple rule may be involved. Bjork (1968) constructed numerical sequences based on three separate rules, as shown in Box 2-12. The sequence given here, 042153264375, was based on the subrules "add 4," "subtract 2," and "subtract 1" for each set of three numbers. The subjects saw the numbers in order, one at a time, and were asked to anticipate the next number. The same sequence was continued until they correctly anticipated the numbers five times in a row up to a maximum total of twenty-five trials. The overall results were that the proportion of correctly anticipated numbers gradually increased with more trials; however, Bjork found that if he focused on one subrule at a time (as in trials 1, 4, 7, 10, 13, etc.) the learning was not gradual but rather jumped in all-or-none fashion from a very low level on one trial to a very high level on the next, and remained high. Thus although the overall

*The first few numbers for base 3 were 0, 1, 2, 10, 11, 12, 20, 21, 100, and for base 4 were 0, 1, 2, 3, 10, 11, 12, 13, 20, 21, 22, 23, 30, etc.

BOX 2-12   COMPLEX RULES FOR SERIAL PATTERN LEARNING

Position	1	2	3	4	5	6	7	8	9	10	11	12
Subrule 1	+4			+4			+4			+4		
Subrule 2		-2			-2			-2			-2	
Subrule 3			-1			-1			-1			-1
Sequence	4	2	1	5	3	2	6	4	3	7	5	....

Based on Bjork (1968)

learning of sequence appeared to be very complex, a more careful analysis by subrule indicated an orderly and all-or-none process.

Restle (1970) has further investigated how a complex set of rules is induced by subjects solving serial pattern problems made up of numbers from 1 to 6. Restle designed serial patterns based on *structural trees*, like the diagram in Box 2-13. Structural trees represent a hierarchy of rules such as:

mirror (M)—subtract each of the numbers in the preceding chunk from 7 (change 1234 to 6543);

BOX 2-13   STRUCTURAL TREES FOR SERIAL PATTERN LEARNING

M means subtract number from 7, R means repeat number, T means add 1 to number. To read: begin at first (left) position in sequence (1), go to lowest applicable rule (T) and apply (2 for position 2); then use next lowest rule (R) to get 12 for positions 3 and 4; continue, always using lowest applicable rule.

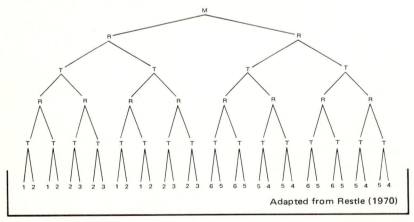

1 2   1 2   2 3   2 3   1 2   1 2   2 3   2 3   6 5   6 5   5 4   5 4   6 5   6 5   5 4   5 4

Adapted from Restle (1970)

transpose (T)—increment numbers in the preceding chunk by 1 (change 1234 to 2345);

repeat (R)—reproduce the numbers in the preceding chunk (1234 becomes 1234).

Restle's subjects were seated in front of a set of six lights with a response button under each light. A light would go on, the subject had to predict which one would go on next by pushing a button, then the next light would appear, and so on. Although sequences were based on a hierarchy of rules like that in Box 2-13, the subjects were not told of the rules and saw only a sequence of stimuli. In investigating the pattern of errors for the first twenty repetitions of the sequence, Restle found that subjects tended to learn the rules in order starting with the lowest level and working up to the most complex. For example, the sequence 121223231212232365655454654644545 is made up of the hierarchy of rules shown in Box 2-13. The highest level rule was M—with the most errors for the first 6 at the seventeenth position in the sequence—and the easiest rule was the lowest T—with subjects making fewest errors on the even numbered positions. Analysis of the errors for the first twenty repetitions of the sequence revealed an average of 50 percent correct for the highest rule, M, 55 percent for the second highest R, 65 percent for the third highest T, 80 percent for the fourth highest R, and 85 percent for the lowest T. Other patterns based on a five-level hierarchy of rules produced similar results. Apparently, when many rules must be induced, subjects work on the lowest, most obvious level first and build up to more complex ones.

Evaluation

The concept learning and rule induction task has been a major paradigm (or method) in the study of human thinking. One advantage of concentrating on an agreed-upon task and method is that researchers have been able to amass an impressive amount of detailed and thorough information about human thinking with respect to concept learning. A disadvantage, however, is that the concept learning task is just one kind of problem solving situation and it is not clear how far one can generalize from laboratory studies on concept learning to the full range of human thought. A second problem concerns the finding that subjects tend to use "rules" and "strategies" in problem solving; in the concept learning task the rules and structure are built into the task by the experimenter (e.g., defining red as positive, or making a structural tree), and therefore it is not entirely surprising that the subjects display some effects of the experimenter's rules and structure. In problem solving tasks that are less structured, an entirely different set of strategies may be observed. Finally, there is the problem of individual differences in which different people may show different reasoning processes in the concept learning task. The Kendlers have demonstrated that preverbal children do not share the strategies of adult college students, but further research is needed to determine whether the performance of college students (who have typically been the subjects in concept learning experiments) is representative of all adult subjects. A challenging new area of research involves analyzing concept learning behavior in different cultures, such as Rosch's (1973) work on "natural categories" in Stone Age tribes.

Suggested Readings

Bourne, L. E., Jr. *Human conceptual behavior.* Boston: Allyn & Bacon, 1966. Describes research on concept learning.

Bourne, L. E., Jr., Ekstrand, B. R., & Dominowski, R. L. *The psychology of thinking.* Englewood Cliffs, N.J.: Prentice-Hall, 1971. Chapters 9, 10, 11, and 12 provide an excellent review of current research and theory in concept learning.

Bruner, J. S., Goodnow, J. J., & Austin, G. A. *A study of thinking.* New York: Wiley, 1956. Describes a classic set of experiments on concept learning.

Duncan, C. P. *Thinking: Current experimental studies.* Philadelphia: Lippincott, 1967. Papers by Bower & Trabasso, by Levine, by Laughlin, and by Hovland & Weiss provide a good survey of theories and research in concept learning.

Johnson, D. M. *A systematic introduction to the psychology of thinking.* New York: Harper & Row, 1972. Chapters 2 and 3 provide a detailed survey of recent experimental work.

3

Gestalt:
Thinking as Restructuring Problems

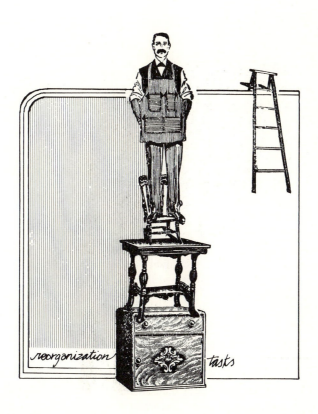

reorganization *tasks*

Preview of Chapter 3

Introduction

Reorganization Tasks

Suppose you were given six identical matchsticks and asked to make four identical, equilateral triangles with them. Find six matchsticks (or toothpicks, etc.) and try it. What are you doing? According to the Gestalt psychologists, you are trying to *reorganize* the problem solving elements—in this case, the six sticks—so they fit together in a new way.

An important contribution of the Gestaltists is the idea that people get stuck solving problems because they cannot change their *problem solving set*—since they cannot look at the situation in a new way, they cannot see a new way to fit the elements together. For example, when trying to solve the six-stick problem, many people have trouble changing their problem solving set from two dimensions to three. Giving a hint like this (or as some Gestaltists have called it, giving *direction*) is important in problem solving because it helps people to break out of their old ways of organizing the situation. The new way of looking at this problem afforded by thinking in three dimensions is called *insight*—the "magical" flash that occurs when you suddenly see how to fit the sticks together. (Some Gestaltists have pointed out that the solution and flash of insight are often accompanied by the word, "Aha!")

If you still have not solved the problem, leave it for a while and come back to it later. This process is called *incubation,* and while no one is sure why it helps, it often does. One reason may be that the time lapse allows

BOX 3-1 THE SIX-STICK PROBLEM

The Problem
Given six sticks, arrange them to form four triangles that are equilateral and with each side one stick long.

The Solution
Some subjects take the six sticks,

and form a square with an X in it, such as,

However, this solution is not acceptable because the triangles are not equilateral—each has a 90 degree angle. In order to solve the problem, the solver must think in three dimensions, making a pyramid with a triangle base. For example, an overhead view is,

with the middle point raised from the triangle base.

confusing ideas to be forgotten. See if this helps you, but if you cannot solve it, then you may "cheat" by looking at Box 3-1.

Let's try another example. During World War I, Wolfgang Kohler, one of the founders of the Gestalt school of psychology, was stranded on the island of Tenerife in the Atlantic Ocean. Being a good scientist, Kohler was determined not to waste his time and so he spent seven years studying problem solving in the island's most willing subjects, some chimpanzees. Eventually he got home and later published a monograph on his research, *The Mentality of Apes* (1925). Here was a typical problem as he reported it: given that you are an ape in a cage, that there are some crates in your cage, and that there is a banana hanging from the ceiling out of reach, how do you get the banana?

What Kohler wanted was for the apes to place the crates on top of each other to form a stairway to the banana. This solution, like the solution to the six-stick problem, required that the problem elements be reorganized. Kohler reported that solutions were preceded by a period of intense thinking by the ape, followed by what appeared to be a flash of insight.

These two problems—the six-stick problem and Kohler's banana problem—are examples of the type of problem solving the Gestalt psychologists tried to understand. Their problems usually supply all the needed parts—either in the form of pieces of information or as concrete objects—and the solver's task is to arrange them in a certain way to solve the problem. The Gestaltists felt that these kinds of problems involved creative or novel solutions—although some later evidence has indicated that without appropriate past experience (in the case of the apes, for example, moving crates) such problems cannot be solved (Birch, 1945).

Gestalt Definition of Thinking

What is problem solving? According to Gestalt psychologists, the process of problem solving is a search to relate one aspect of a problem situation to another and it results in *structural understanding*—the ability to comprehend how all the parts of the problem fit together to satisfy the requirements of the goal. This involves *reorganizing* the elements of the problem situation in a new way so that they solve the problem.

Thus, although the Gestaltists limit themselves to one class of problems, and use certain imprecise terms such as "insight" and "structural understanding," they are trying to comprehend and explain a very high level and creative type of mental process. Their emphasis on *organization*—on how elements fit together to form a *structure*—is consistent with the contributions of the Gestalt psychologists to the study of perception. The famous laws of perceptual organization, for example, were based on the Gestalt idea that perception involves the mind imposing an order or structure on incoming stimuli.

The differences between the Gestalt approach to thinking and the associationist approach are summarized in Box 3-2. These two approaches do not deal with the same kinds of problems—Gestalt is concerned with creating novel solutions to new situations while the associationists are concerned with applying solution habits from past experience. Where the Gestalt theory views thinking as rearranging problem elements, the associationist view is that problem solving involves trying possible solutions until one works. In analyzing thinking into its component parts, the Gestaltists rely on mental structures or organizations as the unit of thought while the associationists describe thinking in terms of associa-

BOX 3-2   DIFFERENCES BETWEEN GESTALT AND ASSOCIATIONIST THEORIES

	Associationist	Gestalt
1. Type of Task	Reproductive	Productive
2. Mental Activity	Try S-R links	Reorganize elements
3. Unit of Thought	S-R links	Organizations
4. Detail of Theory	Precise	Vague

tions among stimuli and responses. And finally, although the Gestaltists deal with a more complicated kind of thinking than do the association-ists, their theory is more vague and thus more difficult to test scientifically.

Distinction Between Two Kinds of Thinking

One of the basic concepts in the Gestalt approach is that there are two kinds of thinking. One, based on creating a new solution to a problem, is called *productive* thinking because a new organization is produced; the other, based on applying past solutions to a problem is called *reproductive* thinking because old habits or behaviors are simply reproduced. The distinction between productive and reproductive thinking (Wertheimer, 1959; Maier, 1930, 1931, 1933, 1945) has also been called a distinction between "insight" and "trial and error" (Kohler, 1925; 1929), "meaningful apprehension of relations" *vs.* "senseless drill and arbitrary associations" (Katona, 1940), and "structural understanding" *vs.* "rote memory" (Wertheimer, 1959). Unfortunately, however, the Gestaltists have never clarified their various distinctions, have often confused differences in instructional method with differences in subsequent problem solving approach, and have provided little or questionable empirical support for their claims.

The flavor of Gestalt distinction between productive and reproductive thinking can be found in an example by Wertheimer (1959) suggesting two methods of teaching students how to find the area of a parallelogram. One method emphasizes the geometric or structural property that the triangle on one end of the figure could be placed on the other end of the figure thus forming a rectangle (see Box 3-3). The other method emphasizes a sort of cookbook recipe of steps to calculate the area by dropping the perpendicular and multiplying its height times the length of the base.

Although students taught by both methods should perform equally well on criterion tasks that involve finding the area of parallelograms like those they had learned about, Wertheimer reported that they differed in their ability to transfer what they had learned to new tasks. For example, the students who learned "by understanding" (the first method) were able to find the area of unusual parallelograms and shapes and to recognize uncalculable situations such as are shown in the figure, while the students who learned in a mechanical way (the second method) usually said something like, "We haven't had this yet."

In an example of memorizing digit strings, Katona (1940) claimed that learning by "understanding the structural relationships" not only im-

Understanding Method

The "understanding" method encouraged students to see the structural relations in the parallelogram, e.g., that the parallelogram could be rearranged into a rectangle by moving a triangle from one side to the other. Since the students knew how to find the area of a rectangle, finding the area of a parallelogram was easy once they discovered the appropriate structural relations.

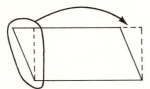

Rote Method

In the "rote" method, students were taught to drop a perpendicular and then apply the memorized solution formula,

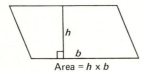

Area = $h \times b$

Transfer

Both groups performed well on typical problems asking for the area of parallelograms; however, only the "understanding" group could transfer to novel problems, such as,

or distinguish between solvable and unsolvable problems, such as,

The response of the "rote" group to novel problems was something like, "We haven't had that yet."

Based on Wertheimer (1945)

proved subjects' ability to transfer but also improved their ability to retain information over time. He had one group learn the digit string 581215192226 by understanding the structural pattern of "add 3, add 4" as indicated by the organization 5-8-12-15-19-22-26, while another group learned by rote memorization of the string organized as 581-215-192-226. Although both groups performed equally well on immediate retention, Katona reported that the first group remembered the string longer.

Katona (1940) provided another set of problem solving situations in the form of card tricks and matchstick problems. A typical card trick problem (trick No. 3 in the series) involved figuring out how to arrange eight cards in such a way that if the subject dealt the top card of the deck face up on the table, put the next card from the remaining seven in the pack at the bottom without determining what it was, placed the next card face up on the table, the one after that at the bottom and so on until all the cards were dealt; the cards put on the table would follow the sequence: red, black, red, black, red, black, red, black. The problem was to find the order of the red and black cards in the original deck.

The solution was taught by two methods: (a) *learning by memorizing*, in which the specific order of the cards required for solution (RRBRRBBB) was given in its entirety for the solver to memorize, and (b) *learning by understanding*, in which the solver was given a diagram to help him figure out the "structure" of the problem situation for himself. The diagram system involved writing down the required color for each card for each run through the deck as shown in Box 3-4.

In one experiment, subjects in the memorization group learned this card trick and card trick No. 4 (in which they produced a chain of spades from ace to eight by dealing out every other card) by memorizing the required order for four minutes. Subjects in the understanding group had the same time to learn, by means of the suggested diagram, how to arrange the deck for trick No. 3 only. A control group received no training. An immediate transfer task consisted of the previously learned task (trick No. 3), an easy variation of trick No. 3 (trick No. 1, output BRBRBR by dealing every other card), and a difficult variation (trick No. 2, output same as trick No. 3 by dealing every third card); a four-week retention transfer task consisted of trick Nos. 3, 4, and 5 (same output as trick No. 1 but by dealing out every third card).

The results summarized in Box 3-4 show the proportion correct with asterisks indicating where subjects had prior practice. As you can see, the memorization subjects (Group Mem) performed slightly better on immediate retention but much worse on transfer and long-term retention than understanding subjects (Group Und).

Katona also reported studies in which subjects learned to solve matchstick problems by several instructional methods. Two of these methods were: (a) Group Mem, in which the experimenter presented the

The Problem
Deal out every other card onto the table, putting every skipped card on the bottom of the deck until all eight cards are on the table. The order of appearance on the table is RBRBRBRB. What was the order of the original deck?

Rote Method (Group Mem)
Subjects may be taught the solution by rote memorization: "The order of the original deck was RRBRRBBB."

Meaningful Method (Group Und)
Or they may learn by a more meaningful method involving a diagram:

1st run	R	?	B	?	R	?	B	?
2nd run		R		?		B		?
3rd run				R				?
4th run								B
Original	R	R	B	R	R	B	B	B

Results
Typical proportions correct on retention and transfer tests were as follows:

	Transfer Problems			Retention Problems		
Group	No. 1	No. 2	No. 3	No. 3	No. 4	No. 5
Mem	.23	.08	.42*	.32*	.36*	.18
Und	.44	.40	.44*	.48*	.62	.52
Con	.09	.03	.09	.09	.14	.09

*Subjects had practice on the problem prior to the test.

Adapted from Katona (1940)

complete series of solution steps in order, moving one stick at a time, and repeating the series six times, and (b) Group Help, in which the experimenter presented a series of hints to help the subjects understand the structure of the problem, such as by shading in the squares that were essential and pointing to the sticks that had to be moved. For example, in the problem shown in Box 3-5, the subject was shown five squares made of matchsticks and was required to move three sticks to make four squares; no sticks could be removed and all squares had to be one stick wide and one stick long. The first method (memorization) involved showing the required moves to the subject repeatedly and the second method (understanding) encouraged the subject to discover the principle that some sticks served as the sides of one square and some bordered two squares by having the experimenter give a series of hints and saying, "Try to understand what I am doing."

In a typical experiment, all the subjects were given (1) a pretest to assure their initial state of inexperience, (2) practice on two tasks by one of the two methods, and (3) delayed tests (some after one week and others after three weeks) on the learned problems as well as on the two new transfer tasks.

The results, in terms of percent correct, are given in Box 3-5. The Group Mem subjects performed quite well—better than the Group Help subjects—on retention of the solution for practiced tasks both after one week and after three weeks; however, Group Help subjects excelled (as did Group Und subjects with card tricks) on transfer tasks.

BOX 3-5   TWO KINDS OF LEARNING AND THINKING ABOUT KATONA'S MATCHSTICK PROBLEM

The Problem
Given matchsticks which form five squares, move three sticks to form four squares.

Rote Method (Group Mem)
The complete solution steps are presented to the subject in order, moving one stick at a time, and repeating six times. For the above problem, the required moves shown are:

Meaningful Method (Group Help)
The second method involves giving a series of hints to the subject accompanied by the comment, "Try to understand what I am doing."

Results
Typical proportion correct on retention and transfer tests were as follows:

Group	Test After 1 Week Practiced Tasks	New Tasks	Test After 3 Weeks Practiced Tasks	New Tasks
Mem	.67	.25	.53	.14
Help	.58	.55	.52	.55
Con	.12	.12	.12	.12

Note: The subjects who took the test after three weeks were a different group than those who took it after one week.

From Katona (1940)

The experimental design, the lack of clear definitions, and particularly, the lack of statistical analysis have all been criticized (Melton, 1941; Katona, 1942) and to the extent that these criticisms are justified, an interpretation of Katona's results is difficult. However, there is some evidence for the idea that giving solvers hints so they can discover the "structure of the problem situation" does aid in transfer—what the Gestaltists would call productive problem solving. For example, in a similar experiment performed under more controlled conditions, Hilgard, Irvine, and Whipple (1953) found that the understanding group took significantly longer than the memorizing group to solve the two practice problems, performed no differently from the memorizing subjects on a one-day retention test, and performed significantly better on a set of transfer problems.

A major practical question raised by this work is how to help learners "understand" so they will be productive thinkers who are able to transfer their experience to novel problems. For example, Hilgard et al. (1953) pointed out that many so-called understanding subjects did not really understand the diagraming device in the full sense. In another experiment, Hilgard, Ergren, & Irvine (1954) taught subjects by one of five variations of the learning by understanding. Although there were no overall differences on a transfer task, the errors the subjects made were related to the type of method used, suggesting a mechanical or rote application of the various "helps." Similarly, Corman (1957) found that giving subjects a statement of the "double function principle"—that a stick can be a part of one square or of two squares—did not aid in productive thinking on transfer although the diagram method did. Apparently, a supposedly meaningful principle such as the diagram or double function method can be learned in a mechanical way.

In more recent years, the distinction between these two kinds of learning to solve problems has taken the equally ambiguous form of a separation between "discovery" and "expository" methods of instruction (Shulman & Keisler, 1966). Bruner (1961, 1966, 1968) has been a major proponent of the discovery method. Although educators often describe discovery as an instructional method and as a desired outcome of learning, and seldom empirically define either, they have produced several examples of Bruner's preferred method of instruction (see Shulman, 1968).

For example, Dienes' (see Bruner & Kenney, 1965) method of teaching children the concept of the quadratic equation involved allowing students to manipulate the shapes shown in Box 3-6 in such a way that they could see that the area of a square with sides of length X was X^2, of sides $(X + 1)$ was $X^2 + X + X + 1$, of sides $(X + 2)^2$ was $X^2 + 4X + 4$, etc. The discovery method shares with the Gestalt learning by understanding method the promise of superior transfer and retention performance by the learner; in short, the road to productive thinking is paved with discovery

BOX 3-6   DISCOVERY LEARNING OF QUADRATIC EQUATION

Children are encouraged to manipulate shapes like these

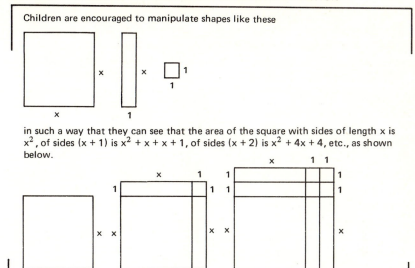

in such a way that they can see that the area of the square with sides of length x is x^2, of sides $(x + 1)$ is $x^2 + x + x + 1$, of sides $(x + 2)$ is $x^2 + 4x + 4$, etc., as shown below.

From Bruner & Kenney (1965)

of the structure of the problem situation. Although it is vague and hard to apply, psychologists and educators are still trying to clarify the idea of structural understanding and to determine if it does provide better transfer and retention of knowledge and if so, how.

Stages in Problem Solving

General Phases

There have been many attempts to analyze the thinking process down into several smaller stages. In his classic book, *The Art of Thinking,* Wallas (1926) suggested four phases:

preparation—the gathering of information and preliminary attempts at solution;

incubation—putting the problem aside to work on other activities or sleep;

illumination—the key to the solution appears (this is where the "flash of insight" and the "aha" occur);

verification—checking out the solution to make sure it "works."

Unfortunately, these four stages are based on introspections by Wallas and others about what they think they are doing when they solve problems, rather than on psychological experimentation. However, McKeachie and Doyle (1970) have shown how the analyses can be applied with partial success to reports of the thinking process such as the introspections of the mathematician Henri Poincaré (1913) shown in Box 3-7. The first fifteen days of thinking are Poincaré's preparation period; preparation continues as ideas "collide[d] until pairs interlocked," and is followed immediately by illumination and verification. In the second phase, preparation is followed by illumination and verification, apparently without a sudden burst of insight. The third part of the introspection completes Wallas' four stages, including an incubation period (during the geological excursion) and a sudden burst of insight in the illumination period.

BOX 3-7 WALLAS' PHASES OF PROBLEM SOLVING: AN EXAMPLE FROM POINCARÉ

"For fifteen days I strove to prove that there could not be any functions like those I have since called Fuchsian functions. I was then very ignorant; every day I seated myself at my work table, stayed an hour or two, tried a great number of combinations and reached no results. One evening, contrary to my custom, I drank black coffee and could not sleep. Ideas rose in crowds; I felt them collide until pairs interlocked, so to speak, making a stable combination. By the next morning I had established the existence of a class of Fuchsian functions, those which come from the hypergeometric series; I had only to write out the results which took but a few hours.

"Then I wanted to represent these functions by the quotient of two series; this idea was perfectly conscious and deliberate, the analogy with elliptic functions guided me. I asked myself what properties these series must have if they existed, and I succeeded without difficulty in forming the series I have called theta-Fuchsian.

"Just at this time I left Caen, where I was then living, to go on a geologic excursion under the auspices of the school of mines. The changes of travel made me forget my mathematical work. Having reached Countances, we entered an omnibus to go some place or other. At the moment when I put my foot on the step the idea came to me, without anything in my former thoughts seeming to have paved the way for it, that the transformations I had used to define the Fuchsian functions were identical with those of non-Euclidean geometry. I did not verify the idea; I should not have had time, as, upon taking my seat in the omnibus, I went on with a conversation already commenced, but I felt a perfect certainty. On my return to Caen, for conscience' sake I verified the result at my leisure."

From Poincaré (1913)

More recently, Polya (1957, 1968) has introduced a series of steps in problem solving based on observations he has made as a teacher of mathematics. Polya's four steps—first described in his classic book, *How to Solve It* (1957)—are:

> *understanding the problem*—the solver gathers information about the problem and asks, "What do you want (or what is unknown)? What have you (or what are the data and conditions)?"

> *devising a plan*—the solver tries to use past experience to find a method of solution and asks, "Do I know a related problem? Can I restate the goal in a new way based on my past experience (working backwards) or can I restate the givens in a new way that relates to my past experience (working forward)?" (Here's where insight flashes.)

> *carrying out the plan*—the solver tries out the plan of solution, checking each step.

> *looking back*—the solver tries to check the result by using another method, or by seeing how it all fits together, and asks, "Can I use this result or method for other problems?"

Polya's steps are similar to Wallas' in general form. Polya's "understanding" step is similar to Wallas' preparation phase, his "devising a plan" step includes some of Wallas' preparation phase and both the incubation and illumination phases, and the "carrying out the plan" and "looking back" steps relate to Wallas' verification.

Box 3-8 gives an example of Polya's (1968, p. 2) four phases of problem solving based on a mathematical problem. The "understanding the problem" phase requires that the solver ask what is given (*a, b,* and *h* are given) and what is unknown (*F* is unknown). The "devising a plan" phase requires the solver to "look around for an appropriate related problem" (let's assume the solver already knows how to find the volume of a pyramid). In addition, the solver must try to restate either the goal or the givens to fit the related problem. In the frustum problem, the solver may restate the goal to find the volume of the big pyramid minus the volume of the smaller pyramid and to then use the givens to produce the needed variables. The "carry out plan" phase requires the solver to make the calculations by using the formula for volume of a pyramid. The "looking back" phase requires the solver to see the logic of what he or she has done and to check to see if the method works on other problems.

As you can see, Polya's idea of restating the goal (working backward from the unknown to the givens) and restating the givens (working forward from the givens to the goal) are examples of the Gestalt idea of "restructuring." While Polya gives many excellent intuitions about how the

BOX 3-8   STAGES IN SOLUTION OF POLYA'S FRUSTUM PROBLEM

The Problem

Find the volume F of the frustum of a right pyramid with square base. Given the altitude h of the frustum, the length a of a side of its upper base, and the length b of a side of its lower base.

The Solution Process

1. Understanding the problem. Solver asks: What do you want? Answer: The volume of frustum F. Solver asks: What have you? Answer: a, b, and h.

2. Devising a plan. If you cannot solve the proposed problem, look around for an appropriate related problem. Solver asks: What is a related problem that I can solve? Answer: The volume of a full pyramid. Solver asks: Can I restate the goal or the givens differently? Answer: Restate the goal as the volume of the full pyramid minus the volume of the smaller pyramid in the upper portion. Restate the givens to yield the height of the full pyramid and the height of the smaller pyramid in the upper portion.

3. Carrying out the plan. Use known formulas to find the height of the full pyramid, the height of the smaller pyramid, and the volumes of each.

4. Looking back. Solver asks: Can I use this method for other problems? Do I see the overall logic of this method?

Based on Polya (1965)

restructuring event occurs and how to encourage it, the concept is still a vague one that has not been experimentally well studied.

Functional Solutions and Reformulations

Duncker (1945) attempted to study the stages in solving a problem empirically by giving a problem to a subject and asking him to report his thought process aloud as he was thinking. The problem Duncker used was the tumor problem shown in Box 3-9, and was stated as follows: "Given a human being with an inoperable stomach tumor, and rays which destroy organic tissue at sufficient intensity, by what procedure can one free him of the tumor by these rays and at the same time avoid destroying the healthy tissue which surrounds it?" The protocol of a typical subject led Duncker to conclude that problem solving proceeds by stages, going from general solutions to more specific ones, with the original problem being continually reformulated. An example of how problem solving moves from *general solutions* to *functional solutions* to *specific solutions* is shown in the solution tree for the tumor problem. For example, a general solution might be "avoid contact between rays and healthy tissue"; once solvers had thought of this they would generally hit upon several functional solutions such as "use free path to the stomach," or "insert protecting wall," or "remove healthy tissue from path" and ultimately reach specific solutions such as "use esophagus" or "insert a cannula." If that general plan or those functional solutions failed, solvers would think up new general and functional solutions such as "lower intensity of rays on their way through healthy tissue"; more specific ideas that followed from this general idea were "turn down ray when it gets near healthy tissue and turn it up when it gets to the tumor" (wrong), or "use focused lens" (right).

BOX 3–9   SOLUTION TREE FOR ONE SUBJECT WORKING ON DUNCKER'S TUMOR PROBLEM

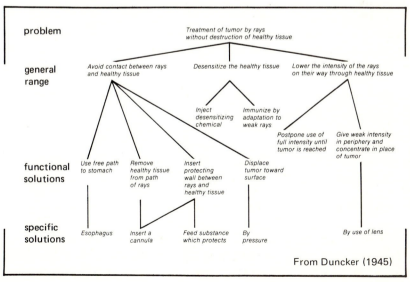

From Duncker (1945)

Like Polya and the other Gestalt psychologists, Duncker noted several basic phenomena in the process of problem solving.

Functional solution or *value*—elements of the problem must be seen in terms of their general or functional usefulness in the problem and general or functional solutions precede specific solutions.

Reformulating or *recentering*—problem solving involves successive stages of reformulating (or restructuring) the problem with each new partial solution creating a new, more specific problem. In this example, the general solution of desensitizing healthy tissue is a reformulation of the original goal.

Suggestion from above—reformulating the goal to make it closer to the givens, e.g., thinking of protecting the healthy tissue by somehow desensitizing it, similar to Polya's "working backward."

Suggestion from below—reformulating the givens so they more closely relate to the goal, e.g., thinking of using the rays somehow in a weak form, similar to Polya's "working forward."

Another example comes from Duncker's (1945) 13 problem; "Why are all six place numbers of the form 276,276 or 591,591 or 112,112, etc., divisible by 13?" The solution, according to Duncker, involves a suggestion from below to reformulate or recenter the originally given material from *abcabc* to *abc* $\times$ 1001. Once the solver restates the givens in this form it can be argued that any number divisible by 1001 is also divisible by 13. In his experiments, Duncker found that when he told subjects "The numbers are divisible by 1001," over 59 percent of the subjects solved the problem but when he gave the general rule or no help the solution rate was 15 percent or below. Thus, as Duncker noted, "the real difficulty of the 13 problem is overcome as soon as the common divisor 1001 emerges"—that is, as soon as the givens are reformulated.

Subgoals

More recently, there have been more sophisticated attempts to investigate how problems are reformulated into smaller problems or *subgoals* as Duncker suggested. One technique, developed by Restle and Davis (1962) is based on the idea that problem solving involves an individual's going through a number of independent and sequential stages and solving a subproblem at each stage which allows the solver to start work on the next stage (see Box 3-10). The number of stages, k, for any given problem

**BOX 3–10   DETERMINATION OF THE NUMBER OF STAGES IN PROBLEM
SOLVING**

Assumptions
1. Problem solving involves completing a sequence of stages. When one stage is completed, the solver goes on to work on the next.
2. Each stage is independent.
3. Each stage is equally difficult. Average time to move from any one stage to the next is constant.

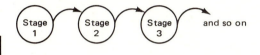

Stage 1   Stage 2   Stage 3   and so on

Based on Restle & Davis (1962)

can be roughly determined, according to the Restle and Davis argument, by the square of the average time to solution, t, divided by the square of the standard deviation of the time to solution, s. The theory is summarized in the formula, $k = t^2 \div s^2$.

Data from three different problems were used. The rope problem asks how it is possible for a prisoner to escape from a tower using a rope which is half as long as he needs by dividing the rope in half and tying the halves together. The answer—that he divides the rope lengthwise—takes an average of 131 seconds and a standard deviation of 115 seconds, yielding a value of $k = 1.3$. Thus the rope problem is a one-stage problem. A second problem was the word tangle: "If the puzzle you solved before you solved this one was harder than the puzzle you solved after you solved the puzzle you solved before you solved this one, was the puzzle you solved before you solved this one harder than this one?" The answer—yes—took an average of 265 seconds with a standard deviation of 154 seconds so that k, the number of stages, is roughly three. Finally, the gold dust problem asks subjects to figure out how to get exactly 77 units of gold dust using containers of size 163, 14, 25, and 11. The answer—163 minus 25 minus 25 minus 14 minus 11 minus 11, or 163 minus 25 minus 25 minus 25 minus 11, etc.—took an average of 373 seconds with a standard deviation of 167, yielding approximately five stages. Although the Restle and Davis technique allows an empirical determination on the number of stages, it does not tell what those stages are, nor does the model's assumption that all stages in the problem are equally difficult seem to be correct.

BOX 3-11   HAYES' SPY PROBLEM

The Problem
Subjects memorized a list of connections for spies who can pass messages from one to the other, such as:

SHOWER to CLERK
DROUGHT to HILL
LARYNX to BETH
ADJECTIVE to SHOWER
HILL to HORSE
BEEF to LARYNX
ADJECTIVE to PARCHESI
DROUGHT to KEVIN
SHOWER to BEEF
LARYNX to DROUGHT
BEEF to TAFT

The connections form the network (not shown to subjects):

ADJECTIVE → SHOWER → BEEF → LARYNX → DROUGHT → HILL
  ↓   ↓   ↓   ↓   ↓   ↓
PARCHESI CLERK TAFT BETH   KEVIN   HORSE

Results
The average time for each move is shown below for subjects given subgoals (broken line) and subjects not given subgoals (solid line).

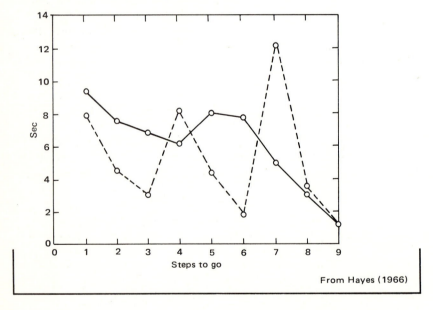

From Hayes (1966)

A method for studying subgoals in problem solving that overcomes some of these problems was developed by Hayes (1965, 1966) in his study of spy problems (see Box 3-11). Subjects memorized a list of connections among spies and were then asked to tell out loud how to get a message from one spy to another. Hayes gave subgoals to some subjects such as, "Get a message from JOE through APE and WATERFALL to CAT," while other subjects were not given subgoals but were told only, "Get a message from JOE to CAT." The average times taken to make each of the nine required steps to solution for a typical problem are shown in Box 3-11. As the graph shows, the subgoals seemed to break the problem into three smaller chunks—from JOE to the third spy, APE, from the third spy to the sixth, WATERFALL, and from the sixth to the last, CAT. The subjects worked faster as they approached a subgoal and more slowly on the steps that followed subgoals. Apparently, after they reached one subgoal, there was a period in which the subjects thought about how to carry out the next subproblem which was followed by their going rapidly through the steps to the next subgoal; then they slowed again while figuring out how to solve the next subproblem, and so on. The subjects who were not given subgoals seem to have cut the problem into two main subproblems—their solution times fell moving from the given spy, JOE, to the fourth spy, there was a pause, and then the times speeded up moving from the fifth to the final spy, CAT. The fact that solution times tended to accelerate as a subject approached a subgoal, and to slow on the steps following a subgoal suggests that the subjects restructured or chunked the problems into smaller ones and tried to solve the subproblems.

Thomas (1974) used a similar procedure to determine whether subjects imposed subgoals on a more difficult problem—the Hobbits and Orcs problem. The problem is to get three hobbits and three orcs across a river using a boat that can hold only one or two creatures at a time with at least one creature in the boat during each crossing. The other condition is that orcs must never outnumber hobbits on either bank of the river. An analysis of mean time to make each move and of errors on each move shows peaks at state 321 and 110. (See Box 3-12). The difficulties at these stages in the solution process are not completely determined by the number of alternative responses which seems to indicate that subjects cut the problem into three subproblems—from the start at 320 to state 310 or 220, from that point to 300 or 311, and from there to the goal, 000. As in Hayes' study, the subjects tended to divide problems into subproblems; their error rates and times seemed to fall as they neared a subgoal and to rise on the steps that directly followed subgoals.

BOX 3-12   STEPS IN SOLVING THE HOBBITS-ORCS PROBLEM

The Problem Space
"Each state is specified by a three-digit code: (1) the number of hobbits on the
starting side, (2) the number of orcs on the starting side, (3) the location of the
boat—1 if it is on the starting side and 0 if it is on the opposite side."

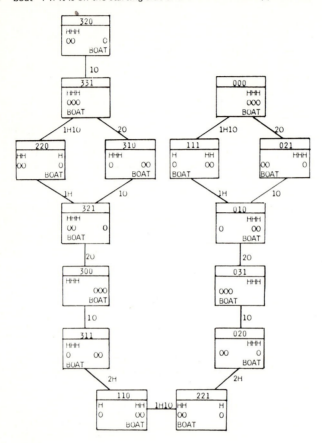

Mean Time Spent and Errors Made at Each State

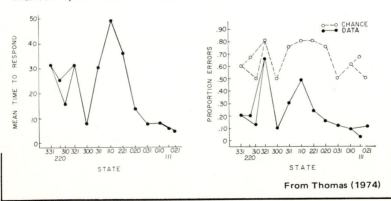

From Thomas (1974)

BOX 3-13   LUCHINS' WATER JAR PROBLEM

Problem	Given Jars of the Following Sizes			Obtain the Amount
	A	B	C	
1.	29	3		20
2. E1	21	127	3	100
3. E2	14	163	25	99
4. E3	18	43	10	5
5. E4	9	42	6	21
6. E5	20	59	4	31
7. C1	23	49	3	20
8. C2	15	39	3	18
9.	28	76	3	25
10. C3	18	48	4	22
11. C4	14	36	8	6

From Luchins (1942)

Rigidity in Problem Solving

Problem Solving Set

A nother major contribution of the Gestalt psychologists is their finding that prior experience can have negative effects in certain new problem solving situations. The idea that the reproductive application of past habits inhibits productive problem solving has been called *functional fixedness* (Duncker, 1945), *einstellung** or *problem solving set* (Luchins, 1942), and *negative transfer* (Bartlett, 1958).

The Luchins' work (Luchins, 1942; Luchins & Luchins, 1950) provides an often-cited example of how prior experience can limit an individual's ability to develop a solution rule of sufficient breadth and generality. Their water jar problem involved presenting subjects with the hypothetical situation of three jars of varying sizes and an unlimited water supply, and asking them to figure out how to obtain a required amount of water. The problems, in order of presentation (about two minutes allowed for each), are reproduced in Box 3-13.

Item 1 is an example-practice problem. The experimental group was given Problems 2 through 11 in order, one at a time, to be solved by each subject without aid from the experimenter. The control group was given the same introduction and practice problem but began working on Problems 7 through 11. Luchins called Problems 2 through 6 *einstellung* problems because they all evoked the same problem solving set of $b - a - 2c$

Einstellung is a German word meaning "attitude."

as a solution. Problems 7, 8, 10, and 11 were critical problems because they could be solved by either a shorter, more productive method ($a - c$ or $a + c$) or by the longer method used to solve 2 through 6. Problem 9 was inserted to help the subjects "recover" from their mechanized or einstellung response, since the $b - a - 2c$ formula would not work on this problem; the recovery, if any, could be noted by a greater tendency to use the shorter solution on 10 and 11 than on 7 and 8. Luchins performed this experiment on over nine hundred subjects ranging from elementary-school students to students in his graduate seminars.

Typical results are shown in Box 3-13. The control group almost always discovered the short, direct solution whereas the experimental group frequently used the longer, einstellung solution even on Problems 10 and 11. Luchins summarized the findings as follows (Luchins & Luchins, 1950): "This basic experiment and its variations have been administered by the author to over 900 subjects. Most of these subjects showed considerable Einstellung effect. Recovery from mechanization was in general not large for adult groups, and was negligible in most elementary school groups." Based on these findings, Luchins (1942, p. 15) preached the evils of mechanized thinking and even implied that the Allies could defeat the Nazis if they could avoid einstellung: "Einstellung—habituation—creates a mechanized state of mind, a blind attitude towards problems; one does not look at the problem on its own merits but is led by a mechanical application of a used method."

This monumental work provided the basis for the Gestalt claim that reproductive application of past habits could be a detriment to effective and productive problem solving in a new situation. There is, of course, another explanation which is often cited by associationist-oriented psychologists: that the experimental subjects who used the einstellung method to solve new problems were actually more efficient because they did not have to waste time trying to create a new method for each problem. However, it does seem clear that Luchins' results provide evidence that past experience can limit the type of solution a subject devises in a new situation.

Bartlett (1958) noted a similar effect, which he called *negative transfer,* when he observed how subjects solved the DONALD + GERALD = ROBERT problem shown in Box 3-14. The task was to substitute numbers for the letters, given that D = 5, that every number from 0 to 9 has its corresponding letter, and that each letter must be given a number different from any other number. In observing his subjects, Bartlett (1958, p. 59) noted that much of the difficulty they had was due to their past habits or methods of solving addition and subtraction problems, such as working from right to left: "Several more students tried the problem, but couldn't do it. They substituted 5 for D and zero for T, but since no direct clue is provided for L and R, they said they couldn't get any farther. It seems

BOX 3-14   BARTLETT'S DONALD + GERALD = ROBERT PROBLEM

DONALD
GERALD
ROBERT

"This is to be treated as an exercise in simple addition. All that is known is: (1) that D = 5; (2) that every number from 0-9 has a corresponding letter; (3) that each letter must be assigned a number different from that given for any other letter. The operation required is to find a number for each letter, stating the steps of the processes and their order."

From Bartlett (1958)

that the habit of starting to make an addition sum from the right-hand column and continuing to the left with succeeding columns was so deeply ingrained that they couldn't conceive of any other method of approach and they soon tired of trying to find L and R by trial and error."*

Functional Fixedness

Using a slightly more experimental approach, Duncker (1945) also investigated how past experience could limit problem solving productivity. For example, he devised a diagram for his tumor problem with an arrow (representing the ray) going thru a black dot (representing the tumor) surrounded by a circle (representing the healthy tissue). When the diagram was shown with the problem, the solution rate was 9 percent as compared with 37 percent when no diagram was given. This finding suggested to Duncker that the diagram helped to fix the function of the ray as a single line going through the body, and thus blocked the ability of the subject to think of it as several rays focused on the tumor. Duncker called this phenomenon *functional fixedness* because the past experience of seeing the diagram acted to limit the number of different functions a subject could devise for the ray.

Duncker (1945) thus defined functional fixedness as the "inhibition in discovering an appropriate new use of an object owing to the subject's previous use of the object in a function dissimilar to that required by the present situation." In order to investigate this phenomenon more carefully, he devised a series of problems which he thought might involve functional fixedness and presented them to subjects in his laboratory. For example, in the box problem (see Box 3-15), the subject was given three cardboard boxes, matches, thumb tacks, and candles. The goal was to

---

*The solution, by the way, is: T = 0, G = 1, O = 2, B = 3, A = 4, D = 5, N = 6, R = 7, L = 8, E = 9.

mount a candle vertically on a nearby screen to serve as a lamp. Some subjects were given a box containing matches, a second box holding candles, and a third one containing tacks—pre-utilization of the boxes—while other subjects received the same supplies but with the matches, tacks, and candles outside the boxes—no pre-utilization. The solution—to mount a candle on the top of a box by melting wax onto the box and sticking the candle to it and then tacking the box to the screen—was much harder to discover when the boxes were given filled rather than empty. Duncker's explanation, like Luchins' and Bartlett's, was that the placement of objects inside a box helped to fix its function as a container, thus making it more difficult for subjects to reformulate the function of the box and think of it as a support.

In the paperclip problem, the subject was given one large square, four small squares, several paperclips, and an eyelet screwed to an overhead beam. The task was to attach the small squares to the large one and hang it from the eyelet. The pre-utilization group had to use some of the paperclips to attach the small squares to the large one first, but for the no pre-utilization group the small squares were already stapled to it. The solution—bending one paperclip to form a hook from which to hang the

BOX 3-15   MATERIALS IN DUNCKER'S BOX PROBLEM

Based on Duncker (1945)

large square—was much harder for the pre-utilization group to discover. Again, Duncker suggested that using the clip as an attacher made it more difficult for subjects to conceive of it in a different function, namely, as a hook. In all, half a dozen tasks of this sort were given; typical results were for the pre-utilization group to solve 58 percent and the no pre-utilization group to solve 97 percent.

Although these results are consistent with Luchins', they are suspect because there were only fourteen subjects in Duncker's original study, the experiment was poorly specified, and no statistical analysis was performed. To overcome some of these problems, Adamson (1952) reran several of Duncker's experiments, including the box problem and the paper clip problem. Fifty-seven subjects were divided into two groups—pre-utilization and no pre-utilization—and each subject received three different problems for a maximum of twenty minutes each. The results were similar to Duncker's original study. For example, with the box problem, 86 percent of the subjects solved the problem within twenty minutes when the boxes were presented empty but only 41 percent solved the problem when the boxes were presented as containers. All subjects solved the paperclip problem but those in the pre-utilization group (the group that had to first use the paperclips to attach the squares together) took almost twice as much time.

Adamson's replication seemed to confirm Duncker's original idea—that subjects who utilize an object for a particular function will have more trouble in a problem solving situation which requires a new and dissimilar function for the object. One drawback to the Duncker and Adamson experiments was that since the same situation was used both for pre-utilization and for the new task, it was difficult to locate the source of the problems the pre-utilization subjects had; furthermore, there was no control for the experience the subjects had with the objects prior to the experiments. Birch and Rabinowitz (1951) conducted an experiment which attempted to overcome these two criticisms with a problem different from those used by Duncker. The two-cord problem was adapted from an experiment by Maier (1930; 1931) and is shown in Box 3-16. In this experiment a subject was given a room with two cords hanging from the ceiling to the floor just out of reach of one another and two heavy objects, an electrical switch and an electrical relay, placed nearby. The goal was to tie the cords together. Some subjects, group S, were given a pretest task of completing an electrical circuit on a "breadboard" by using a switch; other subjects, Group R, were given the same pretest task but were given a relay to use to complete the circuit; and a third group, the control Group C, was given no pretest experience. The solution required a subject to tie one of the cords to a heavy object, swing it as a pendulum and, while holding the other cord, catch the pendulum on the upswing. If the subjects had not solved the problem within nine minutes the experimenter gave a help-

BOX 3-16   FUNCTIONAL FIXEDNESS IN MAIER'S TWO-CORD PROBLEM

The Problem
Given two cords hanging from the ceiling and heavy objects around the room, tie the cords together.

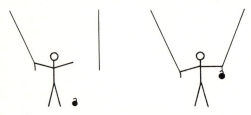

Frequency of Choice of Objects in Problem Solving

Group	N	Number Using Relay	Number Using Switch
Pre-utilization with Relay	10	0	10
Pre-utilization with Switch	9	7	2
No Pre utilization	6	3	3

Based on data from Birch & Rabinowitz (1951)

ful hint by walking by one of the cords and "accidentally" setting it in motion. The results are shown in Box 3-16. All of the subjects solved the problem, but the Group R subjects tended to use the switch as a weight and the Group S subjects tended to use the relay as a weight. When asked why they used one heavy object instead of the other, subjects in both groups replied, "Anyone can see this one is better."

These results seem to fit nicely with those of Duncker and with the idea of functional fixedness. Previous experience with the object as a relay made it much more difficult to think of it as a weight—previous experience had fixed the function of the object. The Gestalt psychologists would not, of course, claim that all previous experience is detrimental to problem solving. Broad, nonspecific, general experience and certain basic past learning "represents an essential repertoire of behavior which must be available for restructuring when the new situation demands"; however, "on the other hand, productive thinking is impossible if the individual is chained to the past," and in cases where a subject relies on very specific, limited habits, "past experience may become a hindrance" (Birch & Rabinowitz, 1951, p. 121).

There are the additional questions of how long the effects of functional fixedness last, and whether functional fixedness with respect to a certain object tends to affect similar objects. Adamson and Taylor (1954) investigated these questions with a variation of the two-cord problem described above. Before the subjects tackled this problem, they were given a task of working on an electrical circuit board with a pair of pliers. Then, when they tried to solve the two-cord problem, Adamson and Taylor found they were far less likely than control subjects to use those same pliers as a weight for the pendulum; in addition, they had more difficulty than control subjects in using another pair of pliers or even a pair of scissors as weights which, however, they preferred to using the original pliers. Apparently the effect of functional fixedness does spread to objects that are similar to the fixed object. However, the effect seems to fade with time, as Adamson and Taylor (1954) showed by giving the two-cord problem at varying intervals following the initial experience of their subjects with the pliers and the circuit board. They tested subjects immediately following the experience, one hour later, one day later, and one week later. The longer the time elapsed between the use of the pliers on the circuit board and the introduction of the two-cord problem, the larger the number of subjects who used the pliers as the weight.

Positive Effects of Past Experience

The work of Luchins, Duncker, and others has often been cited as evidence that reapplication of very specific, rigid, past habits can hinder productive problem solving. There is, of course, complementary evidence that in some cases specific past experience may aid problem solving. For example, Maier (1945) asked subjects to solve the string problem as shown in Box 3-17: given several wooden poles, clamps, and a string, the goal was to hang the string from the ceiling without defacing it. The solution consisted of tying the string around one stick and bracing it horizontally against the ceiling at both ends with two long sticks made by clamping the wooden poles together. Another problem subjects were asked to solve was the hatrack problem: given objects similar to those in the preceding experiment, to make a hatrack. The solution to the hatrack problem consisted of clamping two sticks together to make a pole that reached from the floor to the ceiling and using the handle of the clamp to hang the hat. Of subjects with no prior experience with the string structure, only 24 percent solved the hatrack problem; of subjects who had solved the string problem which had been removed from their sight, 48 percent solved the hatrack problem; and of subjects who had solved the string structure problem and could still see the solution, 72 percent solved the new problem.

Maier's results seem to conflict directly with those of Duncker and the others who found that past experience limited future problem solving

BOX 3-17   MATERIALS IN MAIER'S STRING AND HATRACK PROBLEMS

String Problem
Given several wooden poles, clamps, and string, hang the string from the ceiling to the floor without defacing the ceiling.

The solution is to tie the string around a pole and then brace the pole against the ceiling using poles clamped together.

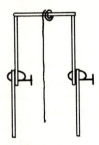

Hatrack Problem
Given poles and clamps, make a hatrack.

The solution is to clamp two poles together from floor to ceiling and use a clamp as a hook from which to hang a hat.

Based on Maier (1945)

effectiveness. Instead of negative transfer, Maier found strong evidence for *positive transfer*—the fact that past experience with the string structure helped subjects in a new problem solving situation. In trying to reconcile the Maier experiment with those in the previous section, three facts seem to be important: (a) The change from function one to function two is very small in Maier's experiment since the hatrack is part of the string structure, but the two functions of box as container and box as support are very different in the experiments by Duncker. (b) The change from the normal use to function one is great in Maier's experiment in that using a braced pole to hang a string is a little uncommon, but small in Duncker's experiments as boxes are often used as containers. (c) The first function facilitates the second function in Maier's experiment but in the Duncker experiment the functions are mutually exclusive. Apparently, specific habits and experiences are useful in situations which require those specific ideas applied in much the same form, but are a hindrance in situations which require using objects in a new way.

One interpretation of the value of past experience is that in some cases it can make functions of objects available, especially if the past experience with a certain function of an object and the required function in a new situation are similar. Saugstad and Raaheim (Raaheim, 1965; Saugstad & Raaheim, 1960) presented subjects with the following problem (Box 3-18): given newspapers, string, pliers, rubber bands, and a nail, figure out a way to transfer a few steel balls from a glass jar on a wheeled platform to a bucket 260 cm away from you without crossing a chalk line. The solution, believe it or not, is to bend the nail with the pliers to make a

BOX 3-18   MATERIALS IN SAUGSTAD AND RAAHEIM'S TRANSFER PROBLEM

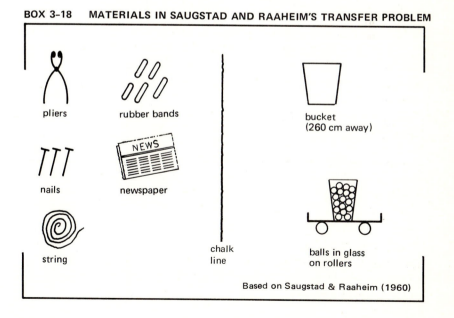

pliers

rubber bands

bucket
(260 cm away)

nails

newspaper

string

chalk
line

balls in glass
on rollers

Based on Saugstad & Raaheim (1960)

hook, attach the hook to the string, throw it out to catch the movable glass full of steel balls and pull it toward you, roll the newspapers into tubes which you hold in shape with the rubber bands, and drop the balls through the tubes into the bucket.

Suppose you gave the subjects, before starting the experiment, a bent nail and said, "This object could be used to catch things with. Could you give some examples?" and suppose you showed them the newspaper rolled into a tube and said, "This object you may use to conduct something through. Can you give me some examples?" Saugstad and Raaheim (1960, p. 97) called this "making the functions of objects available"; Duncker would probably have called it giving the problem away. After thirty minutes on this problem, 95 percent of the subjects solved it if they had the experience described above, but only 22 percent of the subjects solved the problem if they had no prefamiliarization with the two new functions of the nail and the newspaper.

In a similar, slightly more subtle experiment, subjects were given the nail and the newspaper prior to the experiment and asked to think of all possible uses for them. They were then given the task of transporting the steel balls. Of the subjects who mentioned both the hook as possible function of the nail and the tube as a possible function of the newspaper during the pretest, 89 percent solved the problem; of subjects who mentioned either the hook or the tube function during the pretest but not both, 42 percent solved the problem; and of subjects who thought of neither function during the pretest, only 19 percent solved the problem. Again, Saugstad and Raaheim claimed that success in problem solving sometimes depends on appropriate functions being available to the solvers at the appropriate time.

"Making the functions available" may result from general experience with the solution objects. For example, Birch (1945) examined the role of "insight" in apes—over twenty years after Kohler—by placing some food out of reach outside the cage and giving them a hoe with which to rake it in. Only two out of four chimpanzees could solve this task, so Birch allowed them to play with short sticks for the next few days. The chimps invented many new uses for the sticks while playing with them, including prying, shoveling, and noisemaking. After a few days of such play the apes were given the hoe problem again and this time they solved it quite easily. Apparently, insight is aided by and builds on useful past experiences.

Taken together, the work of Maier, of Saugstad and Raaheim, and Birch seem to supplement the idea of functional fixedness described by Duncker: in situations where similar functions are required, past experience is an aid. It should be noted, however, that the type of problem solving that Maier and Saugstad and Raaheim are discussing is very close to the definition of reproductive thinking. To put it a little more gently, what these results seem to show is that problems which seem to require productive solutions—reorganization of the problem elements—are more easily solved by a mind that is prepared with appropriate general past experiences. On the other hand, if those past experiences specifically tend to fix the function of objects in one way, creative problem solving can be hurt.

One way to resolve this problem, and one that most good teachers aim for, is to provide learners with certain basic, specific facts coupled with more general problem solving techniques. Although Luchins successfully demonstrated that past experience solving problems can limit problem solving ability, there is also evidence that such practice can lead to a more general ability to deal with all sorts of problems. For example, Harlow gave monkeys problems (Box 3-19) in which they were given two (or three) objects on a tray and had to pick one up. If they picked up the "correct" object they received a piece of banana. (When three objects were presented, the correct object was the odd object.) The monkeys were given the same problem over and over again, with the position (right or left, etc.) of the objects randomly arranged on each trial. Then a new problem was presented, and so on for hundreds of problems (monkeys are more patient than human subjects). Harlow found that the monkeys performed better on new problems as the experiment progressed; while it took them many trials to respond consistently to the early problems, they never made a mistake after the second trial on the problems presented towards the end of the experiment. Although the specifics of problems at the end were different or even opposite from those at the beginning, the monkeys had apparently picked up a *general* strategy for responding. They seemed to follow a rule which we can express as, "If you get food for picking that object keep picking it, and if you do not then pick the other object." Harlow called this use of general past experience, "learning set" or "learning to think." His work shows that general experience as well as specific can be an aid in problem solving if the problem situation is like the prior ones.

Direction

The experiments by Maier, Saugstad and Raaheim, and by Harlow indicate that part of solving a problem is finding out how it relates to past experience. Polya cited "finding a related problem" as a main factor in devising a solution plan, and Birch and Rabinowitz talked about using "an essential repertoire" of past behaviors and experiences in solving Duncker's problems. How does a problem solver find the relationship between past experience and the needed reformulation of the problem? According to Maier (1930; 1931; 1933) the leap to solution requires *direction*.

From Harlow & Harlow (1949)

Since past experience alone is not enough for an original solution, a subject needs some organizing principle, some new way of looking at the problem situation, in short, some direction. Maier provided an example of the crucial importance of direction in his two-cord problem. In one experiment, he waited some time as the subject tried to solve the problem and then provided hint 1: he walked by the string, thus setting it in gentle motion. He waited a little more time, and if there was still no solution, gave hint 2: he handed the subject a pair of pliers and said, "This is all you need."

He waited again and if no solution occurred, repeated hint 1. Of sixty-one college student subjects, 39 percent solved before any hints were given and 38 percent solved with hints. Those in the group who solved with hints, generally did so almost immediately after the hints were given—an average of forty-two seconds from the last hint to solution. The solution appeared suddenly and in complete form and many subjects were not consciously aware of hint 1. From this experiment, Maier concluded that direction is needed in problem solving—that subjects need some clue, which may be either externally or internally generated, as to how to re-formulate the problem. Putting the string in motion helped the subjects to reformulate the function of the string as a swing on a pendulum. Apparently, direction can be very subtle and in some cases the problem solver does not realize it has occurred: "When an idea suddenly appears what sets it off may be lost to consciousness" (Maier, 1933, p. 192).

In an even more subtle use of direction, Cofer (1951) used the same two-cord situation but had his subjects memorize lists of words before they were given the problem. Subjects who had memorized lists with words such as rope, swing, and pendulum produced more solutions than subjects who had memorized "neutral" words.

In another variation of the same problem, Battersby, Teuber, and Bender (1953) provided direction by restricting the number of potential solution objects among three groups of subjects. The "restricted" group were told they could only use objects the experimenter put on the table; the objects were added to the table every two minutes for a total of five objects with any one capable of serving as a weight for the pendulum. The "less restricted" group could use any object in the room including the five objects the experimenter was adding at the same rate. Finally, the "un-restricted" group could use any object in the room including the five objects which were already placed upon the table with no attention drawn to them. The average solution times were much faster for the restricted group (2.4 minutes) than for the less restricted (7.5 minutes) or the unre-stricted group (15.2).

Evaluation

The Gestaltists attempted to understand some very complex mental processes—what they called "productive thinking." They enriched the study of thinking by introducing several provocative ideas: the distinction between productive and reproductive thinking, the idea that thinking occurs in stages, and the demonstration of rigidity of problem solving set. Their main tool for understanding such processes was the idea that problem solving involves reorganizing or restructuring the problem situation. Most critics point out, however, that the theory is much too vague to be tested directly in experiments. More recently, cognitive psychologists have been partially successful in clarifying some of the ideas of the Gestaltists and their work will be discussed in Chapter 6 on information processing.

Suggested Readings

Johnson, D. M. *A systematic introduction to the psychology of thinking.* New York: Harper & Row, 1972. Chapters 4, 5, and 7 survey the Gestalt approach.

Katona, G. *Organizing and memorizing.* New York: Columbia University Press, 1940. This monograph describes Katona's experiments on learning to solve matchstick and card problems.

Kohler, W. *The mentality of apes.* New York: Harcourt, 1925. Kohler's famous study of problem solving and insight in apes.

Luchins, A. S., & Luchins, E. H. *Rigidity of behavior: A variational approach to Einstellung.* Eugene, Oregon: University of Oregon Press, 1959. Discusses rigidity in problem solving.

Polya, G. *How to solve it.* Garden City, N.Y.: Doubleday, 1957. A mathematician explains "how to" solve problems.

Wason, P.C., & Johnson-Laird, P.N. *Thinking and reasoning.* Baltimore: Penguin, 1968. Articles by Duncker, by Maier, by Luchins & Luchins, and by Adamson provide an excellent collection of basic Gestalt research and theory in problem solving.

Wertheimer, M. *Productive thinking.* New York: Harper & Row, 1959. A Gestalt view of problem solving and how to teach it.

4

Meaning: Thinking as Assimilation to Schema

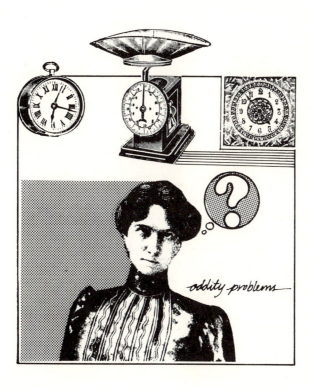

oddity problems

Introduction

Suppose you were solving "oddity problems" in which your job was to circle the word that does not belong. Try this problem:

SKYSCRAPER   CATHEDRAL   TEMPLE   PRAYER

If you circled PRAYER, your response is consistent with the results that have generally been obtained in experiments with this kind of problem (Judson & Cofer, 1956). Now try the following problem:

CATHEDRAL   PRAYER   TEMPLE   SKYSCRAPER

If you circled SKYSCRAPER, your response is also consistent with Judson & Cofer's (1956) results.

In fact, these researchers found that in many ambiguous oddity problems like these, the order of presentation of the words was very important. The first problem, for example, evoked the concept of "building" while the second evoked the idea of "religion." One explanation of this shift is that problem solving requires assimilation of the problem into the past experience of the subject; that is, the subject must find what part of his or her past experience will help in the interpretation of the problem.

Let's try another example. Read the story in Box 4-1. What do you think it means? Bransford and Johnson (1972) gave a comprehension test on this paragraph to a group of subjects and found they performed rather poorly. But what if I tell you the title of the story is "Washing Clothes"? Now the paragraph makes a lot more sense. The title seems to help the readers to figure out how the words relate to their past experiences and what set of past experiences they should use to interpret the story.

BOX 4-1   AN UNTITLED STORY

The procedure is actually quite simple. First you arrange things into different groups depending on their makeup. Of course, one pile may be sufficient depending on how much there is to do. If you have to go somewhere else due to lack of facilities that is the next step, otherwise you are pretty well set. It is important not to overdo any particular endeavor. That is, it is better to do too few things at once than too many. In the short run this may not seem important, but complications from doing too many can easily arise. A mistake can be expensive as well. The manipulation of the appropriate mechanisms should be self-explanatory, and we need not dwell on it here. At first the whole procedure will seem complicated. Soon, however, it will become just another facet of life. It is difficult to foresee any end to the necessity for this task in the immediate future, but then one can never tell.

From Bransford and Johnson (1972)

This chapter will focus on the issue of how we interpret and relate a problem situation to a particular aspect of our individual past experience.

Meaning Theory Definition of Thinking

You will remember from Chapter 3 that the Gestalt psychologists view thinking as restructuring or relating the elements of a problem in a new way. According to Duncker, this process often involves what he called finding the *function* of problem solving elements and what Maier reported as the importance of *direction* in restructuring. Many of these Gestalt ideas are closely tied to a slightly different view of thinking which we call here *meaning theory*. The Gestalt view of thinking involves finding how problem elements relate to one another, i.e., internal relations among elements; the meaning view of thinking involves finding how the present problem relates to those concepts and ideas that already exist in a problem solver's memory, i.e., external relations between elements and schemata. The problem must be assimilated or incorporated into the thinker's own experience and must be translated into familiar terms. According to this view, thinking is mainly a process of figuring out which schema or set of past experiences the new problem situation should be related to and then interpreting and restructuring the new situation in accord with the particular schema that is selected. When a problem situation is assimilated to schemata that are not useful, the result is what the Gestalt psychologists call the "functional fixedness" we discussed in Chapter 3.

Obviously, the meaning theory adds a new element to the Gestalt interpretation—the idea, albeit vague, of schemata and of assimilation.

Bartlett (1932, p. 201) popularized the concept of the schema and attempted to define it as follows:

> Schema refers to an active organization of past reactions which must always be supposed to be operating in any well-adapted organic response.

Bartlett expressed the idea of assimilation as a search for the appropriate "setting" or "schema" in past experience:

> Whenever such settings are found, facts of 'meaning' emerge . . . all the cognitive processes, from perceiving to thinking, are ways in which some fundamental 'effort after meaning' seeks expression. Speaking very broadly, such effort is simply the attempt to connect something that is given with something other than itself (page 227).

Two Kinds of Cognitive Structure

More recently, the concept of assimilation to schema has been expressed as "assimilation to cognitive structure" (Ausubel, 1968). Although there are various ways to define "schema" and "cognitive structure," a lack of precise operational definitions for any of them suggests that it is not useful to detail the differences at this time. A major contribution of the meaning theory, however, is a distinction between two types of cognitive structure—two types of knowledge in a problem solver's memory:

> *meaningful* (Ausubel, 1968), or *propositional* (Greeno, 1973) knowledge, which is made up of concepts from general experience such as, "Collies are dogs."

> *rote* (Ausubel, 1968) or *algorithmic* (Greeno, 1973) knowledge, which is made up of mechanical formulas or rules for how to operate on concepts, such as $a + b - 2c$.

Problem solving information may be assimilated to different types of schemata and thus result in different types of problem solving performances. For example, with a story like that in Box 4-1, Bransford and Johnson (1972) found that giving their subjects the title *before* reading greatly increased performance on a comprehension test but giving the title *after* reading had little effect. Knowing the title in advance apparently informed the subjects as to how to assimilate the material and hence allowed an encoding that was useful for later problem solving.

In a study on solving binomial probability problems, Mayer and Greeno (1972) varied the sequencing of instruction in the following manner: Group 1, the Concepts Group, began by learning about general concepts such as "trial," "success," and "probability of success" in terms of their past experience with batting averages or the probability of rain, and gradually learned to put the concepts together into a formula, while Group 2, the Formula Group, began with the formula and gradually learned how the component concepts figured in calculating with it. Although both groups received the same general information—albeit in different ordering and emphasis—and the same examples, they showed completely different patterns of performance on a subsequent problem solving test. The Formula Group performed best on solving problems that were very much like those in the instruction booklet (near transfer), but very poorly on questions about the formula and on problems they should have recognized as impossible to solve (far transfer); the Concepts Group showed the reverse pattern. These results were taken as evidence that the two instructional methods produced "structurally different learning outcomes"—one, the Formula Group, which supported good near transfer and the other, the Concepts Group, good far transfer. Mayer and Greeno (1972) discussed these findings using the idea that the two groups had assimilated the problem solving concepts to different schemata: ". . . new learning involves development of cognitive structure that results from relating new ideas and accommodating existing structures. According to this idea about learning, different instructional procedures could activate different aspects of existing cognitive structure. And since the outcome of learning is jointly determined by the new material and the structure to which it is assimilated, the use of different procedures could lead to the development of markedly different structures during the learning of the same new concept." Apparently, the Formula Group assimilated the new information to a narrow range of past experience with computation and formulas (algorithmic) while the Concepts Group connected the new information to more general experience with probability situations.

In a related study, Mayer (1975) taught a simple computer programming language to subjects using a standard ten-page text. Some of the subjects were introduced to a concrete model of the computer expressed in familiar terms (the memory was a scoreboard, the program was a shopping list with a pointer arrow, input was a ticket window and output was a telephone message pad) prior to learning and were allowed to use this model during learning; other subjects were introduced to the same model *after* they had received the instruction. On a subsequent transfer test, the After group was better at writing simple programs like those taught in the booklet, but the Before group was better at tasks that had not been specifically taught, such as interpreting what a program would do or writing complex "looping" programs. Apparently, the model served as a meaningful cognitive structure which allowed the subjects to relate new information to other knowledge they already had in memory; this broader learning outcome produced better transfer performance.

Concretizing

As the previous studies suggest, another contribution of the meaning theory is the idea that representing the problem in a concrete way may result in a different method of solution than when it is expressed in abstract words. For example, Box 3-6 gave an example of a method used by Dienes to make the quadratic formula concrete. The supposed advantage of concretizing a difficult abstract problem is that it enables the problem solver to represent it in familiar terms—concretizing provides a quick route to a meaningful cognitive structure.

Brownell and Moser (1949) investigated the effects of making arithmetic problems "meaningful" to third-grade children. One group of several hundred children was taught a procedure for subtraction by using concrete objects like bundles of sticks with the subtraction rules of "borrowing" and grouping by tens shown in terms of rearranging the sticks; another group was taught in "purely mechanical rote fashion" by being given the rules verbally at the outset of learning with no further explanation. Although both groups were taught to perform equally well, the "meaningful" group—the children that had learned with the stick bundles—performed much better on later tests with different problems (Box 4-2).

Using results obtained from similar earlier research, Brownell (1935) developed what he called a "meaning theory" of arithmetic learning based on the idea that students must understand how problem solving rules relate to their past experiences and not simply memorize responses for quick computations. "If one is to be successful in quantitative thinking, one needs a fund of meanings, not a myriad of automatic responses" (p. 10). "Drill is recommended when ideas and processes already understood are to be practiced to increase proficiency" (p. 19). Brownell's view of problem solving was based on "full recognition of the value of children's experiences" and aimed at making "arithmetic less a challenge to the pupil's memory and more a challenge to his intelligence" (p. 31). Unfortunately, an understanding of what is "meaningful" problem solving and how to produce it are still not well known, and most mathematics teachers probably must rely on a set of intuitions about quantitative thinking that involves both the importance of "meaning"—however defined—and "computation."

Another attempt to foster better problem solving performance by concretizing a problem situation was reported by Luchins and Luchins (1950). They made the jar problems discussed in Chapter 3 (Box 3-13) concrete by supplying their subjects with cups and water. When sixth-graders were given these problems, all but two of them calculated the solution on paper and pencil first before they used the cups, and 68 per-

BOX 4–2   HOW TO MAKE ARITHMETIC MEANINGFUL

Standard Method (Mechanical)

```
  65      I can't take 8 from 5 so I think of 5 as 15.
- 28      8 from 15 is 7, and I write 7.
          Since I thought of 5 as 15, I must think of 6 as 5.
          2 from 5 is 3, and I write 3.
```

Meaningful Method

65 = (bundles) (bundles) (bundles) (bundles) (bundles) (bundles) /////

65 = (bundles) (bundles) (bundles) (bundles) (bundles) ////////// /////

28 = (bundles) (bundles) // // // //

65 – 28 = (bundles) (bundles) (bundles) //////

```
  65      I can't take 8 from 5, so I borrow a ten from the 6 tens.
- 28      I cross out the 6 and write a little "5" to show that I borrowed a ten.
          I write a little "1" in front of the 5 to show that I now have 15 instead of 5.
          Then I subtract.
```

Weaver and Suydam (1972) point out that in the meaningful instruction for this subtraction problem, the "teachers led pupils to understand the procedures by: (1) using actual objects (e.g., bundles of sticks) and drawings if necessary, (2) writing the example in expanded notation, (3) writing the 'crutch' digit, (4) delaying the learning of the verbal pattern until they understood what it means."

Adapted from Brownell and Moser (1949)

cent gave einstellung solutions on the first two critical problems. Of the two who did not choose to use paper and pencil, a much lower einstellung effect was found, thus suggesting some aid due to making the task concrete. However, when the sixth-graders were not allowed to use paper and pencil, many were not able to solve the problems using only the concrete objects. When college students were given the same problem with concrete objects, 60 percent showed the einstellung effect on the first two critical problems if they were allowed to use paper and pencil and 55 percent if they were not. Apparently, concretizing the situation slightly reduced but did not eliminate the einstellung effect or mechanization of thought in this case. One reason for the difficulty in eliminating the einstellung effect, according to Luchins and Luchins, was that the subjects carried over school-learned attitudes toward problem solving that counteracted the experimental manipulations.

Activity

There has been much interest in the idea that when students discover for themselves how to solve a problem, they learn something different than when they are simply given the solution. One explanation for this supposed difference is that when people actively work at solving problems they are trying to fit them into their own meaningful cognitive structures, but when they are given the solution rules they relate them to a much narrower set of past experiences with rote-learned cognitive structures. Although active discovery learning is generally believed to result in better transfer and retention, there has been little experimental research to confirm it. As Wittrock (1966, p. 33) points out, "Many strong claims for learning by discovery are made in educational psychology. But almost none of these claims has been empirically substantiated or even clearly tested in an experiment."

Gagné and Smith (1962) investigated the role of active participation on the part of the problem solver in solving the disc problem (Ewert & Lambert, 1932) or what Ernst and Newell (1969) called the tower of Hanoi problem. This problem, shown in Box 4-3, is as follows: given three pegs with a number of discs on peg 1 arranged in order of size with the smallest on top, move the discs from peg 1 to peg 3 in the least number of moves, moving them one at a time and never putting a larger disc on top of a smaller one.

The subjects solved this problem using 2, 3, 4, and 5 discs in order under the following conditions: (1) Group V-SS, in which the subjects were instructed to state the reason for each move and to think of a general principle involved, (2) Group V, which received only the instruction to verbalize, (3) Group SS, which received only the instruction to think of a general principle, and (4) Group No, which received none of these instructions. All the subjects eventually found the solutions to all four problems with Group SS and Group No taking less time but making more moves. However, on a transfer problem using 6 discs in which no verbalizations were required, the subjects who had verbalized during the previous four problems performed significantly better than the nonverbalization subjects. The effect of the instruction to think of a general principle was not significant. (See Box 4-3.) Apparently, the active verbalizations given for each move provoked subjects to think more about the basic rule involved in the problem, so that they were better able to transfer to a new situation.

In another study, Gagné and Brown (1961) allowed subjects to solve series sum problems such as, "What is the sum and formula for the sum of $1 + 3 + 5 + 7 + 9 \ldots$?" Some of the subjects (Guided Discovery Group) were allowed to solve a set of problems with the help of some hints while others were given the same examples but were provided with the

BOX 4-3   THE DISC PROBLEM

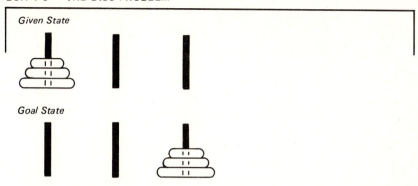

Given State

Goal State

Allowable Moves
Move only one disc at a time; take only the top disc on a peg; never place a larger disc on top of a smaller one.

Performance on 6-Disc Problem

	Groups			
	V-SS	V	SS	No
Mean Excess Moves	7.9	9.3	48.1	61.7
Mean Time to Solution (min.)	4.2	3.8	10.1	10.0

Based on Gagné and Smith (1962)

rules and answers. Although the Guided Discovery Group took longer to learn, they performed much faster and made many fewer errors on subsequent transfer tasks that involved similar but different series sum problems.

Similar results were obtained by Roughead and Scandura (1968) who gave some subjects, the Rule-Discovery Group, three series sum examples *with* rules, followed by three examples to be solved using the same rule. Other subjects, the Discovery-Rule Group, received the same problems but in reversed order; that is, this group had to make up their own rules for the first three problems and were then given the rule with the second three problems. Although the Discovery-Rule Group had more trouble with the original problems, it outperformed the Rule-Discovery Group on a transfer task. The results obtained by Gagné and Brown and Roughead and Scandura seem to show that some activity on the part of the problem solver results in a broader learning. However, it should be noted that activity per se does not guarantee this productive problem solving; for example, a learner who fails to solve a problem by discovery will have nothing to add to memory no matter how actively he or she has been thinking.

Imagery

Another way a person can relate a problem situation to past experience is to form an image. DeSoto, London, and Handel (1965), for example, have suggested that subjects solve linear ordering syllogisms by imagery. A subject who is told that "A is better than B" forms an image of A above B, and if he or she is then told "A is worse than C," puts C above A on the image. When asked, "Is B better than C?" the subject can refer to this image, and respond "No." Further refinements (Huttenlocher, 1968) and objections (Clark, 1969) to this "spacial paralogic" theory of syllogistic reasoning are discussed in Chapter 7.

Paige and Simon (1966) investigated whether the kind of visual representations used to solve mathematical problems influenced perfor-

---

BOX 4-4   ALGEBRA STORY PROBLEMS

The Problem
A board was sawed into two pieces. One piece was two-thirds as long as the whole board and was exceeded in length by the second piece by four feet. How long was the board before it was cut?

The Diagrams
Subjects who failed to recognize the contradictions tended to draw unintegrated diagrams such as,

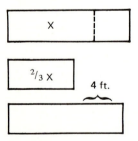

Subjects who recognized the contradictions tended to draw integrated diagrams such as,

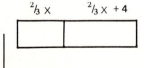

From Paige and Simon (1966)

mance. They gave a group of tenth-graders a series of algebra story problems that included several contradictions and ambiguities like the one in Box 4-4. In addition, they asked the subjects to draw diagrams representing the information in the problem. The students who solved the problem correctly (or recognized the contradictions) were more likely to produce integrated diagrams. Nonsolvers tended to produce a series of diagrams, each representing a translation of a sentence in the story problem, or to change the information in the story into a diagram that "made sense" but which was different from what was presented.

These results suggest that translation of problem information to a visual representation may involve a sort of assimilation, and that integrated visual diagrams may be useful tools in certain types of problem solving.

Problem Representation

The meaning theory suggests that subtle differences in the way a problem is presented could have vastly different effects on how a subject assimilates the problem and thus on problem solving performance. For example, consider the problem shown in Box 4-5 based on a similar example by Kohler (1969). The problem is to determine the length of line *l*

BOX 4–5   THE CIRCLE PROBLEM

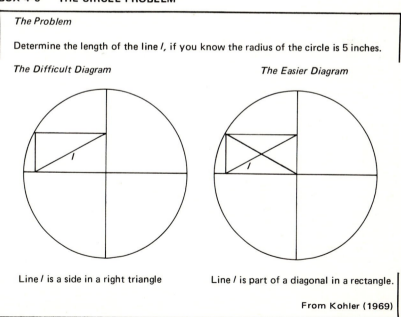

The Problem

Determine the length of the line *l*, if you know the radius of the circle is 5 inches.

The Difficult Diagram   *The Easier Diagram*

Line *l* is a side in a right triangle   Line *l* is part of a diagonal in a rectangle.

From Kohler (1969)

in the circle. The figure on the left half of the box generally encourages subjects to work on manipulating the triangle—and often makes the problem quite hard to solve. However, if instead the problem is represented as trying to find an equivalent for line *l,* as in the figure on the right of Box 4-5, it becomes much easier. In the latter case the subjects work on manipulating the rectangle which includes a radius. Kohler's (1969) example suggests that apparently minor differences in representation can influence how a problem is assimilated, in this case, as a problem about a triangle or as a problem about a rectangle.

Consider another example, this time an algebra story problem: "Two train stations are fifty miles apart. At 2 P.M. one Saturday afternoon two trains start towards each other, one from each station. Just as the trains pull out of the stations, a bird springs into the air in front of the first train and flies ahead to the front of the second train. When the bird reaches the second train it turns back and flies toward the first train. The bird continues to do this until the trains meet. If both trains travel at the rate of twenty-five miles per hour and the bird flies at one hundred miles per hour, how many miles will the bird have flown before the trains meet?" As Posner (1973) points out, if subjects interpret this problem in terms of the bird's flight pattern, the computations to determine the distance on each hop between the trains can become very difficult. However, if the problem asks instead, ". . . how many hours will have elapsed, and how many miles will the bird have flown before the trains meet?" then the

BOX 4-6   THE HORSE PROBLEM

Representation 1
A man bought a horse for $60 and sold it for $70. Then he bought it back again for $80 and sold it for $90. How much did he make in the horse business?
a. lost $10
b. broke even
c. made $10
d. made $20
e. made $30

Representation 2
A man bought a white horse for $60 and sold it for $70. Then he bought a black horse for $80 and sold it for $90. How much money did he make in the horse business?
a. lost $10
b. broke even
c. made $10
d. made $20
e. made $30

Adapted from Maier and Burke (1967)

problem will more likely be interpreted as determining the elapsed time; since the bird travels at one hundred miles per hour, it can easily be determined that the bird flew one hundred miles. Again, a very minor change in representation can influence whether subjects assimilate the problem to the bird's path or to elasped time.

Maier and Burke (1967) investigated different ways of representing story problems and found that minor changes in wording had important effects. As an example, look at the horse problem in Box 4-6. Subjects in Maier and Burke's experiment performed quite poorly on this problem when they were given the first representation, getting the correct answer ($20) less than 40 percent of the time. However, when the problem was changed as shown in the bottom half of Box 4-6 and given to a new group of subjects, the solution rate was 100 percent. Apparently, the first representation encouraged the subjects to think about *one* horse; whereas, the second representation encouraged them to interpret the problem as two separate and independent transactions.

These examples suggest that seemingly minor factors influence how a subject represents a problem and thus affect problem solving.

Evaluation

The meaning theory is closely related to Gestalt theory, and is often not explicitly separated from it. While Gestalt theory emphasizes internal structure—how problem solving elements relate to one another—meaning theory contends that this restructuring process is guided by an additional process—finding external relations between the present problem solving elements and other concepts in the thinker's memory. Unfortunately, the meaning theory suffers from several of the main defects of Gestalt theory, including lack of clarity and lack of experimental testability. Developments in the field of human verbal learning have some promise of "spilling over" into this area; for example, Ausubel's concept of "advance organizer" suggests that presenting learners with outlines or previews before learning will guide and aid them in the assimilation process. However, the task facing supporters of the meaning theory of thinking at present is to distinguish it clearly from Gestalt theory and express it in ways that invite testability.

Suggested Readings

Ausubel, D. P. *Educational psychology: A cognitive view.* New York: Holt, Rinehart & Winston, 1968. Chapters 2, 3, 14, 15, and 16 provide a statement of the assimilation-to-schema idea and its relationship to problem solving.

Bartlett, F. C. *Remembering.* London: Cambridge University Press, 1932. Bartlett's experiments and the theory of assimilation to schema.

5

Question Answering: Thinking as a Search of Semantic Memory

abstraction of meaning

Preview of Chapter 5

Introduction

Question Answering Task

How do people understand and retrieve the answers to questions? Look at the following question and then try to describe how you went about answering it.

> Query: In the house you lived in three houses ago, how many windows were there on the north side?

Rumelhart, Lindsay, and Norman (1972) found that most people are able to solve this problem; they do so by first visualizing their present dwellings, then moving back in time to visualize their previous homes, determining the north wall, and counting the windows.

Although this example may tap a trivial piece of information, it does point to the amazing ability we have to use our memories to answer questions. Let's try another one.

> Query: What were you doing on Monday afternoon of the third week of September two years ago?

A hypothetical set of responses given by Lindsay and Norman (1972) is shown in Box 5-1. How does this protocol mesh with yours? The interesting aspect of such examples is that human beings are capable of answering a wide variety of complex questions and that we do so, not always by direct recall, but by working on a series of subquestions that bring us progressively closer to the answer. In observing the process of question answering, Lindsay and Norman were struck by the observation that their subjects engaged in productive thinking, and thus it was possible to discuss "retrieval as problem solving." The problem for psychologists, of course, is to describe how this process of answering questions occurs.

Let's try one last question.

Query: Draw a diagram of the floor plan of your place of residence. In a typical study conducted by Kovarsky and Eisenstadt (cited by Anderson & Bower, 1973), the errors made by graduate students who had occupied the same apartments for years did not occur randomly but were systematic. A common error was for the students to include structural features which were part of most apartments but not of their own particular dwelling. One possible conclusion that may be reached is that in recall we tend to rely primarily on our general experiences or knowledge rather than entirely on specifics. Were there any such errors in your diagram?

Semantic Memory Theory
Definition of Thinking

The previous chapter relied heavily on the idea that a person's understanding of a problem depends on how the problem situation is represented in the memory of the individual. This chapter follows the same memory representation approach but emphasizes how the memory representation is used to answer questions. Thus, while both chapters deal with the structure of knowledge in memory, the focus of Chapter 4 is on how external information is assimilated to memory, and of Chapter 5 on how it is retrieved or recalled. The idea of schematic memory representation is central to both chapters, but where Chapter 4 emphasizes thinking as assimilation to schemata, this chapter emphasizes thinking as a search and retrieval from the store of meaningful knowledge we call semantic memory.

Since problem solving depends heavily on how knowledge is organized in memory, the nature of memory representation is a particularly important issue. When we ask someone a question on a subject of which he or she has knowledge, there are several aspects of the recall task that we as psychologists may be interested in: How is the information represented in the memory, and how is it retrieved? The next section of this chapter will deal primarily with how people store and use information they have recently acquired while the following section on semantic memory will investigate how they store and use their existing general knowledge.

Abstraction of Meaning from Text

Bartlett's Experiment

Bartlett (1932) was one of the first psychologists to address the question of what processes people use to remember. As an example, consider "The War of the Ghosts" in the first part of Box 5-2. Read it over once, at your normal pace, then put the text away and try to reproduce on paper, from memory, what you have just read.

This example comes from the pioneering work of Bartlett and is summarized in his delightful little monograph, *Remembering* (1932). In his experiments, Bartlett used a version of the child's game of "telephone," in which a message is passed along a chain of people, changing a bit in each retelling. Bartlett called his procedure the "method of serial reproduction," and employed it as follows: he presented folk stories (or pictures) from unfamiliar cultures to British college students, asking Subject #1 to read the story, put it aside, reproduce it from memory, and to pass this reproduction on to Subject #2, who would in turn read the reproduced version, put it aside, reproduce his own version and pass it on to Subject #3, and so on.

Bartlett noticed that something quite curious happened in these studies. The stories (and pictures) changed as they were passed along but they changed in systematic ways. The version of the story reproduced by Subject #10, given in Box 5-2, is one of many examples on which Bartlett based the following observations:

Leveling or *flattening.* Most of the details such as proper names (Egulac, Kalama), titles (The War of the Ghosts), and the individual writing style tended to fall out of the passage. Bartlett attributed this loss to the fact that British college students had no prior experience with folk

BOX 5-2   THREE VERSIONS OF *THE WAR OF THE GHOSTS*

Original Version

The War of the Ghosts

   One night two young men from Egulac went down to the river to hunt seals, and while they were there it became foggy and calm. Then they heard war-cries, and they thought: "Maybe this is a war-party." They escaped to the shore, and hid behind a log. Now canoes came up, and they heard the noise of paddles, and saw one canoe coming up to them. There were five men in the canoe, and they said:
   "What do you think? We wish to take you along. We are going up the river to make war on the people."
   One of the young men said: "I have no arrows."
   "Arrows are in the canoe," they said.
   "I will not go along. I might be killed. My relatives do not know where I have gone. But you," he said, turning to the other, "may go with them."
   So one of the young men went, but the other returned home.
   And the warriors went on up the river to a town on the other side of Kalama. The people came down to the water, and they began to fight, and many were killed. But presently the young man heard one of the warriors say: "Quick, let us go home: that Indian has been hit." Now he thought: "Oh, they are ghosts." He did not feel sick, but they said he had been shot.
   So the canoes went back to Egulac, and the young man went ashore to his house, and made a fire. And he told everybody and said: "Behold I accompanied the ghosts, and we went to fight. Many of our fellows were killed, and many of those who attacked us were killed. They said I was hit, and I did not feel sick."
   He told it all, and then he became quiet. When the sun rose he fell down. Something black came out of his mouth. His face became contorted. The people jumped up and cried.
   He was dead.

Version Reproduced by First Subject

The War of the Ghosts

   There were two young Indians who lived in Egulac, and they went down to the sea to hunt for seals. And where they were hunting it was very foggy and very calm. In a little while they heard cries, and they came out of the water and went to hide behind a log. Then they heard the sound of paddles, and they saw five canoes. One

tales native to other cultures or to spirits and ghosts; thus, since learning in this case required assimilating new material to existing concepts, the students were at a loss. According to Bartlett (1932, p. 172): "Without some general setting or label as we have repeatedly seen, no material can be assimilated or remembered."

Sharpening. A few details may be retained and even exaggerated. Apparently subjects can store a schema plus a few selected details.

Rationalization. Passages tended to become more compact, more coherent, and more consistent with the readers' expectations. All references to spirits and ghosts faded away and the story became one of a simple fishing trip. Bartlett called this process *rationalization* and arcanoe came toward them, and there were five men within, who cried to the two Indians, and said: "Come with us up this river, and make war on the people there."

But one of the Indians replied: "We have no arrows."

"There are arrows in the canoe."

"But I might be killed, and my people have need of me. You have no parents," he said to the other, "you can go with them if you wish it so; I shall stay here."

So one of the Indians went, but the other stayed behind and went home. And the canoes went on up the river to the other side of Kalama, and fought the people there. Many of the people were killed, and many of those from the canoes also.

Then one of the warriors called to the young Indian and said: "Go back to the canoe, for you are wounded by an arrow." But the Indian wondered, for he felt not sick.

And when many had fallen on either side they went back to the canoes, and down the river again, and so the young Indian came back to Egulac.

Then he told them how there had been a battle, and how many fell and how the warriors had said he was wounded, and yet he felt not sick. So he told them all the tale, and he became weak. It was near daybreak when he became weak; and when the sun rose he fell down. And he gave a cry, and as he opened his mouth a black thing rushed from it. Then they ran to pick him up, wondering. But when they spoke he answered not.

He was dead.

Version Reproduced by the Tenth Subject

The War of the Ghosts

Two Indians were out fishing for seals in the Bay of Manpapan, when along came five other Indians in a war-canoe. They were going fighting.

"Come with us," said the five to the two, "and fight."

"I cannot come," was the answer of the one, "for I have an old mother at home who is dependent upon me." The other also said he could not come, because he had no arms. "That is no difficulty," the others replied, "for we have plenty in the canoe with us"; so he got into the canoe and went with them.

In a fight soon afterwards this Indian received a mortal wound. Finding that his hour was coming, he cried out that he was about to die. "Nonsense," said one of the others, "you will not die." But he did.

From Bartlett (1932)

gued that the reader was actively engaged in "an effort after meaning"—an attempt to make the story fit in with the individual's expectations. Since mystical concepts are not a major factor in Western culture, the mystical aspects of the story were not well remembered; instead, many subjects tended to tack on a "moral" which was a widely accepted practice in other stories they were familiar with.

Although Bartlett's work lay dormant for many years as the behaviorist movement swept across the study of psychology in the United States, he is now recognized as the major forerunner of modern cognitive psychology because he suggested two fundamental ideas about human mental processes:

Learning and memory. The act of comprehending new material requires "an effort after meaning": in reading a complex text, or acquiring any new information, humans must assimilate the new material to existing concepts or schemata. The outcome of learning (i.e., what is stored in memory) does not duplicate exactly what was presented, but rather depends on both what was presented and the schema to which it is assimilated. People change the new information to fit their existing concepts, and in the process, details fall out and the knowledge becomes more coherent to the individual.

Remembering and memory. The act of remembering requires an active "process of construction"; during recall, an existing schema is used to generate or construct details which are consistent with it. Memory is not detailed, but rather is schematic, that is, based on general impressions. Although recall produces specific details which seem to be correct, many of them are, in fact, wrong.

Carmichael, Hogan, and Walter (1932) provided complementary evidence for Bartlett's theory by using pictorial figures and providing subjects with a method for interpreting them. They showed their subjects a series of twelve figures like those in Box 5-3 and gave each one a name. Before presenting Figure 1, for example, the experimenter might say, "This figure resembles eyeglasses," or "This figure resembles a dumbbell." For Figure 4, the experimenter might suggest "a gun" or "a broom." When the subjects were asked to reproduce these figures from memory, their drawings tended to be influenced by the labels they had been given during the presentation. These results were consistent with Bartlett's idea that memory for figures or passages involves assimilation to schemata—in this case, the labels may have served as schemata.

Bartlett's work was tantalizing because it demonstrated that memory is "schematic"—that both learning and remembering are based on general schemata rather than specifics. However, Bartlett's work did not yield clear or powerful predictions; for example, it could not predict which details would "fall out" of a passage or in what ways a subject would make a passage more coherent. In a sense, the work of modern cognitive psychologists has been to clarify the ideas of Bartlett and the Gestalt psychologists (discussed in Chapter 3) and to test and refine their theories. The basic method that has been used for this is known as the "recall method" in which subjects are presented with complex verbal material and are then asked questions about it.

Memory structure of sentences

The modern rebirth of interest in psycholinguistics, and especially in the study of how sentences are comprehended and stored, was touched

BOX 5-3 EFFECTS OF VERBAL LABELS ON MEMORY FOR AMBIGUOUS FIGURES

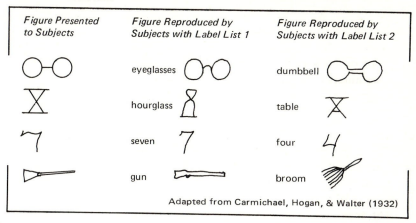

Figure Presented to Subjects	Figure Reproduced by Subjects with Label List 1	Figure Reproduced by Subjects with Label List 2
○—○	eyeglasses ○○	dumbbell ○—○
X	hourglass	table X
7	seven 7	four 4
(broom)	gun	broom

Adapted from Carmichael, Hogan, & Walter (1932)

off by Chomsky's "generative" theory of language (1957, 1959, 1965, 1968). Although Chomsky's theory is very complex, and although it is a linguistic theory rather than a tested psychological theory, it includes three basic ideas that have attracted psychologists:

the distinction between surface structure and deep structure—the surface structure of a sentence is the way it is written or spoken; its deep structure is the way it is represented in memory. For example, the sentence "The ball was hit by John" may be stored in deep structure as "John hit ball." Thinking, apparently, is based on the deep structure of language.

transformation rules—language consists of a set of rules for converting surface structure into deep structure (comprehension) and deep structure into surface structure (recall and communication).

universal grammar—some general characteristics are shared by all language users.

Chomsky's cognitive approach to language came as an alternative to the idea B. F. Skinner expressed in his book, *Verbal Behavior* (1957), that language is a learned behavior subject to the laws of conditioning. By introducing the idea of deep structure and transformation rules, Chomsky suggested that memory structure—how sentences are stored and used—is not necessarily the same as surface structure. Unfortunately, Chomsky's theory was not based on psychological research, but rather on logical arguments. For example, consider the sentence: They are eating apples. According to Chomsky, the meaning of this sentence depends on how one transforms it to deep structure; if one assumes that "they" refers to people, the deep structure is quite different than if "they" refers to the apples. (The author spotted a similar example hanging in a laundromat: Not responsible for clothes you may have stolen.) The importance of such examples is that they show the same surface structure may lead to different deep structures; apparently, the study of surface structure or verbal behavior alone may not adequately explain human comprehension of language.

Another important distinction with respect to sentences is between:

syntax—the order of language units, as specified by grammatical rules; and

semantics—the meaning or referents of a sentence.

Considerable research has been done on the importance of both syntax and semantics in comprehending and recalling sentences.

For example, Miller and Selfridge (1950) investigated the role of syntax in memory for sentences by varying the "approximation to English" sentences for strings of words. Word strings were constructed based on a random sampling of words (Zero-Order Approximation), a random sampling of words from a typical passage (First-Order), an actual text lifted from a typical passage (Text), or by making a Second-, Third-, Fourth-, Fifth-, or Seventh-Order approximation to English. The procedure for developing the Second-Order, for instance, was to ask a subject to complete a sentence starting with a word supplied by the researchers. A second subject in turn was asked to complete a sentence starting with the word that immediately followed the one that had been supplied for the first subject. Then the second subject's first new word was passed on to a third subject, and so on. The first new words produced by each successive subject were put together into a string that was called Second-Order approximation to English; to obtain Third-Order, Miller and Selfridge took the first *two* words given by each subject, and so on. Examples are given in Box 5-4.

Lists of ten, twenty, thirty, or fifty words were constructed using these methods; new subjects were asked to listen to the string and then recall it in order. The results shown in Box 5-4 indicate that as the word strings more closely approximated English, more words were recalled. Miller and Selfridge concluded that in reading normal prose, people use their knowledge of syntax (grammatical rules) as an aid in comprehension and remembering rather than simply storing and recalling each word individually.

There has also been much work on the role of semantics in memory for sentences. For example, Miller (1962) has suggested that comprehending and storing a sentence involves transforming it into a "kernel" sentence (K) plus a mental "footnote" about the syntactic structure. This theory predicts that a sentence such as "The boy hit the ball" would serve as the kernel (along with some footnote) for passive (P) surface structures, such as "The ball was hit by the boy," for interrogative (Q) surface structures, such as "Did the boy hit the ball?" for negative (N) surface structures, such as "The boy did not hit the ball," or for any combination of passive, interrogative, and negative structures.

BOX 5-4   MEMORY FOR WORD STRINGS THAT ARE APPROXIMATIONS TO ENGLISH

Word Strings (10-Word Lists)
0–order approximation: byway consequence handsomely financier flux cavalry swiftness weatherbeaten extent
1–order approximation: abilities with that beside I for waltz you the sewing
2–order approximation: was he went to the newspaper is in deep and
3–order approximation: tall and thin boy is a biped is the beat
4–order approximation: saw the football game will end at midnight on January
5–order approximation: they saw the play Saturday and sat down beside him
7–order approximation: recognize her abilities in music after he scolded him before
Text: the history of California is largely that of a railroad

Percentage of Words Recalled for Different Word Strings

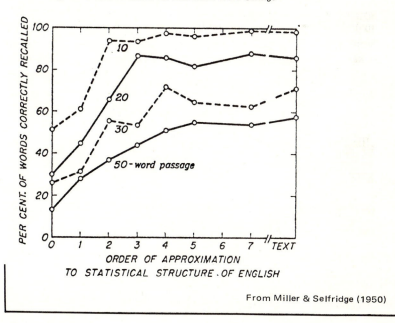

From Miller & Selfridge (1950)

In a promising study, Mehler (1963) presented lists of sentences in kernel form, sentences transformed into passive, interrogative, and negative forms, and all combinations of these. Recall was best for the lists of kernel sentences and worst for the passive-interrogative, interrogative, and passive-interrogative-negative sentences. This result seemed consistent with Miller's and Chomsky's idea that sentences are converted into deeper structure like K sentences. However, when Martin and Roberts (1966) replicated the Mehler study but controlled for sentence length, they obtained the opposite results and concluded that Mehler's findings could be explained by the fact that K sentences were shorter and thus easier to recall.

After reviewing the studies of sentence memory, Adams (1976, p. 355) concluded: "There is no evidence that Miller's hypothesis about sentences, derived from generative theory, is valid . . . Generative theory may have a short theoretical life in psychology because it is not a psychological theory." In other words, although the concept of deep structure has been useful to psychologists, the particular theory that the kernel sentence represents the meaning of a sentence is based on logical or linguistic analysis rather than on psychological study. It is now the task of psychologists through empirical studies to determine exactly how a sentence is represented in memory. Or, to put it another way, the search continues for the "schema" of a sentence.

Memory Structure of Text Passages

Cognitive psychologists have recently been trying to study more carefully Bartlett's idea that subjects *abstract* the general meaning from prose during reading, and *construct* their answers during recall. In an already classic study, Bransford and Franks (1971) read the sentences shown in the first part of Box 5-5 to the subjects and then asked the recognition questions shown in the second part of the box. Take a few minutes now to read the sentence list and then take the recognition test. In the original study the subjects were asked to rate on a 10-point scale how sure they were that the test sentence had been in the original list but you can skip the rating for your test.

In order to make up the sentences given in the top of Box 5-5, Bransford and Franks used four basic "idea sets":

"The scared cat running from the barking dog jumped on the table."
"The old car pulling the trailer climbed the steep hill."
"The tall tree in the front yard shaded the man who was smoking his pipe."

"The girl who lives next door broke the large window on the porch."

Each idea unit was broken down into four single ideas (called ONES), such as:

"The cat was scared."

"The dog was barking."

"The cat was running from the dog."

"The cat jumped on the table."

The ONES could be combined to form TWOS, such as:

"The scared cat jumped on the table."

The ONES could be combined to form THREES, such as:

"The scared cat was running from the barking dog."

Finally, the ONES could be combined to form an entire idea unit, like the examples given above, and called a FOUR.

The subjects heard a long list of sentences consisting of some ONES, TWOS, and THREES but no FOURS from the idea sets, presented in random order.

Now comes the surprise. In your test, the sentences in the second part of Box 5-5 are all "new," so each "old" you checked is a "false recognition"—you thought you had seen it in the original but it was not there. In a related study, Bransford and Franks presented the same kind of study sentences but this test consisted of some sentences that had been in the original list (old), some that had not been in the original list but could be inferred from one of the idea sets (new), and some (called NONCASE) that were based on putting parts of different idea sets together.

The ratings of the subjects for the test sentences are given in Box 5-6. As you can see, they could not tell the difference between sentences which had actually appeared in the original list and those which were simply consistent with an idea set. In fact, they were most confident about having seen FOURS although no FOURS were ever presented. Bransford and Franks concluded that during reading, the subjects abstracted the four general linguistic ideas, and that during recall, they used these general abstract ideas but had no memory of the specific sentences from which they were abstracted.

Further evidence for "abstract" memory of prose was obtained by Sachs (1967). She asked subjects to read a passage about the invention of the telescope like the one shown in Box 5-7; then she presented a test sentence and asked them to tell whether or not it had occurred verbatim in the text. The test sentence was based on a sentence from the text and the test was given immediately after a subject had read the sentence (zero syllables), after the subject had read eighty syllables beyond the sentence, or one hundred sixty syllables beyond the sentence. The test sentence contained either a change in meaning (semantic change), a change in voice (active/passive change), a change in a minor detail that did not alter meaning (formal change), or no change (identical) from the text sentence. For example, the text sentence, "He sent a letter about it to Galileo, the great Italian scientist," was presented in the test in one of the following forms:

Identical: same as above.

Formal change: He sent Galileo, the great Italian scientist, a letter about it.

Active/Passive change: A letter about it was sent to Galileo, the great Italian scientist.

Semantic change: Galileo, the great Italian scientist, sent him a letter about it.

BOX 5-5   THE BRANSFORD AND FRANKS EXPERIMENT: A TYPICAL SET OF SENTENCES

Sentence	*Question*
Acquisition sentences: Read each sentence, count to five, answer the question, go on to the next sentence.	
The girl broke the window on the porch.	Broke what?
The tree in the front yard shaded the man who was smoking his pipe.	Where?
The hill was steep.	What was?
The cat, running from the barking dog, jumped on the table.	From what?
The tree was tall.	Was what?
The old car climbed the hill.	What did?
The cat running from the dog jumped on the table.	Where?
The girl who lives next door broke the window on the porch.	Lives where?
The car pulled the trailer.	Did what?
The scared cat was running from the barking dog.	What was?
The girl lives next door.	Who does?
The tree shaded the man who was smoking his pipe.	What did?
The scared cat jumped on the table.	What did?
The girl who lives next door broke the large window.	Broke what?
The man was smoking his pipe.	Who was?
The old car climbed the steep hill.	The what?
The large window was on the porch.	Where?
The tall tree was in the front yard.	What was?
The car pulling the trailer climbed the steep hill.	Did what?
The cat jumped on the table.	Where?
The tall tree in the front yard shaded the man.	Did what?
The car pulling the trailer climbed the hill.	Which car?
The dog was barking.	Was what?
The window was large.	What was?

STOP—Cover the preceding sentences. Now read each sentence below and decide if it is a sentence from the list given above.

Test set. . . . How many are new?

The car climbed the hill.	(old ___, new___)
The girl who lives next door broke the window.	(old ___, new___)
The old man who was smoking his pipe climbed the steep hill.	(old ___, new ___)
The tree was in the front yard.	(old ___, new ___)
The scared cat, running from the barking dog, jumped on the table.	(old ___, new ___)
The window was on the porch.	(old ___, new ___)
The barking dog jumped on the old car in the front yard.	(old ___, new ___)
The cat was running from the dog.	(old ___, new ___)
The old car pulled the trailer.	(old ___, new ___)
The tall tree in the front yard shaded the old car.	(old ___, new ___)
The tall tree shaded the man who was smoking his pipe.	(old ___, new ___)
The scared cat was running from the dog.	(old ___, new ___)
The old car, pulling the trailer, climbed the hill.	(old ___, new ___)
The girl who lives next door broke the large window on the porch.	(old ___, new ___)
The tall tree shaded the man.	(old ___, new ___)
The cat was running from the barking dog.	(old ___, new ___)
The car was old.	(old ___, new ___)
The girl broke the large window.	(old ___, new ___)
The scared cat ran from the barking dog that jumped on the table.	(old ___, new ___)
The scared cat, running from the dog, jumped on the table.	(old ___, new ___)
The old car pulling the trailer climbed the steep hill.	(old ___, new ___)
The girl broke the large window on the porch.	(old ___, new ___)
The scared cat which broke the window on the porch climbed the tree.	(old ___, new ___)
The tree shaded the man.	(old ___, new ___)
The car climbed the steep hill.	(old ___, new ___)
The girl broke the window.	(old ___, new ___)
The man who lives next door broke the large window on the porch.	(old ___, new ___)
The tall tree in the front yard shaded the man who was smoking his pipe.	(old ___, new ___)
The cat was scared.	(old ___, new ___)

STOP. Count the number of sentences judged "old."
See text for answer.

From Jenkins (1974)

BOX 5-6   THE BRANSFORD AND FRANKS EXPERIMENT: RESULTS

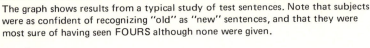

The graph shows results from a typical study of test sentences. Note that subjects were as confident of recognizing "old" as "new" sentences, and that they were most sure of having seen FOURS although none were given.

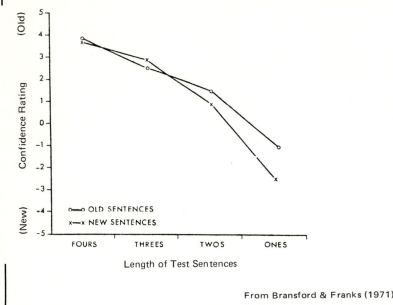

Length of Test Sentences

From Bransford & Franks (1971)

The results of the experiment are given in the lower part of Box 5-7. If the subjects had just read the sentence (zero interpolated syllables), they performed well in saying Yes to the identical sentence and No to each of the changed sentences. However, if the test came after the subject had read eighty or one hundred sixty syllables beyond the target sentence, then performance fell sharply for detecting formal or voice changes but the subjects were still fairly accurate at noticing a change in meaning. In other words, once a sentence from prose had been "digested" by the subject, the subject retained very little information about the original grammatical form of the sentence but did retain the general meaning. Sach's conclusion was that in the course of reading a passage, a subject abstracted the general meaning but not the specific grammatical details.

Paivio (1971) has suggested that subjects may have formed mental images as a way of abstracting meaning of sentences in Sach's study. Since Sachs, and Bransford and Franks used sentences that were relatively concrete, the subjects could have easily formed images that retained the meaning but destroyed the grammatical form of the presented text. In

BOX 5-7   MEMORY FOR THE MEANING OF TEXT

The Passages

Subjects read the following passage and were asked a question about the italicized sentence either immediately after it was presented (0 syllables), 80 syllables later, or 160 syllables later.

There is an interesting story about the telescope. In Holland, a man named Lippershey was an eye-glass maker. One day his children were playing with some lenses. They discovered that things seemed very close if two lenses were about a foot apart. Lippershey began experiments and his "spyglass" attracted much attention. *He sent a letter about it to Galileo, the great Italian scientist.* (0 syllable test here.) Galileo at once realized the importance of the discovery and set out to build an instrument of his own. He used an old organ pipe with one lens curved out and the other curved in. On the first clear night he pointed the glass towards the sky. He was amazed to find the empty dark spaces filled with brightly gleaming stars! (80 syllable test here.) Night after night Galileo climbed to a high tower, sweeping the sky with his telescope. One night he saw Jupiter, and to his great surprise discovered with it three bright stars, two to the east and one to the west. On the next night, however, all were to the west. A few nights later there were four little stars. (160 syllable test here.)

The Results

The proportion of correct response for each type of recognition question is given in the chart below.

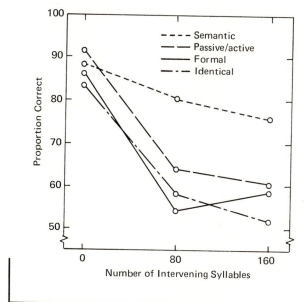

order to test this idea, Begg and Paivio (1969) replicated Sach's study using some passages that tended to evoke vivid images and some that used abstract words that did not tend to evoke imagery. For example, typical sentences were: "The vicious hound chased a wild animal" (concrete), or "The absolute faith aroused an enduring interest" (abstract). For the concrete, high-imagery sentences, Begg and Paivio obtained results similar to Sach's finding: subjects noticed a semantic change more easily than a change in sentence structure; however, for the abstract, low-imagery sentences, the reverse trend was found, with better recognition of lexical changes than semantic changes. Based on such findings, Paivio (1971) developed a "two-process theory of memory"—the idea that knowledge may be stored using imagery codes or verbal codes. Although most of the models of memory described in this chapter assume verbal coding for stored knowledge, Paivio's work has helped to reintroduce the idea that some types of representations may be nonverbal.

These results complement those of Bartlett and help to extend the idea that memory for prose is schematic. However, one important question is whether we can predict in advance what someone will remember about a passage. Johnson (1970) investigated this question by breaking a story down into "idea units" and asking subjects to rate the idea units according to their importance to the story. Then new subjects read the story and were asked to recall it. As predicted, subjects remembered more of the important units, even when the experimenter controlled the study time for each with a slide projector.

Semantic Memory

Tip-of-the-Tongue Phenomena

The previous section investigated recall of newly learned sentences and prose; the present section focuses on recall of one's general knowledge. For example, consider the following dictionary definition and try to think of the word it defines:

"A navigational instrument used in measuring angular distances, especially the altitude of the sun, moon, and the stars at sea."

If the answer does not immediately come to you, try to answer the following questions: What is the first letter of the word? How many syllables does the word have?

If you are ready to give up, the answer that the dictionary gives is: SEXTANT.

Brown and McNeil (1966) gave a series of these problems to subjects in a laboratory setting and found that sometimes the answer came right away, sometimes the subjects had no idea what to say, and in a number of cases subjects were "seized" by a tip-of-the-tongue (TOT) state. In this state the subjects felt that they were on the verge of finding the answer, but had not yet found it; they were in a "mild torment, something like the brink of a sneeze." Brown and McNeil were particularly interested in these cases of TOT, and, in fact, were trying to induce them as a way of studying the structure of human memory and the process of answering questions. The subjects were asked to describe their thought processes aloud (like the introspective methods described in the Overview); in addition, they were asked the two specific questions given above while they were in the TOT state: What is the first letter of the word? How many syllables does it have?

In a typical study, fifty-seven instances of the TOT state were induced and while the subjects "could not for the life of them" state the specific word, they were amazingly accurate at "guessing" the first letter (51 percent correct) and the number of syllables (47 percent correct). Brown and McNeil concluded that in the course of searching one's memory for a piece of information, *generic* recall (or a general memory) may precede the *specific* recall of a word, especially when specific recall is felt to be imminent. (Note the similarity to Duncker's "funneling" view of problem solving we discussed in Chapter 3.)

This type of task, which we could call question answering, provides another important approach to understanding human thinking and problem solving. By emphasizing the role of memory structure, this approach views problem solving as a search of one's meaningful memory. The goal suggested by this view is to develop a theory of how complex information is organized in meaningful fashion in human memory, and what processes are used to retrieve it to answer questions.

Since Brown and McNeil obtained their intriguing results, a number of psychologists have proposed very detailed and precise theories of how human beings organize particular sets of knowledge about the world. These theories have been called models of semantic memory because they try to represent how meaningful, i.e., semantic, knowledge is stored and used. The basic types of models of semantic memory are:

network models, which are based on the idea that memory is made up of elements and the associations among them; this view goes beyond the early associationist ideas (see the Overview) in that (a) the relations may be of many types, (b) the units are "meaningful concepts," and (c) the theories can be tested;

set models, which are based on the idea that memory is made up of features that belong to sets and sets that belong to larger or supersets, and so on.

The basic method used to test these theories is called the reaction time method in which subjects are asked to press a Yes or No button in response to questions about their general knowledge (e.g., Is a collie a dog?). The time to respond is measured in milliseconds (thousandths of a second), and the results are interpreted on the basis of the simple idea that more time means more processes or deeper processes were performed.

Network Models of Semantic Memory

One of the first popular network models was called the *teachable language comprehender* or TLC (Collins & Quillian, 1969; Collins & Quillian, 1972). Although these researchers have revised and amended the specifics of their original model, their goal has been to develop a computer program that simulates how human beings answer factual questions. (The computer simulation approach is discussed more fully in Chapter 6.) According to one version of TLC, the structure of semantic memory is based on:

units—words which represent one thing or subject;
properties—words which represent characteristics of the unit;
pointers—associations of various types among units and properties.

An example of the knowledge a hypothetical adult has about certain animals is given in Box 5-8. In this case, words such as *animal, bird,* and *canary* represent units, whereas word combinations such as *is yellow, has wings, has skin* represent properties, and the arrows represent pointers. According to this hierarchical structure, the properties or characteristics of a unit at any one level apply to things connected by pointers at lower levels. In other words, a bird has wings and so does a canary, but the property of having wings is stored only with the higher unit, bird; it cannot be stored with animals because some animals do not have wings.

According to TLC, the process a hypothetical person uses to respond to the truth or falsity of a statement such as "A canary has skin" is a search process:

1. Find the unit for the target word, *canary.*
2. Check to see if the property, *has skin,* is stored with that unit; if not, follow the pointer to the next higher level on the hierarchy, *bird,* and continue as needed to *animal.*
3. When the pointers lead to a unit that has the target property, respond Yes.

It is a bit more difficult to describe how subjects can figure how to respond No to a sentence such as "A canary has fins," but one idea is that

BOX 5-8 **HYPOTHETICAL ADULT'S KNOWLEDGE ABOUT ANIMALS: COLLINS AND QUILLIAN'S NETWORK HIERARCHY**

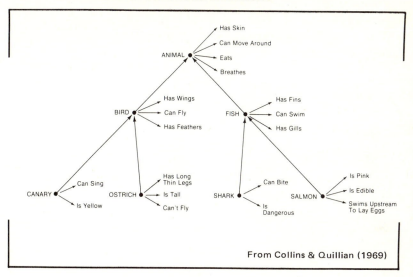

From Collins & Quillian (1969)

subjects terminate their search and give the No answer if they fail to reach the unit with the target property within a certain time period.

While formal models like Collins and Quillian's are elegant and plausible, in order to be useful they must also be testable. Fortunately, this model does offer certain predictions; for example, sentences which require working on just one level of the hierarchy (a canary can sing) should require less processing time than two-level problems (a canary can fly), and a three-level problem (a canary has skin) should take the longest processing time. In order to test these predictions, Collins and Quillian asked their subjects to press a button labeled True or False in response to sentences based on hierarchies such as are shown in Box 5-9. Both true and false statements were presented, but of primary interest was the time it took subjects to respond to various true sentences. You can see that the more levels there were, the longer the response time, and it took a particularly long time to answer False.

These results are clearly consistent with the predictions; however, to the nonpsychologist they may not seem to be very startling. In addition, the Collins and Quillian model is not the only explanation for such findings. For example, Landauer and Meyer (1972) were able to replicate the basic results of Collins and Quillian but they argued that the results could be explained by supposing that it took longer to retrieve information from a large category (e.g., animals) than from a smaller category (e.g., birds).

BOX 5-9   REACTION TIMES FOR ANSWERING QUESTIONS ABOUT ANIMALS

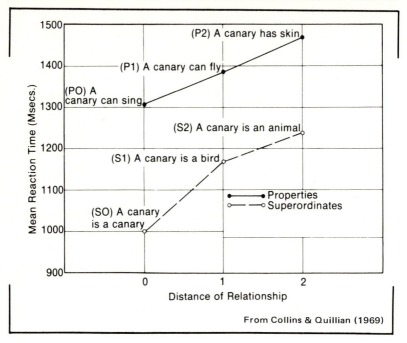

From Collins & Quillian (1969)

In other words, a less complex idea than the hierarchy developed by Collins and Quillian is that the subjects had lists of characteristics for various concepts and that it took more time to answer questions about a long list than a shorter list. One piece of evidence that seems to support the simpler view is that more time is required to answer false to false sentences if they involve a large category (A cliff is an animal) than if they involve a small category (A cliff is a dog).

A second example of a network model of semantic memory has been proposed by Anderson and Bower (1973) in their detailed monograph, *Human Associative Memory*. The HAM (human associative memory) model, like that of Collins and Quillian, can be expressed as a computer program. However, HAM is based on a series of rules for transforming (or "parsing") incoming information into a deeper memory structure like the following:

1. A proposition can be broken down into its context (C) and its fact (F). For example, the proposition "In the park the hippie said the debutante needed a deodorant" can be broken down into

its context (in the park, in the past) and its fact (the hippie saying that the debutante needed a deodorant).

2. The context can be broken down into time (T) and location (L). In this case, the time is "in the past" and the location is "in the park."

3. The fact can be broken down into the subject (S) and the predicate (P). Here the subject is "the hippie" and the predicate is "saying that the debutante needed a deodorant."

4. The predicate in turn can be broken down into relation (R) and object (O). The relation in this example is "saying" and the object is "that the debutante needed a deodorant."

5. The subject or the object can be broken down into subject (S) and predicate (P) or into context (C) and fact (F). The object "that the debutante needed a deodorant" can be divided into subject ("debutante") and predicate ("needed deodorant").

In order to represent a proposition such as the one given above, HAM constructs a "tree diagram" based on three components:

propositions—the overall proposition for which the tree is constructed;

locations—places in the tree for various applications of the above rules;

associations—relations, including several different types, among locations in the tree.

Box 5-10 gives the tree diagram and terminal nodes (the nodes at the bottom of the tree) for the proposition about the hippie and the debutante. These nodes represent the meaning of the words. The process of answering a question that involves semantic knowledge is a matching process; for example, to answer "Where did the hippie say that the debutante needed a deodorant?" HAM would:

1. Translate the input question into a tree diagram, leaving a "?" for the location.
2. Match the terminal nodes of the question with the corresponding locations in the existing memory.
3. Continue along the paths until the same relation (in this case, the L relation) is found.

The HAM model has been subjected to various tests with human subjects; the model is clearly consistent with the research discussed in the

BOX 5-10   **HYPOTHETICAL ADULT'S KNOWLEDGE ABOUT A PROPOSITION:**
ANDERSON AND BOWER'S TREE DIAGRAM

Proposition: In the park the hippie said the debutante needed a deodorant.

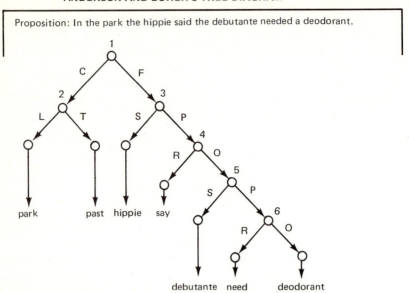

Parsing process:
1. The proposition is divided into context (C) and fact (F).
2. The context is divided into location (L) and time (T).
3. The fact is divided into subject (S) and predicate (P).
4. The predicate is divided into relation (R) and object (O).
5. The object is divided into subject (S) and predicate (P).
6. The predicate is divided into relation (R) and object (O).

From Anderson & Bower (1973)

previous section which indicates that subjects remember the gist (terminal nodes) of sentences rather than the specifics, and it is a concrete model that partly uses Chomsky's distinction between surface and deep structure. However, in summarizing their five hundred pages of research and theory, Anderson and Bower admit that they have failed to "produce decisive evidence" that their particular way of parsing propositions is the one most people use.

A third network model of semantic memory was proposed by Rumelhart, Lindsay, and Norman (1972). Their model was based on the following structural components:

nodes—words which stand for concepts or events;
relations—lines among nodes which are directed (go from one node to another) and labeled (are of different types).

Instead of using a hierarchy like that of Collins and Quillian, or a tree diagram like that of Anderson and Bower, these researchers used the graph representation shown in Box 5-11. As you can see, a sentence or set of sentences can be converted into a graph with nodes and relations. The question-answering process is to go to the nodes that are mentioned in the question and take paths outward from there.

Unfortunately, there has been much more work in developing the Rumelhart, Lindsay, and Norman model than in testing it. Hulse, Deese, and Egeth (1975) suggested that one implication of the model is that verbs are crucial in remembering since the arrows center on verbs; however, they cited a study by Yates and Caramazza in which recall of learned sentences was not better when the cue was a verb than when it was a noun from given sentences.

Set Models of Semantic Memory

Although network models are currently the most numerous, there are other ways of representing semantic memory. For example, Meyer (1970) proposed a model of how subjects answer questions about semantic

BOX 5-11 HYPOTHETICAL ADULT'S KNOWLEDGE ABOUT AN EVENT: RUMELHART, LINDSAY, AND NORMAN'S DIRECTED GRAPH

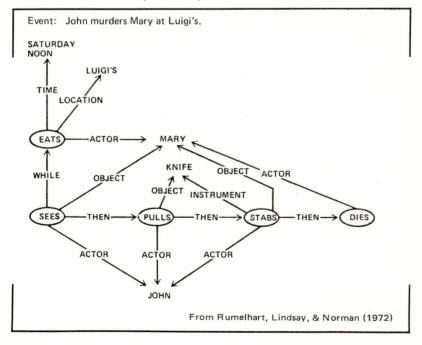

Event: John murders Mary at Luigi's.

From Rumelhart, Lindsay, & Norman (1972)

memory that was not based on networks at all; rather, Meyer assumed that each concept was stored in memory as a list of subsets (or features). When subjects were asked to respond to statements such as "All females are writers" or "Some females are writers," they appeared to go through the following two stages:

Stage 1: Determine all the subsets of "writer," including male and female, and all the subsets of "female," and see if there is any overlap, that is, if there are any subsets in common. If there are no common features (as in a sentence such as "Some typhoons are wheat") answer False; if there are some common features (e.g., writers and females), answer True if the statement calls for "some," and go on to Stage 2 if it calls for "all."

Stage 2: Is each subset of "female" also a subset of "writer"? If yes, answer True; if no, answer False.

Meyer's theory predicted that it would take longer for the subjects to respond to problems of the form "All S are P" than "Some S are P" because two stages were required for the former and only one stage for the latter, and, like Collins and Quillian, Meyer predicted that response time would increase if the size of category P was increased because the list of subsets was now longer. Meyer used experiments similar to those of Collins and Quillian and obtained results consistent with his (as well as Collins and Quillian's) model. However, while the Meyer model based on sets may be just as powerful as Collins and Quillian's network model, neither model can explain results such as why it would take longer to answer Dog-Mammal than Dog-Animal.

Rips, Shoben, and Smith (1973; Smith, Shoben, & Rips, 1974) have developed a set model of semantic memory that accounts for such findings. The main new ingredient in their model was based on a skepticism of Collins and Quillian's assumption that "memory structure mirrors logical structure." In one study, Rips, Shoben, and Smith asked a group of subjects to rate pairs of words in terms of how closely related they were to one another, in order to derive a measure of "semantic distance." For example, they asked the subjects to rate how closely related various kinds of birds were to each other, to the category "bird," and to the category "animal"; or how closely related various mammals were to each other, to the category "mammal," and to the category "animal." The two-dimensional chart that is shown in Box 5-12 was derived from the ratings; note that high relatedness is represented by short distance.

This method of representing semantic memory predicts that reaction time judgments like those used by Collins and Quillian should be related to semantic distance, and these predictions have been upheld. In other

BOX 5-12 ADULTS' KNOWLEDGE ABOUT ANIMALS: A SEMANTIC DISTANCE CHART

The following chart is based on subjects' ratings of how "related" pairs of words were. Short distances represent high relatedness.

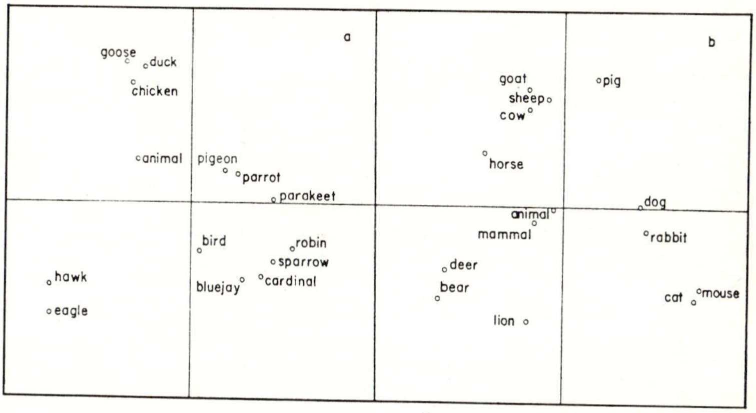

From Rips, Shoben, & Smith (1973)

words, according to the semantic distance idea, the reason it takes longer to press the True button for Robin-Animal than Robin-Bird or longer for Dog-Mammal than Dog-Animal is that the actual semantic distance is greater from Dog to Mammal than Dog to Animal (regardless of logical structure) or from Robin to Animal than Robin to Bird. These authors have further argued that semantic distance is basically a function of how many semantic features the two concepts have in common; in other words, of how much overlap there is between the list of features that make up the sets.

Evaluation

The work with sentence and prose recall extends Bartlett's idea that memory is "abstract," and that responding to questions or problems involves a "construction." The three network models—Collins and Quillian's TLC, Anderson and Bower's HAM, and Rumelhart, Lindsay, and Norman's graph theory—and the two set theories—Meyer's two-stage model, and the "semantic distance" model of Rips et al.—represent five popular attempts to describe specifically how people structure knowledge and answer questions. Because these models are both detailed and broad (the network models are particularly broad), they are useful ways of testing various ideas about human question answering; however, it is still too soon to tell whether or not they will provide a significant advance for cognitive psychology.

Suggested Readings

Bartlett, F. *Remembering.* London: Cambridge University Press, 1932. Presents the work that was the forerunner of modern cognitive psychology, including the "War of the Ghosts" study.

Klatzky, R. *Human memory: Structures and processes.* San Francisco: Freeman, 1975. Chapter 8 deals with semantic memory.

Lindsay, P. H., & Norman, D. A. *Human information processing.* New York: Academic Press, 1972. Chapters 10, 11, and 12 provide an interesting introduction to the structure and processes of memory.

Norman, D. *Memory and attention: An introduction to human information processing.* New York: Wiley, 1969. Chapter 7 presents the original TOT study and related work.

6

Computer Simulation: Thinking as Information Processing

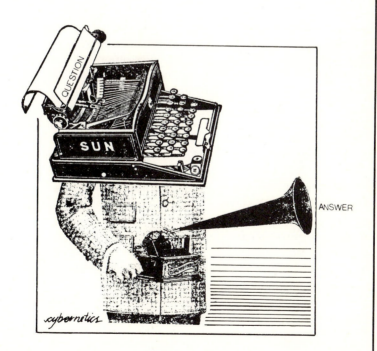

Introduction

Natural Language Tasks

Box 6-1 is the protocol or transcript of part of a therapy session between a doctor (MD) and a patient (P). What is interesting about the discussion is that it took place at a computer terminal keyboard, with the patient typing in statements and the computer responding by teletype or videoscope. Therapist programs like this one, as well as programs that simulate neurotic symptoms, were developed to determine whether it is possible to describe a therapy technique—or a mental syndrome—with enough precision to express it as a computer program (Weizenbaum, 1968; Colby, 1965; Colby, Watt, & Gilbert, 1966). The programmers, of course, did not intend their Rogerian program to replace Carl Rogers (1961) and his disciples, but it does demonstrate a basic advance in theories of human cognitive processing. A theory of what a therapist does while giving therapy, or what a chess player does while playing chess, or what a problem solver does while solving a problem may be specified in very exact terms as a list of things to do—in short, as a computer program. Theories of human cognitive processes may thus be generated and expressed as computer programs, and *tested* by seeing if they work—that is, if they do give therapy, play chess or solve problems the way a person does. Programs which "understand" natural language as in Box 6-1 aid in the development of theories of memory and psycholinguistics; however, programs which solve problems are more specifically important for theories of human thinking.

BOX 6-1   THE COMPUTER AS THERAPIST

P:	Men are all alike.
MD:	In what way
P:	They're always bugging us about something or other.
MD:	Can you think of a specific example
P:	Well, my boyfriend made me come here.
MD:	Your boyfriend made you come here
P:	He says I'm depressed much of the time.
MD:	I am sorry to hear you are depressed
P:	It's true. I am unhappy.
MD:	Do you think coming here will help you not be unhappy
P:	I need some help, that much seems certain.
MD:	What would it mean to you if you got some help
P:	Perhaps I could learn to get along with my mother.
MD:	Tell me more about your family
P:	My mother takes care of me.
MD:	Who else in your family takes care of you
P:	My father.
MD:	Your father
P:	You are like my father in some ways.
MD:	What resemblance do you see
P:	You are not very aggressive but I think you don't want me to notice that.
MD:	What makes you think I am not very aggressive
P:	You don't argue with me.
MD:	Why do you think I don't argue with you
P:	You are afraid of me.
MD:	Does it please you to believe that I am afraid of you
P:	My father is afraid of everybody.
MD:	What else comes to mind when you think of your father
P:	Bullies.
MD:	Does that have anything to do with the fact that your boyfriend made you come here

From Weizenbaum (1968)

Move Tasks

Many of the problems computers can solve have been called "move" problems because they share three basic characteristics: a definite initial state, a definite goal state, and a well-defined set of allowable moves or operators for changing from one state to another. For example, the Hobbits and Orcs problem (Ernst & Newell, 1969), the water jar problem (Ernst & Newell, 1969), or the DONALD+ GERALD = ROBERT problem (Newell & Simon, 1972) fit this description and have been exposed to computer simulation. In order to derive a precise set of procedures for solving such problems, a first step is to closely analyze the performance of one subject by asking the subject to report his or her mental operations aloud, as shown in Box 6-2 for the DONALD + GERALD

problem. Newell and Simon devote an entire chapter to this subject's behavior, including eighteen pages of raw protocol and almost one hundred
pages in all. Can you see any strategy or set of procedures the subject is
using? Newell and Simon note that in step 5 the subject is substituting the
given into the equation, in step 7 the subject is making an inference based
on having two numbers in a column, and in steps 10 and 12 is using a
strategy of searching for "known" letters, etc. By carefully observing the
general procedures used by individual subjects, Newell and Simon were
able to produce a computer program which solved similar cryptarithmetic
problems in a way apparently similar to human methods.

What other types of "thinking" or "problem solving" can computers
engage in? The ever expanding list now includes:

algebra story problems (Bobrow, 1964)—named STUDENT;

geometry problems (Gelernter, 1959);

logical proofs (Newell, Shaw, & Simon, 1957)—named Logic Theorist;

chess (Newell, Shaw, & Simon, 1958; Newell & Simon, 1972; Greenblatt, Eastlake, & Crocker, 1967; Zobrist & Carlson, 1973);

checkers (Samuel, 1963);

concept formation (Gregg & Simon, 1967);

analogy problems (Evans, 1968; Reitman, 1965; Reitman, Grove, & Shoup, 1964)—called Argus;

Rogerian therapy and neurotic personality (Colby, 1965; Colby, Watt, & Gilbert, 1966; Weizenbaum, 1968);

general problem solving (Ernst & Newell, 1969)—called General Problem Solver;

logic and deductive reasoning (Newell & Simon, 1972);

understanding natural language (Winograd, 1970).

Information Processing Definition of Thinking

The information processing approach to thinking assumes that a human being is, among other things, a processor of information. His or her cognitive processes, including thinking, can therefore be represented as either:

a sequence of mental processes or *operations* performed on information in the subject's memory; or
a sequence of internal *states* or changes in information that progress towards the goal.

The goal of the information processing psychologist is to define precisely the processes and states that a particular subject is using to solve a particular problem and to be able to list—e.g., in the form of a computer program—the exact sequence of operations used.

In a sense the information processing approach is a refinement of the associationist view of thinking as selecting the correct response or rule from the response hierarchy, since the subject applies a sequence of moves or operations until he or she has changed the situation to solve the problem. Yet some information processing psychologists suggest that the approach is not a theory at all but rather a method of precisely describing the thinking process; as such, it offers a method of testing competing theories of thinking.

Cybernetics

The cybernetic revolution (Weiner, 1948), which involves the idea of feedback and machine servomechanisms, plus the rapid development of sophisticated computers and computer programs have heavily influenced the information processing approach to thinking. This approach is based on two computer metaphors:

the *human-machine* analogy, in which the human being may be viewed as a complex computer; and
the *thinking-program* analogy, in which the thought processes used by the human being to solve a problem may be viewed as a computer program.

Miller, Galanter, and Pribram (1960) introduced a popular example of a feedback system to describe the cognitive processes involved in hammering a nail (see Box 6-3). The plan shown in the box is called a TOTE, for Test-Operate-Test-Exit, and is simply a hierarchy of operations with feedback. Written as a computer program, the processes should be in the form of a list to be read top down:

1. Test nail. If it sticks up, go to 2; otherwise stop.
2. Test hammer. If down, lift; otherwise go to 3.
3. Strike nail.
4. Go to 1.

Although it may seem peculiar that psychologists are so interested in how to hammer a nail, techniques such as flow charts and programs are important because they allow psychologists to specify their theory of cognitive processes for a certain intellectual task with precision.

Unfortunately, these kinds of representations make no major distinctions between human and nonhuman thought processes. For example, Box 6-4 shows the "thought processes" of a thermostat. The flow chart could also be represented as a program:

1. Test temperature. If under 70°, go to 2, if over 72°, go to 5; otherwise go to 1.
2. Test furnace. If on, go to 1; otherwise go to 3.
3. Turn furnace on.
4. Go to 1.
5. Test furnace. If off, go to 1; otherwise go to 6.
6. Turn furnace off.
7. Go to 1.

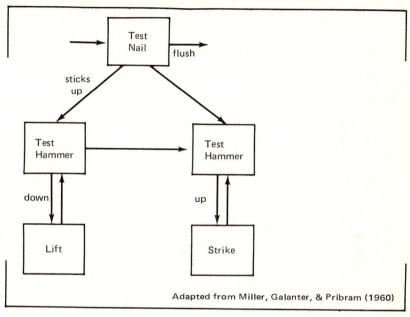

Adapted from Miller, Galanter, & Pribram (1960)

The development of such ways of describing internal cognitive processes is, obviously, heavily dependent on the computer analogy, and in the next section we shall discuss how these kinds of models are used to test theories of thinking.

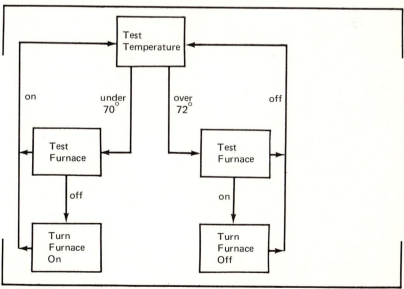

Computer Simulation

Why would anyone want to spend the time to program a computer to solve problems? The motives probably vary, but the reason given for many of the early attempts was to see if machines could solve problems. The development of computer programs that display intelligence by solving problems or engaging in conversation is generally referred to as the field of *artificial intelligence*. A subfield of particular interest to cognitive psychologists is the development of computer systems that display the same problem solving behavior as humans—i.e., behavior which simulates human behavior. This field is referred to as *computer simulation*. If you were interested in building a machine that could serve as an encyclopedia and answer any spoken question, such as HAL in *2001* or COMPUTER in *Star Trek,* you probably would not care if its memory storage system and language perception system were the same as in people as long as the machine "worked"—hence, that would be a problem in artificial intelligence. However, if you had a particular theory of how human beings solve a problem (not necessarily the best or most logical method), you could use computer simulation to test the theory. The logic of computer simulation is simple: if a computer program produces the same problem solving behavior as a human then the series of operations are an accurate representation of the human thought processes.

The experimental method used with computer simulation generally involves asking subjects to solve problems aloud while giving a running description of their thought process and their behavior. From careful analyses of the obtained *protocols* (the transcript of all the subject's comments) the experimenter may derive a description of the mental processes a subject used to solve the problem. By specifying these as a computer program, the experimenter has a precise description that can be tested by feeding it to a computer and observing how closely the computer's protocol matches the subject's. If the match is close, the experimenter may conclude that the description of the processes a subject is using to solve a particular program is accurate; if not, it is necessary to make up a new program and try again.

Although computer simulation offers a new tool for generating and testing theories of human thinking, much popular attention has been directed towards a complementary issue: how can we know whether a machine thinks? Years before the technology for computer simulation existed, the mathematician Turing (1950) wrote an article entitled, "Can Machines Think?" in which he proposed the following test—now called the Turing Test: Put two teletypewriters and a person to act as judge in a room. The judge may ask any questions he likes by typing. One teletype is connected to a person in another room who communicates by typing his answers and one is connected to a computer which also types out its answers. If the human judge cannot tell which teletype is connected to the machine and which is connected to the human, then the computer is thinking.

There is, of course, an interesting flaw in the "logic" of computer simulation. Just because a computer and a human give the same behavioral output, does that really mean they are using the same cognitive processes? In addition, protocol states may not accurately reflect internal states. The idea seems particularly absurd in light of the fact that computers use entirely different components than the human brain; yet, a computer program is a very precise and testable way to state a theory of human thinking and as such offers an opportunity to go beyond the vague theories of the Gestaltists. Talking about programs and states may be no more absurd than talking about thoughts or ideas—all are abstractions which must ultimately be described in a way that provides clear tests.

The Structure of Problem Space

Ernst and Newell (1969) suggested four major components in describing problem solving by computer simulation:

initial state—in which the given or starting conditions are represented;

goal state—in which the final or goal situation is represented;

operators—all the allowable manipulations or moves which may be performed on any one state to change it into another state;

problem states—the intermediate states that result from the application of an operator to a state.

The *problem space* or the *state-action tree* is the set of all possible *problem states* resulting from all possible sequences of the application of operators.

Consider the disc problem (or the tower of Hanoi problem) we discussed in Chapter 4. A problem state can be represented diagrammatically as three pegs labeled A, B, and C with three discs labeled 1, 2, 3 with 1 the smallest and 3 the largest (see Box 6-5). The initial state is simply A = 1, 2, 3; B = 0; C = 0. The goal state is A = 0; B = 0; C = 1, 2, 3. The operation that is allowed is to take the lowest number from one letter and put it on another letter as long as a larger number never goes on top of a smaller number. Part of the problem space is given in Box 6-5. Note that the branches from each node represent different actions that could be selected for that node; thus the same node may appear at many places in the tree.

BOX 6-5   PART OF PROBLEM SPACE FOR THE TOWER OF HANOI PROBLEM

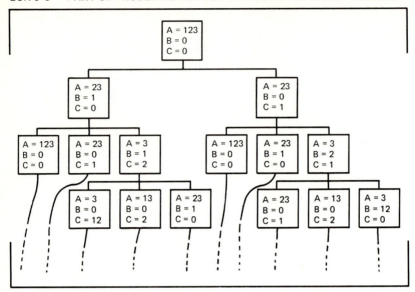

You will find another example of the problem space for the Hobbits and Orcs problems in Chapter 3 in Box 3-12. Here the initial state is: Left = 3H, 3O, BOAT; Right = EMPTY. The goal state is: Left = EMPTY; Right = 3H, 3O, BOAT. The operations are to move a 1H, 2H, 1O, 2O, or 1H and 1O from the side with BOAT to the other side as long as H's are never outnumbered.

Solving a problem can thus be viewed as finding the correct path or route through a problem space. As Wickelgren (1974) pointed out, it is often possible to "prune the tree." For example,

the space can be reduced by thinking in terms of "macroactions" in which different sequences of actions often result in the same problem state,

the space can be reduced by working both forward (from the given state) and backward (from the goal state), and the problem space can be broken down into smaller *subgoals*.

Past Experience

In solving problems—i.e., in moving through a problem space—a subject must also rely on past experience. Lindsay and Norman (1972) have distinguished among several types of relevant past experience used in problem solving:

facts—which are immediately available to the subject;

algorithms—sets of rules that automatically generate the correct answers;

heuristics—rules of thumb or general plans of action.

For example, generating a solution to the question, "What is 8 times 4?" involves a fact; generating a solution for "What is 262 times 127?" involves an algorithm or set of rules; and an heuristic may be to "estimate" the correct answer by rounding to manageable numbers.

Algorithms guarantee correct problem solutions since all that is needed is to apply a past set of rules to a new situation. The set of rules can be stored as a *subroutine,* thus saving memory load. Heuristics, on the other hand, may not solve the problem. For example, the heuristic of finding a related or analogous problem or breaking the problem into subgoals may help but does not guarantee solution. A major heuristic is "means-ends analysis" in whch the present state is compared with the new state that could result from application of an operator in order to determine whether the new state is closer to the goal. If it is, the "move" is made; if not, the solver searches for another move that produces a state closer to the goal state.

The Process of Problem Solving

Ernst and Newell (1969) have provided a simplified description of the problem solving process (see Box 6-6). The INPUT is acted upon by a TRANSLATOR which converts it into an INTERNAL REPRESENTATION (including the initial state, the goal state, and a means of telling which problem states are closer to the goal state) which is acted upon by PROBLEM SOLVING TECHNIQUES which generate the SOLUTION. In spite of the contribution of the assimilation theory of thinking and the idea of functional fixedness from the Gestalt theory, very little attention has been paid to the translation process. The internal representation of a problem can take many forms including the problem space representation we discussed earlier, and the problem solving techniques may be represented as operators, facts, subroutines, and heuristics.

Greeno (1974) has proposed the memory model for problem solving shown in Box 6-7. The three main components of interest in describing problem solving are:

short-term memory, through which the external description of the problem is input;

long-term memory (semantic and factual memory), which stores past experience with solving problems such as facts, algorithms, heuristics, related problems, etc.;

working memory, in which the information from STM and LTM interact and the solution route is generated and tested.

A description of the problem, including the initial state, the goal state, and the legal operators, comes into working memory by way of short-term memory as represented by arrows from STM to WM; and past experience about how to solve the problem enters working memory from LTM, as represented by the arrow from LTM to WM. The arrows from WM to STM and LTM to STM suggest that more information from the outside world may be required as problem solving progresses (the solver may pay attention to different aspects of the presented information) and the arrow from WM to LTM suggests that the generation of new problem states in WM may require more old information from past experience. The concept of working memory, first introduced by Feigenbaum (1970), has special importance in Greeno's model: the internal rep-

BOX 6-6   THE PROBLEM SOLVING PROCESS

Input
(Description of Problem)

Translator

Internal
Representation
of Problem

Problem
Solving
Techniques

Solution
Representation

Adapted from Ernst & Newell (1969)

BOX 6-7   COMPONENTS OF MEMORY

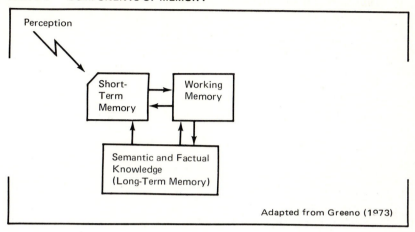

Adapted from Greeno (1973)

resentation of the problem occurs there, the construction of links between givens and unknowns occurs there, and relevant past experience is used to modify the structures held in WM.

For example, Bobrow (1964) developed a program called STU-DENT that attempted to solve algebra story problems. A typical problem is as follows:

> The gas consumption of my car is 15 miles per gallon. The distance between Boston and New York is 250 miles. What is the number of gallons of gas used on the trip between New York and Boston?

The first step is translation from the external representation to an internal representation of the problem. The program derived the following equations from the statement of the problem:

> (Distance between Boston and New York) = ([250] miles)
> (X1) = (Number of gallons of gas used on trip between New York and Boston)
> (Gas consumption of my car) = ([15 miles]/ 1 [gallon])

An additional piece of information added to the internal representation comes from existing knowledge (or LTM):

> (Distance) = (Gas consumption) x (Number of gallons of gas used)

Thus with the preceding information entered into WM—the first three from STM and the latter one from LTM—the program is ready to start manipulating the information in WM. In order to successfully work on this information, several assumptions must be made:

Gas consumption = Gas consumption of my car
Distance = Distance between Boston and New York
Number of gallons of gas used = Number of gallons of gas used on
a trip between New York and Boston

The problem solving techniques, consisting of algebraic and computational algorithms, may now be applied, with the result being that the computer prints out:

THE NUMBER OF GALLONS OF GAS USED ON A TRIP BETWEEN NEW YORK
AND BOSTON IS 16.66 GALLONS.

As you can see, most of the programming effort of STUDENT was devoted to the translation phase—changing natural English into an internal representation that can be operated upon by algebraic and computational subroutines. The internal representation is simply a set of algebraic equations with phrases which must be recognized as equivalent to terms stored in memory.

GPS: An Example

One of the best-known, and most general, programs is known as General Problem Solver or GPS (Ernst & Newell, 1969). GPS was intended as a demonstration that certain general problem solving techniques are involved in a wide spectrum of problems, and that it is possible to state explicitly what these general procedures are in a computer program that will be able to solve a wide variety of different types of problems.

GPS, like other programs, begins by translating a statement of the problem into an internal representation of the initial state, goal state, and set of operators. In addition, GPS has stored in its memory a "Table of Connections" for each problem it will solve; the table of connections contains all possible problem states for that problem with a listing of how far apart any two states are from one another. Problem solving involves *breaking a problem down into subgoals,* and then achieving each subgoal by *applying various problem solving techniques,* each of which changes the problem state in the direction of the subgoal. For example, the program can try a technique and then test whether it changes the problem state to one that is closer to the subgoal by checking the difference on the table of connections; if the technique succeeds the program uses that technique and the process starts over, but if it fails the program tries another technique. Thus, when GPS solves a problem it performs the following:

translates the problem into initial state, goal state, and legal operators;

has the appropriate table of connections in memory in order to tell the differences between the states;

breaks the problem down into a hierarchy of goals and subgoals, each of which brings the problem closer to solution;

applies problem solving techniques based on the principle of means-ends analysis (reducing the difference between the present state and the desired subgoal state); and

when one subgoal is achieved, moves on to the next one until the problem is solved.

The entire process is presided over by the "problem solving executive" which determines the order in which operators will be applied, attempts to achieve subgoals by using means-ends analysis, and develops a new subgoal structure if one does not work.

An example of one problem GPS can solve is the three-coin problem (Filipiak, 1942): three coins are on a table with the first and third coin showing tails and the second coin showing heads (i.e., THT). The problem is to make all three coins show the same—either heads or tails—in exactly three moves with each move consisting of flipping any two coins. The initial state is: THT-3 and the goal state is either TTT-0 or HHH-0 where T refers to tails, H to heads, and 3 to the number of moves remaining.

The problem requires ten goals, attempted in the order shown in Box 6-8 from 1 to 10. The changes in the problem state progress from THT-3 to HTT-2 to TTH-1 to HHH-0.

GPS can also solve a variation of the Hobbits and Orcs problem (missionaries and cannibals), the tower of Hanoi problem, water jar problems, letter series completion problems, calculus problems, and half a dozen other different tasks.

Evaluation

The computer simulation approach is an attempt to study theories of human problem solving in a precise and scientifically testable manner. The approach requires that the theories be stated precisely, in a formal computer program, and provides for the use of sophisticated lab equipment, computers, in testing theories. Thus, computer simulation offers a breakthrough in the psychology of thinking which may ultimately produce a precise reformulation and integration of Gestaltist, associationist, and other ideas. However, the computer simulation approach also has certain basic drawbacks. The human-machine analogy, the description of mental operations as computer operations, is not a perfect analogy. Psychology has been heavily influenced by developments in other sciences, in-

BOX 6-8   SOLUTION TREE FOR THE THREE COIN PROBLEM

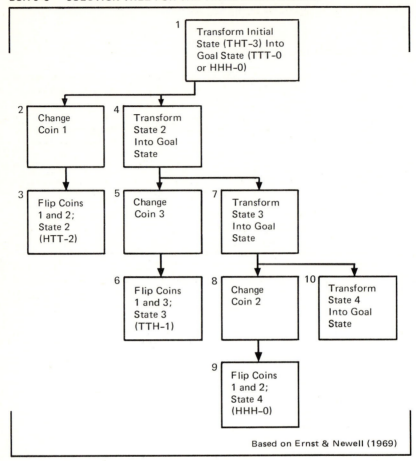

Based on Ernst & Newell (1969)

cluding the breakthroughs in computer technology. However, the information processing view of human beings as machinelike processors of
information—though a currently popular view—is limited and may act to
limit current views of thinking. In addition there is a flaw in the logic of
computer simulation, because although a program may simulate human
thinking behavior, this does not mean it simulates the underlying cognitive processes. Finally, current simulation programs require something
like a table of connections—a list of every possible problem state and a
measurement of its distance from the goal. Thus, in a way, the solution is
given and the thinking process involves what the Gestaltists would call reproductive thinking. But the chapter on computer simulation is a contin-

uing one, and it remains to be seen how far technology and man may go in simulating human thought.

Suggested Readings

Newell, A., & Simon, H. A. *Human problem solving.* Englewood Cliffs, N. J.: Prentice-Hall, 1972. A giant, 900-page book that offers an information processing theory and computer simulation of problem solving in cryptarithmetic, logic, and chess.

Wickelgren, W. A. *How to solve problems: Elements of a theory of problem solving.* San Francisco: Freeman, 1974. A short, basic introduction to the information processing approach to problem solving and how it can be applied to solve numerous interesting problems.

7

Deductive Reasoning: Thinking as Processing a Cognitive Structure

Introduction

Syllogisms

Consider the three problems in Box 7-1 and then pick the conclusion which logically follows each one.

If you think like most people—or at least like most people who participate in psychology experiments—problem 1 was probably the easiest for you (Answer: A). However, problems 2 and 3 generate much higher error rates—75 percent errors for problem 2, with most errors due to subjects' picking C instead of E, and 90 percent errors in problem 3, mainly due to subjects' picking D instead of E.

While these results (based on data from Stratton, 1967, and reported by Johnson, 1972) do not suggest that people are stupid, they do indicate that formal logic and individual mental or psycho-logic are not necessarily the same.

Now try the syllogisms in Box 7-2, and write for each one whether or not the conclusion logically follows.

If you are like most of Lefford's (1946) subjects, you had much more difficulty answering Yes to problem 1 than to problem 3, and more difficulty answering No to problem 2 than to problem 4. Although problems 1 and 3 have the same formal characteristics and length (All A are B, All B are C, Therefore All A are C), and 2 and 4 have the same formal characteristics and length (All A are B, All C are B, Therefore All C are A), problems 1 and 2 are far more difficult. Apparently, human reasoning or psycho-logic is influenced not only by the form of the argument but also by the desirability or amount of agreement with the conclusion.

BOX 7-1   PICK THE CONCLUSION YOU CAN BE SURE OF

1. All S are M
    All M are P
    Therefore,
    A. All S are P
    B. All S are not P
    C. Some S are P
    D. Some S are not P
    E. None of these conclusions is valid

2. As technology advances and natural petroleum resources are depleted, the
    securing of petroleum from unconventional sources becomes more imperative.
    One such source is the Athabasca tar sands of northern Alberta, Canada. Since
    some tar sands are sources of refinable hydrocarbons, these deposits are worthy
    of commercial investigation. Some kerogen deposits are also sources of
    refinable hydrocarbons. Therefore:
    A. All kerogen deposits are tar sands.
    B. No kerogen deposits are tar sands.
    C. Some kerogen deposits are tar sands.
    D. Some kerogen deposits are not tar sands.
    E. None of the above.

3. The delicate Glorias of Argentina, which open only in cool weather, are all
    Sassoids. Some of the equally delicate Fragilas, found only in damp areas, are
    not Glorias. What can you infer from these statements?
    A. All Fragilas are Sassoids.
    B. No Fragilas are Sassoids.
    C. Some Fragilas are Sassoids.
    D. Some Fragilas are not Sassoids.
    E. None of the above.

                                                            From Stratton (1967)

BOX 7-2   DOES THE CONCLUSION LOGICALLY FOLLOW FROM THE
           PREMISES?

1. War times are prosperous times, and prosperity is highly desirable; therefore,
    wars are much to be desired.
2. All communists have radical ideas, and all CIO leaders have radical ideas;
    therefore, all CIO leaders are agents for communism.
3. Philosophers are all human, and all human beings are fallible; therefore,
    philosophers are fallible too.
4. All whales live in water, and all fish live in water too; therefore, all fish must be
    whales.

                                                            From Lefford (1946)

Syllogisms like the ones in the boxes require deductive thinking—deducing or deriving a conclusion from given premises. This contrasts with inductive thinking, discussed in Chapter 2, which involves inducing or formulating or extrapolating a rule based on limited information. In deductive thinking, the propositions or rules are given and the thinker uses this given information to derive a conclusion which can be proven correct. Mathematical proofs, for example, are deductive. Inductive thinking, however, such as concept learning, can never result in a provable rule because new information may come along that violates the induced rule; since induced rules are based on a limited set of information, they require the thinker to "go beyond" that information, to "generalize." Since human beings and many other kinds of animals are capable of solving both induction and deduction tasks, such tasks have received much research attention in psychology. While induction and deduction are tasks rather than theories of thinking, each has an implied view of human thinking. In Chapter 2 we investigated the idea—fostered by examining induction—that thinking involves a constant searching (sampling) for a rule. In this chapter, we shall focus on an approach—suggested by work in deduction—that thinking involves combining information by using a set of psychological/mathematical operations.

Deductive Reasoning
Definition of Thinking

Although the area of deductive reasoning is not a theoretical approach in the same sense that associationism and Gestalt are, deduction implies that thinking involves the combining of existing information by following specific mental operations as in addition or subtraction, etc. This approach is consistent with the information processing approach in that thinking can thus be interpreted as the processing of premises by using specifiable operators—similar but not identical to formal logical operators.

William James (1890) devoted nearly an entire chapter of his classic textbook on psychology to describing the two main processes involved in deductive reasoning: analysis and abstraction. Analysis refers to the process of breaking down an object into its parts and then substituting a part for the object, whereas abstraction refers to subsuming a specific property under a broader, more general rule. As an example of analysis, in order to process the proposition "Socrates is a man," a thinker must think of Socrates only in terms of one property. James argued that analysis requires a "mode of conceiving"—a way of referring to Socrates (as a man). As an example of abstraction, the thinker, to process the proposition "All men are mortal," must subsume Socrates-as-a-man under the general heading of "mortality." While James' conception of the analysis-and-abstraction processes may not necessarily be the best or the most precise (this is really an empirical question to be answered by sound experimental research), it does suggest that deduction may be viewed as a series of specific processes or operations performed on information.

Formal Logic and Logical Errors

Types of Errors

Propositions that concern set-subset relations can be of four main types:

Universal Affirmative: All A are B.
Universal Negative: No A are B.
Particular Affirmative: Some A are B.
Particular Negative: Some A are not B.

Venn diagrams of these four basic "categorical propositions" are given in Box 7-3. Note that universal affirmative (UA) propositions may result from Set A and Set B being identical, or Set A being a subset of Set B. Thus "All A are B" does not necessarily imply "All B are A" but it does not rule it out either. Similarly, the particular negative (PN) proposition may result either from Set A and Set B overlapping, or from Set A and Set B being disjoint, or from Set B being a subset of Set A. Thus "Some A are not B" does not necessarily imply "Some B are not A" although it does not rule it out either.

A syllogism consists of two premises and a conclusion with each being any one of the four types of categorical propositions. For example, the famous syllogism:

All men are mortal.
Socrates is a man.
Therefore, Socrates is mortal.

consists of two premises: a UA and a PA; and a conclusion: a PA.

Box 7-4 gives the form of three types of logical syllogisms and an example of each. Syllogism 1 is a reasonably simple one with the conclusion following from the premises; however, using premises or conclusions which violate a subject's beliefs, attitudes, or expectancies makes accurate deduction more difficult for this and all syllogistic forms. Syllogisms 2 and 3 are presented in more difficult forms, with the conclusions not necessarily following from the premises. Each of these syllogisms is particularly susceptible to one of three predictable types of errors of logic:

content errors, in which (as in the first syllogism) the truth or desirability of the premises or conclusion influence the subject's deductions regardless of the logic involved;

undistributed middle term errors, in which (as in the second syllogism) the subjects may overgeneralize the breadth of the middle term;

particular premises errors, in which (as in the third syllogism) subjects may overgeneralize the breadth of "some" to mean "all."

Errors due to form—the latter two types—and to content may be confounded in any one situation, thus increasing the tendency to error. Since these types of errors are quite common, they have enjoyed a practical value for propagandists and others who wish to affect public opinion. However, they are also of theoretical interest because they suggest that formal logic and human, psycho-logic are not the same and thus these errors have received much research attention.

BOX 7-3   POSSIBLE VENN DIAGRAMS FOR FOUR TYPES OF PROPOSITIONS

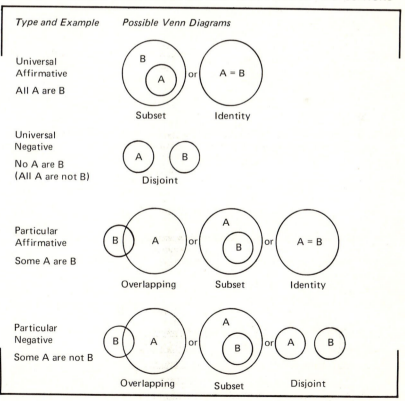

BOX 7-4   THREE TYPES OF LOGICAL ERRORS

Content Errors

Any form of recreation that constitutes a serious health menace will be outlawed by the City Health Authority. The increasing water pollution in this area will make swimming at local beaches a serious health menace. Swimming at local beaches will be outlawed by the City Health Authority.

Content: undesirable conclusion.

From McGuire (1960)

Undistributed Middle Errors

Wallonians dance the polka. My worthy opponent dances the polka. Therefore, it is obvious that my worthy opponent is a Wallonian.

Form: All A are B, All C are B, therefore All C are A.

Particular Premises Errors

Some Republicans have inherited oil wells. Some Wallonians are Republicans. Hence we know that some Wallonians have inherited oil wells.

Form: Some A are B, Some C are A, therefore Some C are B.

From Wilkins (1928)

Content Errors

In order to study content errors, Janis and Frick (1943) presented syllogisms as short paragraphs and asked subjects to rate whether they agreed or disagreed with the conclusion and whether or not the conclusion was valid based on the premises. As expected, a high number of errors were obtained, showing a strong tendency for subjects to judge the conclusions they agreed with as valid and the conclusions they disagreed with as invalid. One explanation for these context effects is that deductive syllogisms do not occur in a vacuum, but rather they are assimilated or fitted into the general cognitive structure of the problem solver. *Cognitive consistency*—the tendency for information in a person's memory to be internally consistent—may play a role in deduction.

The syllogisms used by Lefford (1946), shown in Box 7-1, produced similar results with more errors for conclusions with high emotional content than for less important ones, even though the logical form was identical. Using a different approach, Parrott (1969, cited in Johnson, 1972) presented three types of syllogisms that were identical in logical form but were constructed differently. One type used the symbols X, Y, and Z in the premises, the second contained premises that were true (consistent with the subject's past experience), and the third had premises which were false (not consistent with the subject's past experience). Although the instructions made it clear that the subject was to judge the validity of the conclusion assuming the premises were true, there were large differences in performance. The time to reason, in seconds, was: 21.9 for symbols, 24.2 for true-premise, and 29.4 for false-premise. Apparently, the context-free syllogisms allowed the subjects to reason logically on an independent syllogism and to be less influenced by the need for consistency with other information in their memories.

In a classic experiment on context effects, McGuire (1960) asked a group of subjects to rate a list of propositions for probability of occurrence and for desirability. Nested within the list were the components of several syllogisms with premises and conclusions separated by other propositions. If the subjects were entirely rational (thinking logically), the probability of a conclusion should be equal to the probability of premise 1 times the probability of premise 2. If the subjects were entirely irrational (indulging in wishful thinking) there should be a high correlation between desirability and probability—the subjects should rate highly desirable conclusions as highly probable regardless of the premises. As might be expected, McGuire found evidence for both logical and wishful thinking with a correlation of .48 between the judged probabilities of the conclusions and the products of the probabilities of the premises, and a correlation of .40 between the rated desirabilities of events and the rated probabilities of occurrence.* These results seem to indicate that deductive reasoning involves more than the three propositions in the syllogism, and that subjects try to fit the propositions within their existing cognitive structure or knowledge. Inconsistent or undesirable premises and/or conclusions must be dealt with in a way which may violate the rules of logic for a particular syllogism in exchange for preserving the cognitive consistency of the great mass of existing knowledge and beliefs.

Form Errors

The two main errors due to logical form—the fallacy of the undistributed middle and the fallacy due to particular premises—have also been explained in terms of underlying psychological mechanisms. Woodward and Sells (1935) and Sells (1936) suggested that these errors resulted from an *atmosphere effect* in which the form of the two premises set an atmosphere favorable to accepting conclusions of certain forms. For example, two UA premises create an atmosphere for the acceptance of a UA conclusion, two UN premises for a UN conclusion, two PA premises for a PA conclusion, and two PN premises for a PN conclusion; in addition, any one negative premise creates a negative atmos-

---

*Correlations such as .40 and .48 indicate a moderately strong positive relationship between variables.

phere and any one particular premise creates a particular atmosphere. Predictions based on the atmosphere effect theory have been fairly accurate (Sells, 1936; Morgan & Morton, 1944).

A related psychological explanation of logical errors is *invalid conversion*—the tendency to assume that if "All A are B" then "All B are A" or if "Some A are not B" then "Some B are not A." Note that the conversion of the UA and PN propositions above is not valid while conversion of the UN and PA propositions is valid. Chapman and Chapman (1959) gave two premises, in letter form, and asked their subjects to choose the correct conclusion:

Some L's are K's.
Some K's are M's.
Therefore,
1. All M's are L's.
2. Some M's are L's.
3. All M's are not L's.
4. Some M's are not L's.
5. None of these.

Although the correct answer was always "none of these" for each of forty-two experimental syllogisms, the subjects chose other conclusions over 80 percent of the time. Some typical responses are shown in Box 7-5. As you can see, many of the responses, like the first three in the box, seemed to fit both the atmosphere effect explanation and the invalid conversion explanation; however, the atmosphere effect would predict that the main error for the latter three syllogisms should be "Some S are not P" while the more preferred response was often "All S are not P," a response that could be derived if subjects made invalid conversions. Thus, the results indicated that invalid conversion could account for a large proportion of errors, including some that could not be accounted for by atmosphere effect.

You may note that the problems presented in Box 7-2 result in errors that can be described as atmosphere effect (Syllogism 2 has PA premises that encourage the PA conclusion, #C), and invalid conversion (Syllogism 3's statements that "All Glorias are Sassoids" may be converted to "All Sassoids are Glorias," thus encouraging the conclusion #D). Apparently, some errors may be explained by atmosphere and some by conversion, but while the former is a superficial attempt on the part of the thinker to be consistent, the latter reflects an attempt to be logical that simply is not quite right. Although conversions may be formally illogical, Chapman and Chapman (1959, p. 224) point out that they may be based on consistency with practical past experience since invalid conversions "although logically invalid often correspond to our experience of reality, and being guided by experience are usually regarded as justifiable proce-

Premises	Proportion of Subjects' Conclusions				
	All S are P.	Some S are P.	All S are not P.	Some S are not P.	None of these.
All P are M, All S are M.	.81	.04	.05	.01	.09
All M are P, No S are M.	.02	.03	.82	.05	.08
All P are M, Some M are S.	.06	.77	.02	.06	.07
Some M are P, All S are not M.	.01	.06	.62	.13	.18
Some M are not P, All M are not S.	.03	.07	.41	.19	.30
All M are not P, Some S are M.	.03	.10	.24	.32	.32

Based on data from Chapman & Chapman (1959)

dures. One may realistically accept the converse of many, perhaps most PN propositions about qualities of objects; e.g., some plants are not green and some greens are not plants. The acceptance of the converse of UA propositions is also often appropriate, e.g., all right angles are 90 degrees and also all 90 degree angles are right angles."

Linear Orderings

Another type of logical problem that has been carefully investigated is the cognitive processes that involve reasoning about linear orderings of the form: A is better than B; B is better than C; Is A better than C? For example, DeSoto, London, and Handel (1965) allowed their subjects ten seconds to respond Yes or No to conclusions based on premises like those shown in Box 7-6. According to the traditional view of logical reasoning, problems 1 and 4 ought to be easiest since they proceed from one extreme to the middle to the other extreme in presenting the three terms; however, problem 4 is one of the most difficult and problems 5 and 6, which should be difficult, are among the easiest. The authors concluded that formal logic is not necessarily the system human beings use to reason—"Clearly, an altogether different paralogic is required to account for the findings. We would like to propose two paralogical principles . . . that people learn orderings better in one direction than the other . . . [and] that people end-anchor orderings." The first principle is demonstrated by the fact that the subjects performed better on an evaluative ordering when the terms were presented better-to-worse (as in problem 1) than on a mixed order (as in problems 2 and 3), and worst when presented worse-to-better (as in problem 4). The second principle is indicated by the fact that the subjects performed better with propositions that gave an extreme term first (i.e., the best or worst) followed by middle term than with propositions that stated the middle term first followed by an end term; for example, problems 5 and 6 have two propositions that go from ends-to-middle, and are much easier than

BOX 7–6   PROPORTION CORRECT RESPONSE FOR EIGHT DEDUCTION
PROBLEMS

Premises	Proportion Correct Response	Form of Premises	
		Within Premises	Between Premises
1. A is better than B B is better than C	.61	better-to-worse	better-to-worse
2. B is better than C A is better than B	.53	better-to-worse	worse-to-better
3. B is worse than A C is worse than B	.50	worse-to-better	better-to-worse
4. C is worse than B B is worse than A	.43	worse-to-better	worse-to-better
5. A is better than B C is worse than B	.62	ends-to-middle	better-to-worse
6. C is worse than B A is better than B	.57	ends-to-middle	worse-to-better
7. B is worse than A B is better than C	.41	middle-to-ends	better-to-worse
8. B is better than C B is worse than A	.38	middle-to-ends	worse-to-better

The question for the subjects was stated in each of four ways:
Is A better than C? Is C better than A? Is A worse than C?
Is C worse than A?

From DeSoto et al. (1965)

problems 7 and 8 which have two propositions that each go from middle-to-ends.

DeSoto et al. described the reasoning process as involving *spatial paralogic* in which an up-down or right-left series of spaces is imagined and the terms of the ordering (i.e., A, B, C) are placed in the spaces. Similar results were obtained using "better-worse," "above-below," "lighter-darker," and "left-right" although performance was generally poorer for left-right possibly because it is more difficult to imagine horizontal than vertical ordering. Performance was poorer with "worse" than "better," with "below" than "above," with "right of" than "left of," which suggested that the direction of filling the spatial ordering was important.

Huttenlocher (1968) has summarized a series of experiments which replicated the DeSoto findings but used orderings of the form, "Tom is shorter than Sam. Sam is shorter than Pete. Who is tallest?" Huttenlocher noted that the first premise set up a relationship between two terms, (X is taller than Y or X is shorter than Y) and the second premise told the subject where to place the third term, either "above" or "below" the other two terms. If the subject of the second premise was the third term, such as Tom is taller than John; Sam is shorter than John, or Tom is taller than John; Sam is taller than John, then the error rates and response times to answer "Who is tallest?" or "Who is shortest?" were lower than if the third term was the object of the second premise, such as Tom is taller than John; John is taller than Sam, or Tom is taller than John; John is shorter than Sam. Even when the premises were given in the passive voice, reasoning was better when the third (or mobile) term was the logical subject and grammatical object of the second premise. For example, Tom is leading John, Tom is led by Sam was easier than Tom is leading John, Sam is led by John. Apparently the ability to process the second proposition depends on how it fits into the fixed relation established by the first premise.

Huttenlocher's emphasis on the subject-object grammar of the mobile third term in the second premise added a new type of approach to DeSoto's principle of end-anchoring. In experiments with children, Huttenlocher found that it was easier for the children to place a block in a concrete ladder or array, as shown in Box 7-7, if the subject of the instruction sentence was the to-be-placed block. If the ladder had a red block above a yellow block, the children could more easily place the third block (green) in the ladder when they were given sentences in which the green block was the subject, as in "put green over red," or "put green under yellow," than when the mobile block was the object of the sentence, as in "put red under green," or "put yellow over green." The deductive reasoning process of adults may involve this same sort of placing objects into an imaginary array, with the first proposition setting the fixed relation between two terms and the second proposition telling the thinker

BOX 7-7   HUTTENLOCHER'S BLOCK PROBLEM

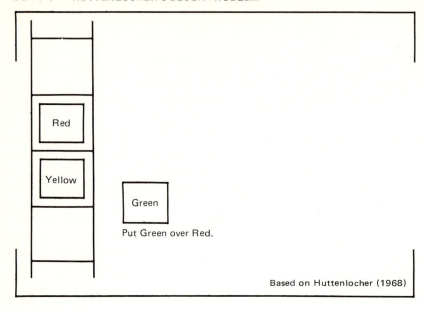

Put Green over Red.

Based on Huttenlocher (1968)

where in the array to place the third term. Answering questions about who is the tallest or shortest involves referring to the constructed spatial array. Thus, while Huttenlocher retained the idea that thinkers construct a spatial linear ordering, she considered that difficulty in placing items in the imaginary array was influenced by the grammar of the second premise or what DeSoto called "ends-to-middle" end-anchoring.

While DeSoto and Huttenlocher described the deductive reasoning process as constructing a spatial image, using principles such as end-anchoring, Clark (1969) attempted to show that reasoning can better be described in terms of nonspatial linguistic processes. Clark asked subjects to respond to problems such as: If John isn't as good as Pete, and Dick isn't as good as John, then who is the best? The overall average response times for eight problem types are given in Box 7-8. The performance on the first eight problems seems to fit nicely with the results of DeSoto and Huttenlocher: performance was better on problems where the propositions went from better-to-worse, such as 1a and 1b, rather than worse-to-better, such as 2a and 2b; and performance was better when the third term was the subject of the second proposition (that is, was end-anchored) as in 1b, 2b, and 3a and b rather than the object, as in 1a, 2a, and 4a and b. However, based on the new information provided by the eight negative examples, Clark proposed three principles to describe reasoning in terms of linguistic processes:

> *the primacy of functional relations*—the idea that it is the logical (or functional) relations in a sentence which are stored rather than the grammatical relations of voice and negatives; for example, "A is led by B" may be translated as "B leads A," or "A is not as good as B" may be translated as "B is better than A."

> *lexical markings*—adjectives that imply both a scale name and a position on the scale (marked adjectives) such as "bad" or "short" require more effort to encode than adjectives which imply only the scale name but no position on the scale (unmarked adjectives) such as "tall" or "good." (To test whether an adjective is marked, you could ask whether there is a difference between "How tall is X?" *vs.* "How short is X?" or "How good was dinner?" *vs.* "How bad was dinner?" The marked adjectives imply that X is short or that dinner was bad.)

BOX 7-8   MEAN SOLUTION TIME (SEC) FOR SIXTEEN DEDUCTION PROBLEMS

Premises	Who is best?	Who is worst?	Mean
1a. A better than B; B better than C	5.4	6.1	5.8
1b. B better than C; A better than B	5.0	5.5	5.2
2a. C worse than B; B worse than A	6.3	6.5	6.4
2b. B worse than A; C worse than B	5.9	5.0	5.5
3a. A better than B; C worse than B	5.4	5.3	5.3
3b. C worse than B; A better than B	4.8	5.8	5.3
4a. B worse than A; B better than C	5.0	6.0	5.5
4b. B better than C; B worse than A	6.1	5.4	5.8
1'a. A not as bad as B; B not as bad as C	6.8	6.0	6.3
1'b. B not as bad as C; A not as bad as B	7.2	6.6	6.8
2'a. C not as good as B; B not as good as A	5.6	6.6	6.1
2'b. B not as good as A; C not as good as B	6.1	6.6	6.4
3'a. A not as bad as B; C not as good as B	6.3	6.7	6.5
3'b. C not as good as B; A not as bad as B	6.7	6.3	6.5
4'a. B not as good as A; B not as bad as C	6.1	6.2	6.1
4'b. B not as bad as C; B not as good as A	5.5	7.1	6.2

From Clark (1969)

Simpler lexicon such as "X is better than Y" is easier to store and process than "Y is worse than X."

the principle of congruence—thinkers compare the question with the functional information in memory and reformulate the question if necessary to make it congruent with this information.

The principle of functional relations correctly predicts that the eight problems with negatives will take longer to solve than the eight sentences without negatives, presumably due to an extra translation step. Similarly, the principle of lexical marking predicts that problems with "bad" or "worse," such as 2 and 1′, should be more difficult than those with good or better such as 1 and 2′. The principle of congruence predicts that if the propositions are given in terms of "worse than," then the question "Who is worst?" will be easier but if the propositions are given in terms of "better than" then "Who is best?" will be easier—a finding that is generally upheld. In addition, the principles of congruence and functional relation suggest that problems 3 and 4′ (with functionally identical sentences) should be easier than problems 4 and 3′ (also with functionally identical sentences), since in the former if A is worse than B then A is worst, and if A is better than B then A is best, but not in the latter. Most of Clark's results are consistent with Huttenlocher's and with DeSoto's findings, and his linguistic interpretation provides a different—albeit not necessarily contradictory—analysis of the reasoning process primarily in terms of how individual propositions are encoded and processed. The fact that there are differences between the a-form and b-form of the eight problems, however, is not well explained by Clark and seems to be best interpreted by the principle of the end-anchoring of functional propositions. For example, problem 2b presents items in the order B, A, C, so that the end term, C, is anchored into the A > B relations; while problem 2a presents items in the order C, B, B, so that first the B > C relation is established but the end term, A, is not mentioned next. As predicted by the end-anchoring idea, 2a takes more time to solve than does 2b.

More recently, Potts (1972) has focused on the cognitive processes a thinker goes through to answer a question about a linear ordering. Potts had subjects read a paragraph about a linear ordering in the form A > B, B > C, C > D as shown in Box 7-9. One interesting finding was that the subjects were more accurate in answering questions about the remote pairs, such as A > C, B > D and A > D, than they were about the adjacent pairs, A > B, B > C, C > D, even though the former were not presented and had to be deduced from the adjacents. This "distance effect" result indicated that subjects did not simply copy the list of three presented propositions (i.e., three separate sentences) in their memories, but rather may have formed a sort of ordering list such as a spatial list.

When the subjects were presented with a question about the ordering of certain animals—bear > hawk > wolf > deer—like "Is the hawk smarter than the deer?" they used a sort of end-anchoring strategy, according to Potts. First they checked to see if either term in the question was an end-term in the ordering (e.g., Is hawk the first or last term in the ordering? and, Is deer the first or last term in the ordering?); if not, then they had to process more deeply by checking, for example, to see if the first term in the question was the second to last term in the ordering. Potts' results are given in Box 7-9. As predicted by the model, for example, questions of the form "Is B > C?" and "Is C > B?" took the longest time to answer since they required deeper processing in the model while questions beginning with the A term ("Is A > C?") took the least time to answer. Potts' work provides a good example of how cognitive models of the reasoning process may be established and in this case, also provides a more detailed description of the end-anchoring effect.

BOX 7-9   MEAN RESPONSE TIME (SEC) FOR TWELVE DEDUCTION PROBLEMS

Typical Passage

In a small forest just south of nowhere, a deer, a bear, a wolf and a hawk were battling for dominion over the land. It boiled down to a battle of wits, so intelligence was the crucial factor. The bear was smarter than the hawk, the hawk was smarter than the wolf, and the wolf was smarter than the deer . . . . In the end, each of the battles was decided in its own way and tranquillity returned to the area.

Typical Results

Question Form	Mean Response Time (Sec)
A > B?	1.1
B > C?	2.1
C > D?	2.0
A > C?	1.1
B > D?	1.8
A > D?	1.0
B > A?	1.8
C > B?	2.2
D > C?	1.7
C > A?	1.8
D > B?	1.7
D > A?	1.3

From Potts (1972, 1974)

Algebra Story Problems

Another type of problem that requires logical deductions is algebraic substitution. For example, if you know that A = B + 10, and B = C + 5, then you can deduce that A = C + 15. These kinds of problems may seem similar to linear orderings but they involve exact quantitative relationships among terms rather than simple nonquantitative relations.

Suppes, Loftus, and Jerman (1969) and Loftus and Suppes (1972) gave children algebra story problems like this one: "Committee members brought 3 jars of candy with 14 ounces in each jar, and 2 boxes of candy with 27 ounces in each box. They put the candy into bags that contained 4 ounces each. How many bags did they fill?" The results indicated that the children had more difficulty as the number of computational operations increased, if conversion of units was required, if the problem sentences were complex, and if the problem was different from the previous one. A greater number of deductive steps tended to decrease performance for quantitative tasks but, as Potts found, the greater the distance between terms in the linear ordering the better the performance with nonquantitative tasks; these results fit nicely with the reports of mathematics instructors that estimation without quantities requires a different reasoning process than exact computation.

Set-Subset Relations

Another task that requires logical deductions involves the set-subset relations we discussed earlier in the section about logical errors. If All A are B, and All B are C, then one may deduce that All A are C. This task seems comparable to the nonquantitative linear orderings in Potts' work; and Restle (1959) has shown that set-subset relations and linear orderings involve some of the same mathematical properties.

Frase (1969, 1970, 1972) presented subjects with paragraphs in the form All A are B, All B are C, All C are D, All D are E, in the following way: "The Fundalas are outcasts from other tribes in Central Ugala. It is the custom in this country to get rid of certain types of people. The outcasts in Central Ugala are all hill people. There are about fifteen different tribes in this area. The hill people in Central Ugala are farmers. The upper highlands provide excellent soil for farming. The farmers of this country are peace loving people, which is reflected in their art work." The underlying structure in the paragraph is: All Fundalas are outcasts, All outcasts are hill people, All hill people are farmers, All farmers are peace loving.

In a recall test, in which the subjects were asked to write down all the given facts (e.g., "All Fundalas are outcasts") and the deducible facts (e.g., "All Fundalas are farmers"), they performed much better on recall of presented information than on recall of deducible information. However, on recognition tests in which the subjects were asked whether a given statement was true (e.g., "All Fundalas are outcasts" or "All Fundalas are farmers," etc.) they performed just as well or, in some cases better, on deducible statements as on presented information. These recognition results are consistent with the findings described by Potts that performance was just as good or better on remote pairs (deduced) as on adjacent pairs (presented). Apparently, the main difference between Frase's task and Potts' task was that in Frase's it may have been more difficult for the subjects to determine the set inclusion relation, perhaps due to the extraneous information and the lack of cues like "All ____ are ____ " or "____ is a subset of ____ ."

Griggs (1974) directly compared recognition for linear orderings and set inclusion in a single set of experiments that used questions such as Is A a B? For linear orderings, performance on deduced information was better than on presented information, as Potts had found. For set inclusion, performance on deduced information was better than on presented information if the answer was No and the reverse was found if the answer was Yes. The performance of the subjects who were given set inclusion relations was strongly influenced by logical errors, especially invalid conversion (if All A are B then All B are A); when the subjects were given special training in avoiding invalid conversions, the difference between performance on Yes and No questions was erased and the set inclusion results were similar to the linear ordering results—better performance on deduced information than on presented information.

Although there were some differences in results and more research is needed, the work with both linear orderings and with set inclusion seems consistent with DeSoto's (1960) observation that human beings have a strong tendency to organize information or to use "ordering schemata" strategy. Both tasks conflict with the idea that people store information in sentences as presented; rather there is evidence that they store it by building a list or some other internal cognitive structure.

Models of Reasoning

Models of Syllogistic Reasoning

The information processing approach has encouraged the reformulation of old theories and the development of new ones based on the operation of specific models of the reasoning processes for various tasks. These models may be represented as computer programs, discussed in the previous chapter, as mathematical equations, mentioned in Chapter 2, or as flow charts. For example, Box 7-10 shows a flow diagram of the processes

**BOX 7-10   AN INFORMATION PROCESSING MODEL OF SYLLOGISTIC
            REASONING**

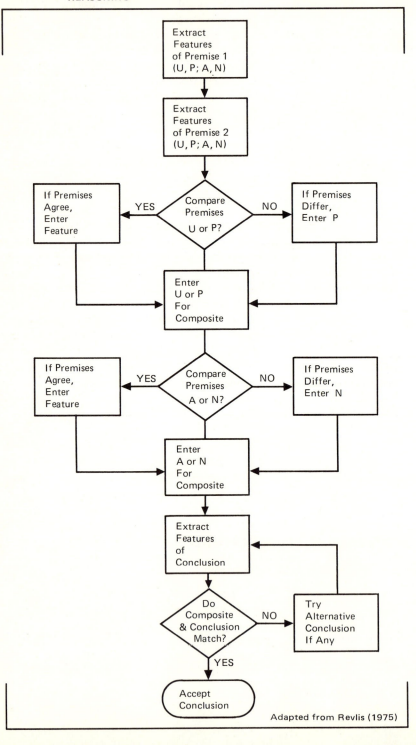

Adapted from Revlis (1975)

involved in syllogistic reasoning based on a reformulation of the idea of atmosphere effect (Revlis, 1975).

In the first stage of the model, the subject extracts two pieces of information from each premise—whether the premise is *universal* (All A are B) or *particular* (Some A are B), and whether the premise is *affirmative* (are) or *negative* (are not). In stage 2, the subject determines the same two characteristics of the composite of the two premises based on two rules: (1) if both premises are universal, the composite is universal; if one or both are particular, then the composite is particular; (2) if both premises are affirmative, the composite is affirmative; if one or both are negative, the composite is negative. The subject then extracts the two characteristics of the conclusion (stage 3). Finally, in stage 4, the subject compares the two characteristics of the conclusion with the two characteristics of the composite and answers Yes if they match and No if they don't.

The advantage of specifying the atmosphere effect as a precise model of information processing stages and rules is that it provides specific predictions that can be tested; as Revlis notes, "The model is sufficiently detailed to make predictions concerning solutions to every syllogism." For example, the model predicts that subjects would never respond that no valid conclusion could be drawn even though many premises were invalid (e.g., All P are M, Some M are S.) Further, of the syllogisms that have valid conclusions, errors are predicted for the following forms: All M are P, All M are S; All P are M, All M are S; No M are P, No M are S; and No P are M, No M are S. Thus, the model can make predictions about error rates in syllogistic reasoning and such predictions are easily tested. In this way, information processing models help in creating testable theories—one of the main conditions for the advance of science (Popper, 1959).

Models of Linear Orderings

A second example, given in Box 7-11, provides the processes involved in making deductions concerning a four-term linear ordering (Potts, 1972). As with the Revlis model, the subject's reasoning process is represented as a flow diagram. When a subject has learned an ordering such as $A > B > C > D$ and is given a question like Is $A > C$?, the model suggests the following stages: The first item in the test question is checked to see whether it is the first item in the ordering (if so, answer True) or the last item in the ordering (answer False). Otherwise, the second item in the test question is checked to see whether it is the first item in the ordering (if so, answer False) or the last item in the ordering (answer True). If none of these tests produces a response, the subject checks to see if the second item in the question pair is the second to last item in

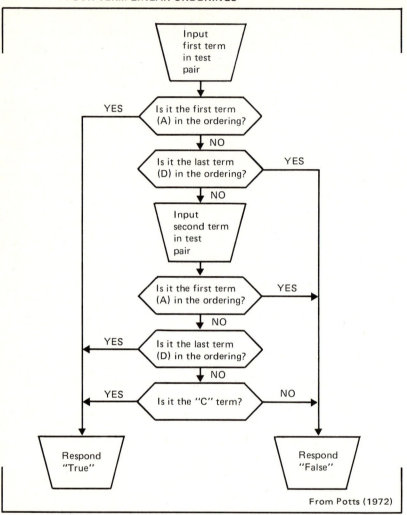

From Potts (1972)

the ordering; if so, the subject answers True and if not, the answer is False. The model provides specific predictions which can be tested, e.g., test questions with A or D as the first item should be answered most quickly, test questions with B or C as the first item but A or D as the second should be a little slower, and test questions with B or C as first and second items should be longest. Potts' model is partially a reformulation of the idea of end-anchoring and provides a new and testable way of presenting the idea.

Evaluation

The syllogistic reasoning or deductive reasoning task, like the inductive reasoning task we discussed in Chapter 2, has been a major method of studying human thinking. Like the rule induction paradigm, the deductive reasoning task has the advantage of being an agreed-upon and well-studied method and the disadvantage of being a specific type of reasoning that may have nongeneralizable characteristics.

The fact that human logic and formal logic do not always coincide has been the source of many interesting insights into the human thought process, but more efforts are needed to connect this work with other theories of human problem solving and memory processes. There is now an increasing literature on memory retrieval processes for set-subset information (Collins & Quillian, 1969; Meyer, 1970) and on memory storage of propositions (Collins & Quillian, 1972; Rumelhart, Lindsay, & Norman, 1972; Kintsch, 1972). These new developments should be integrated with conceptualizations of the deductive reasoning process.

Suggested Readings

Falmagne, R. (Ed.) *Psychological studies of logic and its development.* Potomac, MD.: Erlbaum, 1975. Good selection of readings on current topics in the psychology of deductive reasoning.

Johnson, D. M. *A systematic introduction to the psychology of thinking.* New York: Harper & Row, 1972. Chapter 6 surveys the basic literature in deductive reasoning.

Wason, P. C., & Johnson-Laird, P. N. *Thinking and reasoning.* Baltimore, Md.: Penguin, 1968. Classic papers by Chapman & Chapman, by Henle, and by DeSoto, London, & Handel.

Wason, P. C., & Johnson-Laird, P. N. *Psychology of reasoning: Structure and content.* London: Batsford, 1972. Basic research and theory in syllogistic reasoning.

8

Cognitive Development: Thinking as Influenced by Growth

cognitive development

Preview of Chapter 8

Introduction

Box 8-1 presents words for a free association task. Your job is to read each word, individually and separately, and after each write down the first word that comes to your mind. You may cover the words with a piece of paper and move it down the page one word at a time, giving your association for each word as you come to it. When you have given associations for all the words, look at Box 8-2.

This type of task has been given to subjects of varying ages and several interesting differences in the responses related to age have been noted. For example, Box 8-2 gives the number of children and the number

---

BOX 8-1   FREE ASSOCIATION TEST

Give your first word association for each of the following words.

Table   _____

Dark   _____

Man   _____

Deep   _____

Soft   _____

Mountain   _____

of adults who made each of two basic responses (Woodrow & Lowell, 1916). Don't worry if your responses seem closer to the children's norms or are so bizarre they don't appear on the table—things may have changed a bit since 1916. As Box 8-2 shows, the children tended to give words that would occur with the stimulus word in a sentence (phrase completion) and hence were generally different parts of speech, while the adults tended to give words with the same or opposite meaning and were thus from the same part of speech. More recently, similar differences were obtained by Ervin (1961), Palermo (1963), Palermo and Jenkins (1963), and Brown and Berko (1960). As an example, Palermo and Jenkins asked for associations to such words as Deep, Mutton, Red, Live, Lift, Make; the norm responses for children were, respectively, Hole, Button, Color, House, Heavy, It and the respective norms for adults were Shallow, Sheep, White, Die, Carry, and Build. Brown and Berko (1960), in noting a similar pattern in their data, suggested that the children tended to give "heterogeneous-by-part-of-speech" responses and the adults tended to give "homogeneous-by-part-of-speech respones." The systematic differences between the responses of children and adults implies that there is a basic difference in the way words (and perhaps all concepts) are stored in memory. The fact that children tend to complete phrases suggests that they store strings of words exactly as they would

BOX 8-2   WORD ASSOCIATIONS FOR ADULTS AND CHILDREN

Stimulus	Response	1000 Children	1000 Adults
Table	Eat	358	63
	Chair	24	274
Dark	Night	421	221
	Light	38	427
Man	Work	168	17
	Woman	8	394
Deep	Hole	257	32
	Shallow	6	180
Soft	Pillow	138	53
	Hard	27	365
Mountain	High	390	246
	Hill	91	184

Based on data from Woodrow & Lowell (1916)

be used in ordinary speech whereas adults tend to classify words both by meaning and by part of speech. Such findings suggest that the cognitive processes of children and adults differ, not just in a quantitative way in that adults know more, but also in a qualitative way in that children may not think the same way that adults do.

Take a look at the six sentences in Box 8-3. Read each sentence and after each try to define CORPLUM. Note how your definition is clarified with each new sentence and count how many sentences are required for you to "know" the meaning of CORPLUM. Older children and adults are readily able to abstract the meaning of new words based on their context but Werner and Kaplan (1952) found that younger children behaved differently. They had much more difficulty in figuring out the word meaning; their definitions tended to be tied very closely to the context of the sentence with the meanings of new words completely changing for each new sentence. A typical younger child listened to the sentence, "People talk about the BORDICKS of others and don't like to talk about their own," and then gave the following definition of BORDICKS (faults): "Well, BORDICK means people talk about others and don't talk about themselves, that's what BORDICK means." Apparently, the younger children viewed each sentence separately, with the word meaning changing from sentence to sentence, while the older children and adults could consider several contexts at once, abstracting the common meaning from all.

BOX 8-3   THE CORPLUM PROBLEM

See if you can tell what a "corplum" is:

A corplum may be used for support.

Corplums may be used to close off an open space.

A corplum may be long or short, thick or thin, strong or weak.

A wet corplum does not burn.

You can make a corplum smoother with sandpaper.

The painter used a corplum to mix his paints.

From Werner & Kaplan (1952)

The Cognitive Development Definition of Thinking

According to the theories of cognitive development, thinking depends on how a person represents the world and in what ways a person can manipulate or act upon this internal representation. A major contribution of the cognitive development approach is that different ways of representing the world and different ways of manipulating those representations are present at different stages in development—for example, the way a four-year-old child represents the world is quite different from the way an adult does.

As you may have noticed, the idea that internal mental structures are the substance of our cognitive processes is closely related both to Bartlett's idea of the schema and to the Gestalt idea of organization. In fact, the best known figure in the area of cognitive development, Jean Piaget, calls the internal mental structures or representations "schemata" and the ways we manipulate them when thinking he calls "operations." However, in Piaget's theory, schemata continually grow and develop rather than remaining fixed. Describing thinking at various stages thus becomes a problem of trying to define the schema (or mental structure) and the operations (or internal actions) that a problem solver is using.

Piaget's Theory: Introduction

Piaget is not a psychologist by training nor an American, yet he has made a tremendous impact, perhaps because of his unusual perspective, on American developmental psychology. Piaget is a French-speaking Swiss, a zoologist by training and a philosopher by interest, and since 1927 he and his associates in Geneva have published the world's largest existing source of information and theories on cognitive development.

Piaget's main interest is in "genetic epistemology"—the study of the growth of knowledge in humans. As Elkind (1967) has pointed out concerning Piaget, "He is not fundamentally a child psychologist concerned with the practical issues of child growth and development. He is rather, first and foremost, a genetic epistemologist concerned with the nature of knowledge and with the structures and processes by which it is acquired." However, instead of making armchair theories of how knowledge accumulates in the mind of a human being, he decided he would study the process empirically. Starting with a newborn infant, who presumably had very little knowledge, Piaget would study how knowledge came to be represented in the mind and how it changed with growth. Thus Piaget's study of cognitive development was intended to provide information on an important philosophical question; its effect has also been to stimulate the development of whole new areas in psychology.

Piaget's method of study began as being mainly *clinical*—that is, he has carefully observed how children behave in various "real world" situations, and based on these observations, has developed his theories of cognitive growth. He kept detailed diaries on the early life of each of his three children, which eventually became the basis for his books, *The Origins of Intelligence in Children* (1952), *Play, Dreams and Imitation in Childhood* (1951), and *The Construction of Reality in the Child* (1954). Piaget's method has received a great deal of criticism on two basic accounts—

The clinical method is too loose and lacks good experimental control. For example, Rosenthal and Jacobson (1968) have shown that the experimenter can influence subjects in subtle ways such as by facial expression without being aware of it. In addition, Piaget's method depends heavily on language concepts which young children may not use in the same way as adults.

The theories are too general and vague. Like many of Freud's theories, they are sometimes not even testable in a clear experiment, and those theories which are testable have often been shown not to hold up (Gelman, 1969).

Yet the dozens of books and hundreds of articles by Piaget and his associates continue to stimulate and influence our view of human cognitive growth, including human thinking. Let us now turn to a brief summary of those ideas.

Piaget's Theory: Stage Independent

Piaget's theory may be roughly divided into two parts—the enumeration of the stages of human cognitive development, and the general concepts which are independent of stages.

The premise from which Piaget begins his stage-independent theory is that human beings are alive, striving to survive and to function successfully in their environments. In order to survive, they must take in information from their environments; however, out of all the possible information that exists, only a small part can be taken in by an individual since all new knowledge must be related to existing knowledge. Information from the outside world which is very different from a person's existing knowledge will not be understood or encoded because there is no way to relate it to the existing knowledge just as information which is exactly the same as existing knowledge will have no influence since it adds nothing new. However, outside information which is similar, but not identical, to the existing knowledge structures will be taken in (or assimilated) by the existing mental structures and there will also be some changes in mental organization in order to fit (or accommodate) the new knowledge. The resulting mental structure will be a bit more sophisticated since it includes more knowledge and thus will be able to assimilate even more complex information, restructure to fit that new knowledge, and so on. All cognitive growth, according to this view, depends on our taking in information which is slightly different from what we already know and then restructuring our knowledge to integrate both the old and new information; this process produces an improved cognitive structure which will help us to survive and function better.

As can be inferred from this brief description, Piaget's theory is based on several fundamental ideas:

It is life-based—the accumulation of better and better modes of representing reality is accomplished in order to help us survive and get along in our environment.

Knowledge is mediate rather than immediate—our view of reality is not passively registered but is actively constructed by continually relating new information to existing knowledge.

Motivation for cognitive growth is intrinsic—living things naturally seek out information that is just slightly more complex than their existing knowledge.

It is dialectic—there is a continual interaction between the desire to have a well-organized bank of knowledge (accommodation) and the need for more information (assimilation) which is continuously disrupting existing organizations and evoking slightly more sophisticated ones.

The main terms that Piaget uses to explain his stage-independent theory are given in Box 8-4. The theory is often hard for American psychologists to understand partly because it borrows heavily from unfamiliar biological concepts, partly because it is translated from French, and partly because it is massive, sometimes vague, and difficult. However, a good understanding of some of the basic ideas he uses will help you to understand Piaget's theory and we shall discuss the following terms: structures and schemata; functions, organization, and adaptation; equilibration, assimilation, and accommodation.

According to Piaget, the way a person represents the world—the internal mental structures or schemata—change systematically with development. If the structures did not change there could be no development for there could be no growth in knowledge. For example, the infant structures information based on how the information relates to actions such as sucking. Piaget refers to the "sucking schema" to suggest that knowledge about the world is stored in the form of how objects respond to sucking.

BOX 8-4 PIAGET'S STAGE INDEPENDENT THEORY

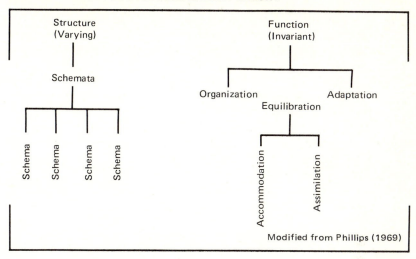

Modified from Phillips (1969)

Although cognitive structures change (e.g., we hope that adults do not represent the world solely in terms of how things taste or feel), our function as living beings remains invariant. There are two basic functions common to all biological systems: the need to stay alive and survive in our environment—adaptation—and the need to have well-organized and orderly internal structure—organization. In terms of cognitive structure, this means that we have a constant need for our representation of the world to be well organized, internally consistent, and orderly while at the same time we have a need to bring in new information which will disrupt the internal organization but will help us better to survive and adapt to the reality of the external world.

The mechanisms for balancing this conflict between the need for organization and the need for adaptation are equilibration, assimilation, and accommodation. Assimilation and accommodation are called "functional invariants" because they are constantly involved in the growth of any biological system—including the growth of knowledge. Assimilation occurs whenever something from outside the system is taken in and incorporated; the most obvious example is the ingestion of food in which something from the environment becomes part of us. In short, input is changed to fit the existing internal structure. Accommodation is the complementary process that always must accompany assimilation—the changing of the existing internal structure to fit the newly assimilated input. Cognitive growth involves continually assimilating new knowledge and accommodating existing knowledge. Piaget cites imitation as a temporary imbalance in which accommodation overpowers assimilation, and playing as a situation in which assimilation overpowers accommodation.

Most of the time, however, in a normally functioning person there is a striving for a balance between assimilation and accommodation; this balancing process is called equilibration and it is actually responsible for all cognitive growth. When new information is assimilated to existing structures, a process of equilibration begins which results in a new cognitive structure—one that incorporates some of the new information but which also retains some of the prior information all organized in a more efficient way. Thus equilibration is never finished because as soon as new information is assimilated the process begins again, resulting in progressively better representations of the world

Piaget's Theory: Stage Dependent

The progressive changes in cognitive structure may vary in rate from person to person but they follow an invariant sequence, always moving in the same order, and the progressive changes in the way children organize information can be characterized as a sequence of stages. The four main periods of cognitive growth are shown in Box 8-5, although in some writings preoperations and concrete operations are considered to be a single period. The ages shown are averages based on Piaget's observations, but they are only approximate and subject to large individual differences; the order of the four periods is, however, fixed and according to the theory, all human beings progress through them in the same order.

The stages are based on two aspects of cognitive life:

structure—how the child represents the world, and
operations—how the child can act upon this representation.

The sequence of stages thus represent progressively better cognitive structures accompanied by progressively more powerful cognitive operations.

BOX 8–5   PIAGET'S STAGE DEPENDENT THEORY

Sensorimotor Period	0–2	years
Preoperational Period	2–7	years
Concrete Operations Period	7–11	years
Formal Operations Period	11–adult	

Sensorimotor Period

For approximately the first two years of life children progress through the six stages of the *sensorimotor period*. Most of Piaget's research on this period came from diaries of careful observations of his own three children—Laurent, Lucienne, and Jacqueline—which were later summarized in his classic books such as *Origins of Intelligence in Children* (1952). At this stage the child represents the world in terms of actions—sucking, shaking, looking, dropping, etc.—and performs operations or manipulations on actual objects rather than on internal representations. The reason for the peculiar name, sensorimotor, is that during this period the infant learns to coordinate its senses with motor behavior such as adapting the sucking reflex to search for a nipple before sucking, coordinating the movement of the hand to the mouth, or visually following an object moving through the environment.

One of the most interesting accomplishments achieved during the sensorimotor period involves the progressive development of the concept of object permanence. At birth, the infant has no concept of object permanence: when objects are out of the visual field they no longer exist; the only reality is the ongoing sensory stimulation. For example, a newborn infant will not search for an object that leaves its field of vision (see the first entry in Box 8-6). Later, the concept begins to develop as an infant will actively search for a vanished object but cannot yet follow a sequence of displacements as is described in the second entry of Box 8-6. Eventually, the child further refines the concept of objects and is able to follow an object through a series of displacements (third entry) and finally to represent the displacements mentally (fourth entry). The ability to represent objects mentally and to move them from place to place mentally (as required in the fourth entry) marks the end of the sensorimotor period.

Another interesting accomplishment of the sensorimotor period is a progressive ability to control and investigate the environment. At first, infants have only reflexes like sucking and grasping which become adapted to the environment (first entry of Box 8-7). Primary circular reactions are attempts by the infant to gain sensorimotor coordination by repeating movements such as hand to mouth, following objects with the eyes, and so on, over and over again. These movements are circular because they are repeated several times; they are primary because they involve a single simple act that is not intentionally initiated by the infant (second entry). Secondary circular reactions are repeated efforts to control the environment that are initiated by the infant—an example is given in the third entry of Box 8-7. Tertiary circular reactions are advances over the previous two because the child actively initiates a series of systematic manipulations such as dropping objects from different heights (entry four). Finally, the beginning of representational thought occurs when, as

On the basis of careful observations of his three children—Lucienne, Laurent, and Jacqueline—Piaget concluded that the concept of object permanence develops during the first two years of life. Excerpts are given below:

7 months, 30 days. (No special behavior.)
Lucienne grasps a small doll which I present to her for the first time. She examines it with great interest, then lets go (not intentionally); she immediately looks for it in front of her but does not see it right away. When she has found it, I take it from her and place a coverlet over it, before her eyes (Lucienne is seated); no reaction.

9 months, 17 days. (Active search for vanished objects without taking account of a sequence of visual displacements.)
Laurent is placed on a sofa between a coverlet A on the right and a wool garment B on the left. I place my watch under A; he gently raises the coverlet, perceives part of the object, uncovers it, and grasps it. The same thing happens a second and a third time . . . . I then place the watch under B; Laurent watches this maneuver attentively, but at the moment the watch has disappeared under B, he turns back toward A and searches for the object under that screen. I again place the watch under B; he again searches for it under A . . . .

11 months, 22 days. (Taking account of visual displacements.)
Laurent is seated between two cushions A and B. I hide my watch alternately under each; Laurent constantly searches for the object where it has just disappeared, that is, sometimes under A and sometimes under B, without remaining attached to a privileged position as during the [above] stage. . . . At 12 months, 20 days, he also searches sequentially in both my hands for a button I am hiding. Afterward he tries to see behind me when I make the button roll on the floor (on which I am seated) even though, to fool him, I hold out my two closed hands.

18 months, 8 days. (Internally representing the visual displacements.)
Jacqueline throws a ball under a sofa. Instead of bending down at once and searching for it on the floor she looks at the place, realizes that the ball must have crossed under the sofa, and sets out to go behind it. . . . She begins by turning her back on the place where the ball disappeared, goes around the table, and finally arrives behind the sofa at the correct place. Thus she has closed the circle [of displacements] by an itinerary different from that of the object.

From Piaget (1954)

in the final entry for example, Lucienne represents the matchbook as her mouth and derives a solution which she then applies.

Preoperational Period

At the end of the sensorimotor and the beginning of the *preoperational period*, the child has made some startling advances including sensorimotor coordination, the ability to represent objects rather than

BOX 8-7 DEVELOPMENT FROM REFLEXES TO REACTIONS TO THOUGHT

0 months, 20 days. (Adaptation of reflexes.)
He bites the breast which is given him, 5 cm from the nipple. For a moment he sucks the skin when he lets go in order to move his mouth about 2 cm. As soon as he begins sucking again he stops . . . when his search subsequently leads him accidentally to touch the nipple with the mucosa of the upper lip (his mouth being wide open), he at once adjusts his lips and begins to suck.

1 month, 1 day. (Primary circular reactions.)
. . . his right hand may be seen approaching his mouth. . . But as only the index finger was grasped, the hand fell out again. Shortly afterward it returned. This time the thumb was in the mouth. . . . I then remove the hand and place it near his waist. . . . after a few minutes the lips move and the hand approaches them again. This time there is a series of setbacks . . . [but finally] the hand enters the mouth. . . . I again remove the hand. Again lip movements cease, new attempts ensue, success results for the ninth and tenth time, after which the experiment is interrupted.

3 months, 5 days. (Secondary circular reactions.)
Lucienne shakes her bassinet by moving her legs violently (bending and unbending them, etc.), which makes the cloth dolls swing from the hood. Lucienne looks at them, smiling, and recommences at once. . . . Lucienne, at four months, 27 days, is lying in her bassinet. I hang a doll [from the hood] over her feet which immediately sets in motion the schema of shaking. But her feet reach the doll right away and give it a violent motion, which Lucienne surveys with delight. Afterward she looks at her motionless foot for a second, then recommences.

10 months, 11 days. (Tertiary circular reactions.)
Laurent is lying on his back . . . He grasps in succession a celluloid swan, a box, etc., stretches out his arm and lets them fall. He distinctly varies the positions of the fall. Sometimes he stretches out his arm vertically, sometimes he holds it obliquely, in front or behind. . . . When the object falls in a new position (for example, on his pillow), he lets it fall two or three times more in the same place . . . then he modifies the situation.

1 year, 4 months, 0 days. (Beginning of thought.)
I put [a] chain into a box and reduce the opening to 3 mm. It is understood that Lucienne is not aware of the functioning of the opening and closing of the matchbox. . . . She only possesses the two preceding schemata: turning the box over . . . and sliding her fingers into the slit to make the chain come out. It is, of course, this last procedure that she tries first: she puts her finger inside and gropes to reach the chain, but fails completely. A pause follows during which Lucienne manifests a very curious reaction. . . . She looks at the slit with great attention; then, several times in succession, she opens and shuts her mouth, at first slightly, then wider and wider!
. . . [Then] Lucienne unhesitatingly puts her finger in the slit and, instead of trying as before to reach the chain, she pulls so as to enlarge the opening. She succeeds and grasps the chain.

From Piaget (1954)

just actions and sensations, and the rudiments of symbolic problem solving. Yet the child at this stage deals with static, concrete images and is limited by the following six problems (Phillips, 1969):

concreteness—the child can deal only with concrete objects that are physically present here and now;

irreversibility—the child is unable to rearrange objects mentally or to conceive of them in some other arrangement;

egocentrism—the child believes that everyone sees the world through his or her eyes, and that what the child is experiencing is what everyone else is experiencing;

centering—the child can attend to only one dimension or aspect of a situation at a time;

states vs. transformations—the child focuses on states, on the perceptual way things look rather than on the operations which produced that state;

transductive reasoning—the child reasons that if A causes B then B causes A.

Examples of these are given in Box 8-8. The child is struck by the perceptual way the world looks and is "preoperational" because it cannot perform mental operations on its representations and cannot change its representation of the world unless the perceptual world also changes.

Concrete Operations

At about age seven, as the child enters into the period of *concrete operations,* Piaget noted a basic change in the child's mental structures and operations. By the end of the preoperational period, the child has achieved or begun to achieve the ability to reverse or decenter (that is, to simultaneously consider two or more dimensions at a time), to focus on transformations rather than static perceptual states, and has begun to lose its egocentrism and transductive reasoning. The world comes to be represented not as a set of static perceptual images, but rather as concrete objects which can be mentally acted upon and changed in logical ways. Reversibility is a newly acquired mental operation which frees the child from being dominated by how things look. The name, concrete operations, comes from this newly acquired ability to mentally operate or change a concrete situation, and to perform logical operations on a situation in one's head.

These new mental operations are displayed in a series of mini-experiments on what Piaget calls *conservation,* including conservation of number, conservation of substance, and conservation of quantity. For example, consider the conservation of number situation shown in the top of Box 8-9. If Piaget showed a handful of pennies, for example, to a preoperational child, the child would base its judgment of quantity on perceptual appearance. The child might say there are "more" pennies when they are spread out than when they are bunched together. Even if the child is asked to count the pennies under each arrangement, it still insists there are more when they are spread out. The child is centering on the dimension of length and cannot mentally reverse the operation of bunching or spreading out the pennies. However, the slightly older child who has acquired concrete operations is certain that it is the same amount of pennies regardless of how they are arranged. When asked how he knows, the child responds that although one arrangement may look bigger he knows he could move them and get the other arrangement, i.e., he can mentally reverse the situation and rearrange the pennies in his head.

The second panel of Box 8-9 gives an example of conservation of substance. A plasticene ball is shown to a child, and then it is stretched out to form a sausage before the child's eyes. The preoperational child generally claims that when the ball is made into a sausage it is now "more" (sometimes the ball is seen as "more" than the sausage shape). In these cases the child is centering on just one dimension such as length (or width), and lacks the ability to perform the mental operation of reversibility—of mentally changing the ball into sausage or sausage into ball. The older child in concrete operations, however, is able to say that the "same" amount of plasticene is part of each shape. Children in this period are not overcome by how things look, and may decenter—consider both length and width simultaneously—and reverse—mentally reshape the plasticene.

The lower panel in Box 8-9 gives an example of conservation of quantity. When liquid is poured from a short-fat glass into a tall-thin glass, the preoperational child may say that there is "more" (or "less") liquid in the tall glass than when it is in the short glass. The child focuses, or centers on the dimension of height (or width) to base the decision, and is unable to reverse. However, the slightly older child who has acquired concrete operations says that the amount of liquid is the "same"; this child can decenter—realize that height and width compensate for one another—and can reverse—can mentally pour the liquid from one glass to another.

Box 8-10 gives an example of the change in egocentrism that occurs at this period—the three mountain problem (Piaget & Inhelder, 1956). A set of three mountains, in three-dimensional relief, is placed on a table as shown. The child sits in one chair and a doll is placed on a chair with a different perspective. The child is asked to draw what the doll "sees" from where it is sitting. The preoperational child draws how the scene looks from her own perspective regardless of where the doll is seated while the concrete operational child is capable of drawing the "correct" per-

BOX 8-8   EXAMPLES OF PREOPERATIONAL THOUGHT

Irreversibility
A four-year-old subject is asked:

"Do you have a brother?" He says, "Yes."

"What's his name?" "Jim."

"Does Jim have a brother?" "No."

From Phillips (1969)

Transductive Reasoning
At two years, 14 days, Jacqueline wanted a doll dress that was upstairs. She said "Dress," and when her mother refused to get it, "Daddy get dress." As I also refused, she wanted to go herself "To mommy's room." After several repetitions of this she was told that it was too cold there. There was a long silence, and then: "Not too cold." I asked, "Where?" "In the room." "Why isn't it too cold?" "Get dress."

From Piaget (1951)

Egocentrism
After interviewing children on how they play the game of marbles, Piaget concludes: ". . .how little children from the same class at school, living in the same house, and accustomed to playing with each other, are able to understand each other at this age. Not only do they tell us of totally different rules . . . but when they play together they do not watch each other and do not unify their respective rules even for the duration of the game. The fact of the matter is that neither is trying to get the better of the other: each is merely having a game on his own, trying to hit the marbles in the square, i.e., trying to 'win' from his point of view. [In other situations, such as sitting around the sandbox] one can observe in children between 2 and 6 a characteristic type of pseudo-conversation or 'collective monologue' during which children speak only for themselves. . .and each is concerned only with himself."

From Piaget (1965)

Centering
When the child is asked to put a set of sticks which vary in length in order, the following arrangement is constructed:

Apparently, the child "centers" on only one aspect of the problem (e.g., the tops of the sticks) and cannot simultaneously consider other aspects (e.g., the bottoms of the sticks).

spective. Apparently, the new mental operations acquired during this period allow children to view the world from many possible perspectives rather than the single static image they are currently receiving.

There are, of course, many other examples of the new mental operations that begin to emerge throughout the period of concrete operations.

Concreteness, irreversibility, centering, and states
A four-year-old is asked: "Have you got a friend?"

"Yes, Odette."

"Well look, we're giving you, Clairette, a glass of orangeade (AI, 3/4 full), and we're giving Odette a glass of lemonade (A2, also 3/4 full). Has one of you more to drink than the other?"

"The same."

"This is what Clairette does: she pours her drink into two other glasses (B1 and B2, which are thus half filled). Has Clairette the same amount as Odette?"

"Odette has more."

"Why?"

"Because we've put less in." (She points to the levels in B1 and B2 without taking into account the fact that there were two glasses.)

(Odette's drink was then poured into B3 and B4.) "It's the same."

"And now?" (Pouring Clairette's drink from B1 and B2 into L, a long thin tube, which is then almost full.)

"I've got more."

"Why?"

"We've poured it into that glass (L) and here (B3 and B4) we haven't."

"But were they the same before?"

"Yes."

"And now?"

"I've got more."

"But where does the extra come from?"

"From in there." (B1)

From Piaget (1952)

However, even these advances have their shortcomings. For example, the child in this period, while freed from the perceptual image of how things look, is still tied to concrete objects thought about and manipulated in the here and now. The concrete operational child, while possessing the powerful operations of reversibility and decentration, is unable to apply them to abstract situations.

BOX 8-9 TYPICAL CONSERVATION TASKS

Conservation of Number

If the experimenter moves the pennies apart, the subject may say "More."

Conservation of Substance

If the experimenter stretches the plasticene ball, the subject may say "More."

Conservation of Quantity

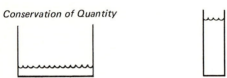

If the experimenter pours the liquid, the subject may say "More."

BOX 8-10 THE THREE MOUNTAIN PROBLEM

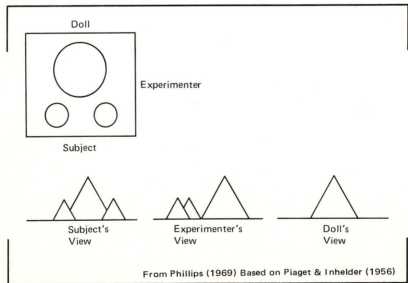

Doll

Experimenter

Subject

Subject's View

Experimenter's View

Doll's View

From Phillips (1969) Based on Piaget & Inhelder (1956)

Formal Operations

By early adolescence, about age eleven, the *formal operations period* begins and with it comes a progressively more sophisticated ability to perform mental operations not only on concrete objects but also on symbols. Although most of Piaget's work has centered on the leap from preoperational to concrete operational thought, formal operations is of some interest because it consists of the mental operations which normal human adults have. During this period the child develops the ability to think in terms of the hypothetical, in terms of probabilities, in terms of the possible rather than the concrete here and now. Given a situation, all possible alternatives can be discovered, and scientific reasoning in its most systematic and sophisticated form begins to emerge.

Box 8-11 shows the pendulum problem which Piaget used to investigate the development of formal operational thought. A pendulum was constructed by hanging an object from a string and the subject had to discover how four factors influenced the frequency of oscillation: the length of the string, the weight of the ball, how high the weight was when it was

BOX 8-11   THE OSCILLATION PROBLEM

Given a pendulum, the subject may vary the length of the string, the weight of the suspended object, the height of the released object, and the force with which the object is released. Which of these influences the rate of oscillation, i.e., how fast the pendulum swings?

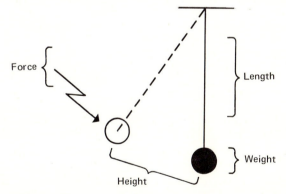

Piaget reports on the performance of a typical adolescent (15 years, 1 month): ". . .after having selected 100 grams with a long string and a medium length string, then 20 grams with a long and a short string, and finally 200 grams with a long and a short, concludes: 'It's the length of the string that makes it go faster or slower; the weight doesn't play any role.' She discounts likewise the height of the drop and the force of her push."

From Inhelder & Piaget (1958)

started, and how hard it was pushed. A typical response is also shown in Box 8-11. Children in the formal operational stage are able to systematically vary conditions—similar to the tertiary circular reactions but more organized—in such a way as to solve the problem.

It may be no coincidence that the cognitive stage of formal operations—the adult ability to think in terms of the hypothetical—is accompanied by social-emotional changes including uncertainty over the meaning of life, the identity crisis, and adolescent idealism. In any case, formal operations is adult thought and Piaget's theory posits no additional stages.

The Big Leap: Bruner's Theory

Perhaps Piaget's greatest contribution is the idea of a qualitative change in cognitive processing between preoperational and concrete operational thought, at about the age of five to seven. Although Piaget relied heavily on the processes of reversibility and decentration as descriptions of new mental powers which occur, there have been many alternative views.

The work of Bruner and his associates (summarized in Bruner, 1964, 1973; Bruner, Olver, & Greenfield, 1966) provides a major supplement to Piaget's theory. For example, instead of four periods of cognitive development, Bruner suggested there are three different modes of representing the world:

> enactive—representing the world in terms of actions (similar to the sensorimotor period);

> iconic—representing the world in terms of static perceptual images (similar to the preoperational period);

> symbolic—the use of language and symbols (similar to operational thinking).

The leap from iconic representation to symbolic representation (or from preoperational to concrete operational thought) is indicated in conservation experiments, but Bruner and Piaget differ on how to explain it. Piaget emphasizes the importance of mental operations such as reversibility as a prerequisite for conservation, and suggests that the child's recognition that identical material must also be equivalent is a side effect. Bruner emphasizes the importance of the child's concept of identity and the linking of identity with equivalence (if it's the "same" it must be "equal") as a prerequisite for conservation, and suggests that reversibility is a side effect. Thus while Bruner's theory closely resembles Piaget's it differs on how to characterize the periods of development (three modes of representation *vs.* four periods) and in how to explain conservation (identity *vs.* reversibility).

Bruner and Kenney (1966) provided an example of the change at about age six from iconic to symbolic representation. Children who were aged five, six, and seven were shown a 3 x 3 matrix of nine glasses with each row getting progressively wider from left to right and each column getting progressively taller from bottom to top, as shown in Box 8-12. A child was asked to look at the matrix and then the experimenter scrambled all the glasses and asked the child to "make something like what was there before." Once the child had successfully reproduced the original array, the experimenter scrambled the glasses again except that the short-thin glass from the lower left corner was now placed in the lower right corner. The child was again asked to "make something like what was there before" but to leave the one short-thin glass in the lower right corner. On the first task (reproduction) there were no differences in errors among the three age groups with all the children performing quite well, although the older children were a bit faster. However, on the second task (transposition) almost none of the younger children and almost all of the older children solved the problem. More careful analysis of the children's comments indicated that the five-year-olds were more likely to represent the matrix iconically—as a spatial image—while the seven-year-olds used language symbols such as height and width.

An experiment by Frank (1966) illustrates Bruner's contention that identity, rather than reversibility, is the basis of conservation. Four-, five-, six-, and seven-year-old children were given a standard conservation of quantity task as a pretest using two standard beakers equally

BOX 8-12   THE NINE GLASS PROBLEM

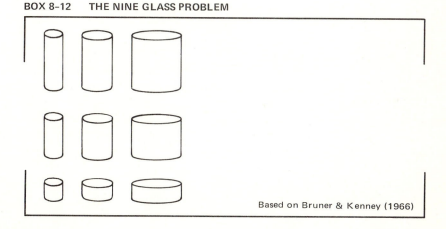

Based on Bruner & Kenney (1966)

filled with water (the children said they were the same). The water was poured from one into another shaped beaker (e.g., short-wide) and the child was asked if the amount of water was still the same. As you can see in Box 8-13, the ability to conserve, indicated by the child's saying that the amount was still the same, increased with age. Next, Frank performed a similar demonstration except that for the pouring, all the beakers were placed behind a screen so that only the tops of the beakers

BOX 8-13   A CONSERVATION EXPERIMENT

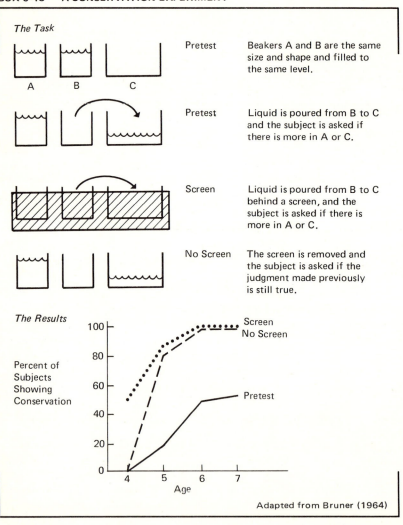

The Task

Pretest — Beakers A and B are the same size and shape and filled to the same level.

Pretest — Liquid is poured from B to C and the subject is asked if there is more in A or C.

Screen — Liquid is poured from B to C behind a screen, and the subject is asked if there is more in A or C.

No Screen — The screen is removed and the subject is asked if the judgment made previously is still true.

The Results

Percent of Subjects Showing Conservation

Screen
No Screen
Pretest

Age

Adapted from Bruner (1964)

were showing. In this case, as is shown in Box 8-13, 50 percent of the four-year-olds, and 90 to 100 percent of the older children predicted that the amount of water in the newly poured beaker was the same. When the screen was removed, all the four-year-olds changed their minds. Apparently the perceptual display overwhelmed them and they decided the wider beaker contained less liquid. However, none of the older children changed their judgments. As one seven-year-old explained, "It looks like more to drink but it is only the same because it is the same water and was only poured from there to there." On a posttest, in which water was poured into a tall-thin beaker along with a standard one, and with no screen, no four-year-olds conserved but the number of older children who conserved increased greatly (see Box 8-13). Apparently, subjects can be correct on reversibility (with screen) but wrong on conservation (without screen); non-conservers may rely on perceptual factors while conservers rely on internal symbolic representations.

Nair (1963, cited in Bruner, 1964) provided a further example of the importance of the concepts of identity and equivalence in conservation. First, children were given a standard pretest for conservation of quantity involving pouring water from one beaker to another. Then, to test for the concepts of identity and equivalence, she added a small toy duck which floated on the water and said that it was moving to a new lake taking its water with it as she poured the water from a tall-narrow beaker into a short-wide one. The children were asked whether the duck now had the same water (identity) and whether it had the same amount of water (equivalence). All the children who conserved in the pretest answered the question about identity correctly; furthermore, reminding the children that the duck was taking its water with it (identity) helped conservation, and reminding them that the new lake must have the same water in it (equivalence) added further help.

Another example of the shift from visual or iconic mode of representation to symbolic came from Olver and Hornsby (1967). Children ranging in age from six to eighteen were asked to tell the similarities and differences among words (e.g., banana, peach, potato, etc.) or among pictures (e.g., bee, balloons, airplanes, etc.) The results indicated that the younger subjects tended to base their judgments on perceptual features such as color, size, and pattern and would say for banana, peach, and potato, "They are curved," while the older children tended to classify objects by their function and would say, in this case, "You can eat them."

The Big Leap: Other Approaches

Bruner's theory accounts for the "big leap" in cognitive processing that occurs at about age five to seven, partly by emphasizing the increased power that language provides—i.e., the shift from iconic to symbolic representation. There are, however, other sources of evidence concerning the big leap from preoperational to concrete operational thought, or from iconic to symbolic representation. Many theorists, like Bruner, emphasize the role of language development rather than Piaget's concept of reversibility and other mental operations.

For example, the introductory section of this chapter provided evidence for a major shift in the way language concepts are stored that occurs at about age six—from heterogeneous to homogeneous word associations (Brown & Berko, 1960). In addition, the work of the Kendlers, discussed in Chapter 2, revealed that reversal shifts were easier for children over six and nonreversal shifts were easier for laboratory animals and children under six. The Kendlers suggested that a set of internal symbols such as language acts as a mediator for the verbal children (e.g., "Pick the large ones") while single perceptual associations are made by the younger children.

In another experiment, Kendler and Kendler (1956, 1962) compared kindergartners and third-grade children on making inferences, as shown in Box 8-14. First, the A-B panel was presented and the children were taught that pressing a button yielded a marble; then, panel A-B was put away and panel X-Y was presented in which pressing a button (X) yielded a ball bearing (Y); then the X-Y panel was put away, and the B-G panel was presented along with a pile of marbles and ball bearings in which putting a marble in the slot produced a toy but putting in a ball bearing produced nothing. After learning how each of the three panels worked sepa-

BOX 8–14   AN INFERENCE PROBLEM

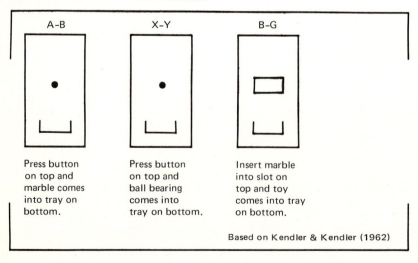

A–B	X–Y	B–G
Press button on top and marble comes into tray on bottom.	Press button on top and ball bearing comes into tray on bottom.	Insert marble into slot on top and toy comes into tray on bottom.

Based on Kendler & Kendler (1962)

rately, the child was given all three panels together. Six percent of the younger children and 50 percent of the older children gave the correct A-B, B-G response. Apparently the ability to mediate—to see the marble as both a result of pressing a button and as a tool for getting the prize—develops with age.

A different kind of evidence comes from the work on eidetic imagery, such as is shown in Box 8-15 (Haber, 1969). When children were shown a picture and then asked about details when the picture was removed, some were able to "see" it in almost perfect detail and to answer questions about it. In a major study, about 8 percent of elementary school children possessed this ability—called eidetic imagery—while almost no adults had it. One explanation (Doob, 1964) is that our society demands that we encode information verbally rather than visually, and that as the ability to read and write increases the use of image representation falls.

Sheldon White (1965) has compiled a list of over twenty changes that occur between the ages of five and seven, including several of those mentioned above. In addition, White notes changes in the following areas:

Resistance to classical conditioning. Susceptibility to classical conditioning—a very simple form of response learning—increases up to age six and decreases thereafter (Razran, 1933; Braun & Geiselhart, 1959).

Far transposition. After learning a simple discrimination task, such as choosing the larger of two squares, older children also succeed in applying the principle to very different situations (squares that are many times larger) while younger children cannot (Reese, 1962; White, 1963).

Discrimination learning. Improvement in discrimination learning increases up to age six and then declines, perhaps because older children develop more complex hypotheses (Weir & Stevenson, 1969; White, 1963).

Development of personal left-right. Children become able to discriminate their left and right sides at about the age of six (Piaget, 1926; Benton, 1959). Since many children with language problems also have trouble distinguishing left and right, this too may be tied to language.

Apparently, there is a major difference in the way the preverbal child and the older child think. The difference is not just a quantitative one, with the older child being "smarter," but rather a qualitative difference in the way thinking occurs. The reason for the differences is still not well understood; for example, it is not clear whether the onset of language is the cause of or the result of these emerging new cognitive powers. As White

BOX 8-15   EIDETIC IMAGERY

Haber (1969), in experiments with eidetic subjects, reported an example of a typical ten-year-old eidetic child who has just seen a color version of the illustration from *Alice in Wonderland* shown here; the picture has been taken away and the child is trying to revisualize it on a blank surface in front of him. What follows is the dialogue between the child and the experimenter.

Experimenter: Do you see something there?

Subject: I see the tree, gray tree with three limbs. I see the cat with stripes around its tail.

E: Can you count those stripes?

S: Yes *(pause)*. There's about 16.

(1965, p. 216) observed, "Surely the move does not take place in one giant step, but the coincidence or sequencing of all the little steps has not yet been investigated and needs to be."

One such careful investigation of the ability to conserve was conducted by Gelman (1969). She gave tests of conservation of length, number, mass, and liquid to five-year-olds; those that failed—i.e., said the line length changed when it was moved, or that the number of pennies differed when rearranged—were given training in how to pay attention to correct aspects of the problem for conservation of length and conservation of number. The training consisted in pointing out what to look for, such as whether the lines were all lined up at the same starting point, and so on. On a posttest, nearly 100 percent of the children conserved length and

E: You're counting what? Black, white or both?

S: Both.

E: Tell me what else you see.

S: And I can see the flowers on the bottom. There's about three stems, but you can see two pairs of flowers. One on the right has green leaves, red flower on bottom with yellow on top. And I can see the girl with a green dress. She's got blonde hair and a red hair band and there are some leaves in the upper left-hand corner where the tree is.

E: Can you tell me about the roots of the tree?

S: Well, there's two of them going down here *(points)* and there's one that cuts off on the left-hand side of the picture.

E: What is the cat doing with its paws?

S: Well, one of them he's holding out and the other one is on the tree.

E: What color is the sky?

S: Can't tell.

E: Can't tell at all?

S: No. I can see the yellowish ground, though.

E: Tell me if any of the parts go away or change at all as I'm talking to you. What color is the girl's dress?

S: Green. It has some white on it.

E: How about her legs and feet?

(The subject looks away from the easel and then back again.)

E: Is the image gone?

S: Yes, except for the tree.

E: Tell me when it goes away.

S: *(pause)* It went away.

From Haber (1969)

number, and 60 percent even gave conservation responses for mass and liquid although they had had no practice on these. One implication is that part of the big leap may be nothing more than learning to pay attention to the relevant cues rather than the development of new mental operations such as reversibility.

Whether the big leap is due to new mental operations (Piaget), or to a better use of language, or to paying closer attention, or just due to the effects of schooling beginning at the age of six is not yet known. However, the curious coincidence of so many cognitive changes, cited by so many different experiments, suggests that "something" is happening and it seems that a better understanding of these changes that lead to adult thinking processes may also help to clarify exactly what adult thinking processes are.

Evaluation

The cognitive development approach provides a unique theory of human thinking and the only one which is explicitly based on the idea that humans are living beings striving to survive and function successfully. Like the information processing approach which is strongly influenced by developments in computer technology, the cognitive developmental approach was heavily influenced by biological concepts. To the extent that the biological analogy is not perfect, theories of human thought based on it are limited.

The cognitive development approach, particularly the work of Piaget, has been criticized on several grounds. Many of Piaget's theories are so vague or ambiguous that they cannot be tested. Some of the theories that are testable fail to be confirmed. Piaget's "experiments" are poorly controlled, lack statistical analysis, and could easily be biased by the experimenter's expectations or by the use of language. However, the unique approach of the cognitive developmentalists offers an emerging source of information which ultimately must be assimilated into the wider area of the psychology of thinking.

Suggested Readings

Bruner, J. S. *Beyond the information given*. New York: Norton, 1973. Articles on cognitive development provide a good summary of the Bruner position.

Ginsburg, H., & Opper, S. *Piaget's theory of intellectual development*. Englewood Cliffs, N.J.: Prentice-Hall, 1969. Summary and interpretation of Piaget's theory for the introductory reader.

Phillips, J. L. *The origins of intellect: Piaget's theory*. San Francisco: Freeman, 1969. Another summary and interpretation of Piaget's theory.

Piaget, J. *Six psychological* studies. New York: Random House, 1967. A collection of some of Piaget's papers, organized and introduced by an American Piagetian psychologist, David Elkind.

References

Ach, N. Determining tendencies. In J. M. Mandler & G. Mandler (Eds. , *Thinking: From association to Gestalt.* New York: Wiley, 1964, 201-7. (Originally published in German in 1905).

Adams, J. *Learning and memory: An introduction.* Homewood, Illinois: Dorsey, 1976.

Adamson, R. E. Functional fixedness as related to problem solving: A repetition of three experiments. *Journal of Experimental Psychology, 1952, 44,* 288-91.

Adamson, R. E., & Taylor, D. W. Functional fixedness as related to elapsed time and set. *Journal of Experimental Psychology, 1954, 47,* 122-216.

Anderson, J. R., & Bower, G. H. *Human associative memory.* New York: Wiley, 1973.

Ausubel, D. P. *Educational psychology: A cognitive view.* New York: Holt, Rinehart & Winston, 1968.

Bartlett, F. C. *Remembering: A study in experimental and social psychology.* London: Cambridge University Press, 1932.

Bartlett, F. C. *Thinking.* London: Allen & Unwin, 1958.

Battersby, W. S., Teuber, H. L., & Bender, M. B. Problem solving behavior in men with frontal or occipital brain injuries. *Journal of Psychology, 1953, 35,* 329-51.

Battig, W. F., & Bourne, L. E., Jr. Concept identification as a function of intra- and inter-dimension variability. *Journal of Experimental Psychology, 1961, 61,* 329-33.

Baum, M. H. Single concept learning as a function of intralist generalization. *Journal of Experimental Psychology, 1954, 47,* 89-94.

Begg, I., & Paivio, A. Concreteness and imagery in sentence meaning. *Journal of Verbal Learning and Verbal Behavior, 1969, 8,* 821-27.

Beilin, H. Developmental determinants of word and nonsense anagram solution. *Journal of Verbal Learning and Verbal Behavior, 1967, 6,* 523-27.

Beilin, H., & Horn, R. Transition probability effects in anagram problem solving. *Journal of Experimental Psychology, 1962, 63,* 514-18.

Benton, A. L. *Right-left discrimination and finger localization: Development and pathology.* New York: Hoeber, 1959.

Berlyne, D. E. *Structure and direction in thinking.* New York: Wiley, 1965.

Birch, H. G. The relation of previous experience to insightful problem solving. *Journal of Comparative Psychology, 1945, 38,* 367-83.

Birch, H. G., & Rabinowitz, H. S. The negative effect of previous experience on productive thinking. *Journal of Experimental Psychology, 1951, 41,* 121-25.

Bjork, R. A. All-or-none subprocesses in learning a complex sequence. *Journal of Mathematical Psychology, 1968, 5,* 182-95.

Bobrow, D. G. Natural language input for a computer problem solving system. In M. Minsky (Ed.), *Semantic information processing.* Cambridge, Mass.: M. I. T. Press, 1968, 135-215.

Bourne, L. E., Jr. *Human conceptual behavior.* Boston: Allyn & Bacon, 1966.

Bourne, L. E., Jr. Knowing and using concepts. *Psychological Review, 1970, 77,* 546-56.

Bourne, L. E. Jr., Ekstrand, B. R., & Dominowski, R. L. *The psychology of thinking.* Englewood Cliffs, N.J.: Prentice-Hall, 1971.

Bower, G. H., & Trabasso, T. R. Reversals prior to solution in concept identification. *Journal of Experimental Psychology,* 1963, *66,* 409-18.

Bower, G. H., & Trabasso, T. R. Concept identification. In R. C. Atkinson (Ed.), *Studies in mathematical psychology.* Stanford, Calif.: Stanford University Press, 1964, 32-94.

Bransford, J. D., & Franks, J. J. The abstraction of linguistic ideas. *Cognitive Psychology,* 1971, *2,* 331-50.

Bransford, J. D., & Johnson, M. K. Contextual prerequisites for understanding: Some investigations of comprehension and recall. *Journal of Verbal Learning and Verbal Behavior,* 1972, *61,* 717-26.

Braun, H. W., & Geiselhart, R. Age differences in the acquisition and extinction of the conditioned eyelid response. *Journal of Experimental Psychology,* 1959, *57,* 386-88.

Brown, R. W., & Berko, J. Word association and the acquisition of grammar. *Child Development,* 1960, *31,* 1-14.

Brown, R. W., & McNeil, D. The "tip-of-the-tongue" phenomena. *Journal of Verbal Learning and Verbal Behavior,* 1966, *5,* 325-37.

Brownell, W. A. Psychological considerations in the learning and teaching of arithmetic. In *The teaching of arithmetic: Tenth yearbook of the National Council of Teachers of Mathematics.* New York: Columbia University Press, 1935, 1-31.

Brownell, W. A., & Moser, H. E. Meaningful *vs.* mechanical learning: A study in grade III subtraction. In *Duke University research studies in education, No. 8.* Durham, N.C.: Duke University Press, 1949, 1-207.

Bruner, J. S. The act of discovery. *Harvard Educational Review.* 1961, *31,* 21-32.

Bruner, J. S. The course of cognitive growth. *American Psychologist,* 1964, *19,* 1-15.

Bruner, J. S. Some elements of discovery. In L. S. Shulman & E. R. Keisler (Eds.), *Learning by discovery.* Chicago: Rand McNally, 1966.

Bruner, J. S. *Toward a theory of instruction.* New York: Norton, 1968.

Bruner, J. S. *Beyond the information given: Studies in the psychology of knowing.* New York: Norton, 1973.

Bruner, J. S., Goodnow, J. J., & Austin, G. A. *A study of thinking.* New York: Wiley, 1956.

Bruner, J. S., & Kenney, H. Multiple ordering. In J. S. Bruner, R. R. Olver, & P. M. Greenfield (Eds.), *Studies in cognitive growth.* New York: Wiley, 1966.

Bruner, J. S., Olver, R. R. & Greenfield, P. M. (Eds.). *Studies in cognitive growth.* New York: Wiley, 1966.

Carmichael, L. L., Hogan, H. P., & Walter, A. A. An experimental study of the effect of language on the reproduction of visually perceived form. *Journal of Experimental Psychology,* 1932, *15,* 73-86.

Chapman, L. J., & Chapman, J. P. Atmosphere effect reexamined. *Journal of Experimental Psychology,* 1959, *58,* 220-26.

Chapman, R. M. Evoked potentials of the brain related to thinking. In F. J. McGuigan & R. A. Schoonover (Eds.), *The psychophysiology of thinking.* New York: Academic Press, 1973, 69-108.

Chomsky, N. *Syntactic structures.* The Hague: Mouton, 1957.

Chomsky, N. Verbal behavior (a review). *Language,* 1959, *35,* 26-58.

Chomsky, N. *Aspects of the theory of syntax.* Cambridge: M.I.T. Press, 1965.

Chomsky, N. *Language and mind.* New York: Harcourt, Brace & World, 1968.

Clark, H. H. Linguistic processes in deductive reasoning. *Psychological Review,* 1969, *76,* 387-404.

Cofer, C. N. Verbal behavior in relation to reasoning and values. In H. Guetz-kow (Ed.), *Group leadership and men.* Pittsburgh: Carnegie Press, 1951.

Colby, K. M. Computer simulation of neurotic processes. In R. W. Stacey & B. D. Waxman (Eds.), *Computers in biomedical research.* New York: Academic Press, 1965.

Colby, K. M., Watt, J., & Gilbert, J. P. A computer model of psychotherapy. *Journal of Nervous and Mental Diseases,* 1966, *142,* 148-52.

Collins, A. M., & Quillian, M. R. Retrieval time from semantic memory. *Journal of Verbal Learning and Verbal Behavior,* 1969, *8,* 240-47.

Collins, A. M., & Quillian, M. R. How to make a language user. In E. Tulving & W. Donaldson (Eds.), *Organization of memory.* New York: Wiley, 1972, 309-51.

Corman, B. R. The effect of varying amounts and kinds of information as guid-ance in problem solving. *Psychological Monographs,* 1957, *71,* Whole No. 431.

Dattman, P. E., & Israel, H. The order of dominance among conceptual capac-ities: An experimental test of Heidbreder's hypothesis. *Journal of Psy-chology,* 1951, *31,* 147-60.

Delgado, J. M. R. *Physical control of the mind.* New York: Harper & Row, 1969.

DeSoto, C. B. Learning and social structure. *Journal of Abnormal and Social Psychology,* 1960, *60,* 417-21.

DeSoto, C. B., London, M., & Handel, S. Social reasoning and spatial para-logic. *Journal of Personality and Social Psychology,* 1965, *2,* 513-21.

Devnich, G. E. Words as "Gestalten." *Journal of Experimental Psychology,* 1937, *20,* 297-300.

Dominowski, R. L., & Duncan, C. P. Anagram solving as a function of bigram frequency. *Journal of Verbal Learning and Verbal Behavior,* 1964, *3,* 321-25.

Doob, L. W. Eidetic images among the Ibo. *Ethnology,* 1964, *3,* 357-63.

Duncker, K. On problem solving. *Psychological Monographs,* 1945, *58:5,* Whole No. 270.

Egan, D. E., & Greeno, J. G. Theory of rule induction: Knowledge acquired in concept learning, serial pattern learning, and problem solving. In L. W. Gregg, (Ed.), *Knowledge and Cognition.* Hillsdale, New Jersey: Erlbaum, 1974.

Elkind, D. Introduction. In J. Piaget, *Six psychological studies.* New York: Random House, 1967.

Ernst, G. W., & Newell, A. *GPS: A case study in generality and problem solv-ing.* New York: Academic Press, 1969.

Ervin, S. M. Changes with age in the verbal determinants of word-association. *American Journal of Psychology,* 1961, *74,* 361-72.

Evans, T. G. A program for the solution of a class of geometry-analogy intel-ligence test questions. In M. L. Minsky (Ed.), *Semantic information pro-cessing.* Cambridge, Mass.: M.I.T. Press, 1968.

Ewert, P. H., & Lambert, J. F. Part II: The effect of verbal instructions upon the formation of a concept. *Journal of General Psychology,* 1932, *6,* 400-411.

Feigenbaum, E. A. Information processing and memory. In D. A. Norman (Ed.), *Models of human memory.* New York: Academic Press, 1970, 451-69.

Filipiak, A. S. *100 puzzles: How to make and how to solve them.* New York: A. S. Barnes, 1942, 20-21.

Frase, L. T. Structural analysis of the knowledge that results from learning about text. *Journal of Educational Psychology,* 1969, *60,* Monograph Supplement 6.

Frase, L. T. Influence of sentence order and amount of higher level text processing upon reproductive and productive memory. *American Educational Research Journal,* 1970, *7,* 307-19.

Frase, L. T. Maintenance and control in the acquisition of knowledge from written materials. In R. O. Freedle & J. B. Carroll (Eds.), *Language comprehension and the acquisition of knowledge.* Washington, D.C.: Winston, 1972, 337-57.

Freibergs, V., & Tulving, E. The effect of practice on utilization of information from positive and negative instances in concept identification. *Canadian Journal of Psychology,* 1961, *15,* 101-6.

Gagné, R. M., & Brown, L. T. Some factors in the programming of conceptual learning. *Journal of Experimental Psychology,* 1961, *62,* 313-21.

Gagné, R. M., & Smith, E. C. A study of the effects of verbalization on problem solving. *Journal of Experimental Psychology,* 1962, *63,* 12-18.

Gelernter, H. Realization of a geometry theorem proving machine. In *Proceedings of 1959 international conference on information processing.* Paris: UNESCO, 1960, 273-82.

Gelman, R. Conservation acquisition: A problem of learning to attend to the relevant attributes. *Journal of Experimental Child Psychology,* 1969, *7,* 67-87.

Greenblatt, R. B., Eastlake, D. E., & Crocker, S. D. The Greenblatt chess program. *Proceedings of the 1967 joint computer conference,* 1967, *30,* 801-10.

Greeno, J. G. The structure of memory and the process of solving problems. In R. L. Solso (Ed.), *Contemporary issues in cognitive psychology: The Loyola symposium.* Washington, D.C.: Winston, 1973, pp. 103-34.

Gregg, L. W., & Simon, H. A. Process models and stochastic theories of simple concept formation. *Journal of Mathematical Psychology,* 1967, *4,* 246-76.

Griggs, R. A. Logical errors in comprehending set inclusion relations in meaningful text. Bloomington, Indiana: Indiana University Mathematical Psychology Program, 1974, No. 74-7.

Guthrie, E. R., & Horton, G. P. *Cats in a puzzle box.* New York: Holt, 1946.

Haber, R. Eidetic images. *Scientific American,* 1969, 36-44.

Harlow, H. H. The formation of learning sets. *Psychological Review,* 1949, *56,* 51-56.

Harlow, H. H., & Harlow, M. K. Learning to think. *Scientific American,* 1949, 36-39.

Hayes, J. R. Problem topology and the solution process. *Journal of Verbal Learning and Verbal Behavior,* 1965, *4,* 371-79.

Hayes, J. R. Memory, goals, and problem solving. In B. Kleinmuntz (Ed.), *Problem solving: Research, method, and theory.* New York: Wiley, 1966, 149-70.

Haygood, R. C., & Bourne, L. E., Jr. Attribute and rule learning aspects of conceptual behavior. *Psychological Review,* 1965, *72,* 175-95.

Haygood, R. C., Harbert, T. L., & Omlor, J. A. Intradimensional variability and concept learning. *Journal of Experimental Psychology,* 1970, *83,* 216-19.

Haygood, R. C., & Stevenson, M. Effects of number of irrelevant dimensions in nonconjunctive concept learning. *Journal of Experimental Psychology,* 1967, *74,* 302-4.

Heidbreder, E. The attainment of concepts: I. Terminology and methodology. *Journal of General Psychology,* 1946, *35,* 173-89.

Heidbreder, E. The attainment of concepts: III. The process. *Journal of Psychology,* 1947, *24,* 93-108.

Hilgard, E. R., Ergren, R. D., & Irvine, R. P. Errors in transfer following learning by understanding: Further studies with Katona's card trick experiments. *Journal of Experimental Psychology,* 1954, *47,* 457-64.

Hilgard, E. R., Irvine, R. P., & Whipple, J. E. Rote memorization, understanding, and transfer: An extension of Katona's card trick experiment. *Journal of Experimental Psychology,* 1953, *46,* 288-92.

Hull, C. L. Quantitative aspects of the evolution of concepts. *Psychological Monographs,* 1920, *28,* No. 123.

Hull, C. L. *Principles of behavior.* New York: Appleton, 1943.

Hulse, S., Deese, J., & Egeth, H. *The psychology of learning.* New York: McGraw-Hill, 1975.

Humphrey, G. *Thinking: An introduction to its experimental psychology.* New York: Wiley, 1963.

Hunt, E. B., Marin, J., & Stone, P. I. *Experiments in induction.* New York: Academic Press, 1966.

Huttenlocher, J. Constructing spatial images: A strategy in reasoning. *Psychological Review,* 1968, *75,* 550-60.

Inhelder, B., & Piaget, J. *The growth of logical thinking from childhood to adolescence.* New York: Basic Books, 1958. (Translated by A. Parson & S. Milgram; original French edition, 1955.)

Jacobson, E. Electrophysiology of mental activity. *American Journal of Psychology,* 1932, *44,* 677-94.

James, W. *The principles of psychology.* New York: Holt, Rinehart & Winston, 1890.

Janis, I. L., & Frick, F. The relationship between attitudes toward conclusions and errors in judging logical validity of syllogisms. *Journal of Experimental Psychology,* 1943, *33,* 73-77.

Jenkins, J. J. Remember that old theory of memory? Well, forget it! *American Psychologist,* 1974, *29,* 785-95.

Johnson, D. M. *A systematic introduction to the psychology of thinking.* New York: Harper & Row, 1972.

Johnson, R. E. Recall of prose as a function of the structural importance of linguistic units. *Journal of Verbal Learning and Verbal Behavior,* 1970, *9,* 12-20.

Judson, A. I., & Cofer, C. N. Reasoning as an associative process: I. "Direction" in a simple verbal problem. *Psychological Reports,* 1956, *2,* 469-76.

Katona, G. *Organizing and memorizing.* New York: Columbia University Press, 1940.

Katona, G. Organizing and memorizing: A reply to Dr. Melton. *American Journal of Psychology,* 1942, *55,* 273-75.

Kendler, H. H., & D'Amato, M. F. A comparison of reversal and nonreversal shifts in human concept information. *Journal of Experimental Psychology,* 1955, *49,* 165-74.

Kendler, H. H., & Kendler, T. S. Inferential behavior in preschool children. *Journal of Experimental Psychology,* 1956, *51,* 311-14.

Kendler, H. H., & Kendler, T. S. Vertical and horizontal processes in problem solving. *Psychological Review,* 1962, *69,* 1-16. (a)

Kendler, H. H., & Kendler, T. S. From discrimination learning to cognitive development: A neobehavioristic odyssey. In W. K. Estes (Ed.), *Handbook of learning and cognitive processes,* Volume 1. Hillsdale, N.J.: Erlbaum, 1975.

Kendler, T. S., & Kendler, H. H. Reversal and nonreversal shifts in kindergarten children. *Journal of Experimental Psychology,* 1959, *58,* 56-60.

Kendler, T. S., & Kendler, H. H. Inferential behavior as a function of subgoal constancy and age. *Journal of Experimental Psychology,* 1962, *64,* 460-66. (b)

Kintsch, W. Notes on the structure of semantic memory. In E. Tulving & W. Donaldson (Eds.), *Organization of memory.* New York: 1972, 247-308.

Kohler, W. *The mentality of apes.* New York: Harcourt, 1925.

Kohler, W. *Gestalt psychology.* New York: Liveright, 1929.

Kohler, W. *The task of Gestalt psychology.* Princeton, N.J.: Princeton University Press, 1969.

Kulpe, O. The modern psychology of thinking. In J. M. Mandler & G. Mandler (Eds.), *Thinking: From association to Gestalt.* New York: Wiley, 1964, 208-16. (Originally published in German in 1912.)

Landauer, T. K., & Meyer, D. E. Category size and semantic-memory retrieval. *Journal of Verbal Learning and Verbal Behavior,* 1972, *11,* 539-49.

Lefford, A. The influence of emotional subject matter on logical reasoning. *Journal of General Psychology,* 1946, *34,* 127-51.

Levine, M. Hypothesis behavior by humans during discrimination learning. *Journal of Experimental Psychology,* 1966, *71,* 331-38.

Lindsay, P. H., & Norman, D. A. *Human information processing: An introduction to psychology.* New York: Academic Press, 1972.

Loftus, E. F., & Suppes, P. Structural variables that determine problem-solving difficulty in computer-assisted instruction. *Journal of Educational Psychology,* 1972, *63,* 531-42.

Luchins, A. S. Mechanization in problem solving. *Psychological Monographs,* 1942, *54:6,* Whole No. 248.

Luchins, A. S., & Luchins, E. H. New experimental attempts at preventing mechanization in problem solving. *Journal of General Psychology,* 1950, *42,* 279-97.

Luchins, A. S., & Luchins, E. H. *Wertheimer's seminars revisited: Problem solving and thinking.* Albany, New York: State University of New York, 1970.

Maier, N. R. F. Reasoning in Humans I: On direction. *Journal of Comparative Psychology,* 1930, *10,* 115-43.

Maier, N. R. F. Reasoning in humans II: The solution of a problem and its appearance in consciousness. *Journal of Comparative Psychology,* 1931, *12,* 181-94.

Maier, N. R. F. An aspect of human reasoning. *British Journal of Psychology*, 1933, *14*, 144-55.

Maier, N. R. F. Reasoning in humans III: The mechanisms of equivalent stimuli and of reasoning. *Journal of Experimental Psychology*, 1945, *35*, 349-60.

Maier, N. R. F. & Burke, R. J. Response availability as a factor in the problem-solving performance of males and females. *Journal of Personality and Social Psychology*, 1967, *5*, 304-10.

Maltzman, I. Thinking: From a behavioristic point of view. *Psychological Review*, 1955, *62*, 275-86.

Maltzman, I., & Morrisett, L. Different strengths of set in solution of anagrams. *Journal of Experimental Psychology*, 1952, *44*, 242-46.

Maltzman, I., & Morrisett, L. Effects of task instructions on solution of different classes of anagrams. *Journal of Experimental Psychology*, 1953, *45*, 351-54.

Mandler, J. M., & Mandler, G. *Thinking: From association to Gestalt*. New York: Wiley, 1964.

Marbe, K. The psychology of judgments. In J. M. Mandler & G. Mandler (Eds.), *Thinking: From association to Gestalt*. New York: Wiley, 1964, 143-52. (Originally published in German in 1901.)

Martin, E., & Roberts, K. H. Sentence length and sentence retention in the free-learning situation. *Psychonomic Science*, 1967, *8*, 535-36.

Max, L. W. Experimental study of the motor theory of consciousness: III. Action-current responses in deaf-mutes during sleep, sensory stimulation, and dreams. *Journal of Comparative Psychology*, 1935, *19*, 469-86.

Max, L. W. Experimental study of the motor theory of consciousness: IV. Action-current responses in the deaf during awakening, kinesthetic imagery and abstract thinking. *Journal of Comparative Psychology*, 1937, *24*, 301-44.

Mayer, A., & Orth, J. The qualitative investigation of association. In J. M. Mandler, & G. Mandler (Eds.), *Thinking: From association to Gestalt*. New York: Wiley, 1964, 135-42. (Originally published in German in 1901.)

Mayer, R. E. Different problem-solving competencies established in learning computer programming with and without meaningful models. *Journal of Educational Psychology*, 1975, *67*, 725-34.

Mayer, R. E., & Greeno, J. G. Structural differences between learning outcomes produced by different instructional methods. *Journal of Educational Psychology*, 1972, *63*, 165-73.

Mayzner, M. S., & Tresselt, M. E. Anagram solution times: A function of letter-order and word frequency. *Journal of Experimental Psychology*, 1958, *56*, 350-76.

Mayzner, M. S., & Tresselt, M. E. Anagram solution times: A function of transition probabilities. *Journal of Psychology*, 1959, *47*, 117-25.

Mayzner, M. S., & Tresselt, M. E. Anagram solution times: A function of word transition probabilities. *Journal of Experimental Psychology*, 1962, *63*, 510-13.

Mayzner, M. S., & Tresselt, M. E. Anagram solution times: A function of word length and letter position variables. *Journals of Psychology*, 1963, *55*, 469-75.

Mayzner, M. S., & Tresselt, M. E. Anagram solution times: A function of multiple-solution anagrams. *Journal of Experimental Psychology*, 1966, *71*, 66-73.

McGuigan, F. J. *Thinking: Studies of convert language processes*. New York: Appleton-Century-Crofts, 1966.

McGuigan, F. J. Electrical measurement of covert processes as an explication of "higher mental events." In F. J. McGuigan & R. A. Schoonover (Eds.), *The psychobiology of thinking*. New York: Academic Press, 1973, pp. 343-86.

McGuigan, F. J., Keller, B., & Stanton, E. Covert language responses during silent reading. *Journal of Educational Psychology*, 1964, *55,* 339-43.

McGuire, W. J. A syllogistic analysis of cognitive relationships. In M. J. Rosenberg & C. I. Hovland (Eds.), *Attitude organization and change*. New Haven, Conn.: Yale University Press, 1960, 65-111.

McKeachie, W. J., & Doyle, C. L. *Psychology*. Reading Mass.: Addison-Wesley, 1970.

Mehler, J. Some effects of grammar transformations on the recall of English sentences. *Journal of Verbal Learning and Verbal Behavior*, 1963, *2,* 346-51.

Melton, A. W. Review of Katona's *Organizing and memorizing*. *American Journal of Psychology*, 1941, *54,* 455-57.

Messer, A. Experimental-Psychological investigations on thinking. In J. M. Mandler & G. Mandler (Eds.), *Thinking: From association to Gestalt*. New York: Wiley, 1964, 148-51. (Originally published in German in 1906.)

Meyer, D. E. On the representation and retrieval of stored semantic information. *Cognitive Psychology*, 1970, *1,* 242-300.

Miller, G. A. Some psychological studies of grammar. *American Psychologist*, 1962, *17,* 748-62.

Miller, G. A., Galanter, E., & Pribram, K. H. *Plans and the structure of behavior*. New York: Holt, Rinehart & Winston, 1960.

Miller, G. A., & Selfridge, J. A. Verbal context and the recall of meaningful material. *American Journal of Psychology*, 1950, *63,* 176-85.

Morgan, J. J. B., & Morton, J. T. The distortion of syllogistic reasoning produced by personal convictions. *Journal of Social Psychology*, 1944, *20,* 39-59.

Nair, P. *An experiment in conservation*. Cambridge, Mass.: Harvard University Center for Cognitive Studies, Annual Report, 1963.

Newell, A., Shaw, J. C., & Simon, H. A. Empirical exploration of the logic theory machine: A case study in heuristics. *Proceedings of the joint computer conference*, 1957, 218-30.

Newell, A., Shaw, J. C., & Simon, H. A. Chess-playing programs and the problem of complexity. *IBM Journal of Research and Development*, 1958, *2,* 320-35.

Newell, A., & Simon, H. A. *Human problem solving*. Englewood Cliffs, N.J.: Prentice-Hall, 1972.

Olver, R. R., & Hornsby, J. R. On equivalence. In J. S. Bruner, R. R. Olver, & P. M. Greenfield (Eds.), *Studies in cognitive growth*. New York: Wiley, 1966.

Osgood, C. E. A behavioral analysis of perception and language as cognitive phenomena. In J. S. Bruner (Ed.), *Contemporary approaches to cognition*. Cambridge, Mass.: Harvard University Press, 1957.

Osgood, C. E. Meaning cannot be an r_m? *Journal of Verbal Learning and Verbal Behavior*, 1966, *5,* 402-7.

Osler, S. F., & Fivel, M. W. Concept attainment: I. The role of age and intelligence in concept attainment by induction. *Journal of Experimental Psychology*, 1961, *62,* 1-8.

Paige, J. M., & Simon, H. A. Cognitive processes in solving algebra word problems. In B. Kleinmuntz (Ed.), *Problem solving: Research, method and theory*. New York: Wiley, 1966, 51-119.

Paivio, A. *Imagery and verbal processes*. New York: Holt, Rinehart & Winston, 1971.

Palermo, D. S. Word associations and children's verbal behavior. In L. P. Lipsitt & C. C. Spiker (Eds.), *Advances in child development and behavior*, Volume 1. New York: Academic Press, 1963.

Palermo, D. S., & Jenkins, J. J. *Word association norms: Grade school through college*. Minneapolis: University of Minnesota Press, 1963.

Parrott, G. L. The effects of instructions, transfer, and content on reasoning time. Unpublished Ph.D. thesis, Michigan State University, 1969.

Penfield, W. *The excitable cortex in conscious man*. Springfield, Illinois: Charles C Thomas, 1958.

Penfield, W. Consciousness, memory, and man's conditioned reflexes. In K. H. Pribram (Ed.), *On the biology of learning*. New York: Harcourt, Brace & World, Inc., 1969, 129-68.

Phillips, J. L. *The origins of intellect: Piaget's theory*. San Francisco: Freeman, 1969.

Piaget, J. *Judgment and reasoning in the child*. New York: Harcourt, Brace & World, 1926. (Translated by M. Worden; original French edition, 1924.)

Piaget, J. *The moral judgment of the child*. New York: Harcourt, Brace & World, 1932. (Translated by M. Gabain.)

Piaget, J. *Play, dreams and imitation in childhood*. New York: Norton, 1951. (Translated by C. Gattegno & F. M. Hodgson; original French edition, 1945.)

Piaget, J. *The child's conception of number*. London: Routledge & Kegan Paul, 1952. (Translated by C. Gattegno & F. M. Hodgson; original French edition, 1941.)

Piaget, J. *The origins of intelligence in children*. New York: International Universities Press, 1952. (Translated by M. Cook; original French edition, 1936.)

Piaget, J. *The construction of reality in the child*. New York: Basic Books, 1954. (Translated by M. Cook; original French edition, 1937.)

Piaget, J., & Inhelder, B. *The child's conception of space*. London: Routledge & Kegan Paul, 1956. (Translated by F. J. Langdon & J. L. Lunzer; original French edition, 1948.)

Poincaré, H. Mathematical creation. In *The foundations of science*. (Translated by G. H. Halstead.) New York: Science Press, 1913.

Pollio, H. R., & Reinhart, D. Rules and counting behavior. *Cognitive Psychology*, 1970, *1*, 388-402.

Polya, G. *How to solve it*. Garden City, New York: Doubleday Anchor, 1957.

Polya, G. Mathematical discovery, Volume II: *On understanding, learning and teaching problem solving*. New York: Wiley, 1968.

Popper, K. R. *The logic of scientific discovery*. New York: Harper & Row, 1959.

Posner, M. I. *Cognition: An introduction*. Glenview, Illinois: Scott, Foresman & Co., 1973.

Potts, G. R. Information processing strategies used in the encoding of linear orderings. *Journal of Verbal Learning and Verbal Behavior*, 1972, *11*, 727-40.

Potts, G. R. Storing and retrieving information about ordered relationships. *Journal of Experimental Psychology*, 1974, *103*, 431-39.

Raaheim, K. Problem solving and past experience. In P. H. Mussen (Ed.), European research in cognitive development. *Monograph Supplement of the Society for Research on Child Development*, 1965, *30*, No. 2.

Razran, G. H. S. Conditioned responses in children: A behavioral and quantitative critical review of experimental studies. *Archives of Psychology*, 1933, No. 14.

Rees, H. J., & Israel, H. E. An investigation of the establishment and operation of mental sets. *Psychological Monographs*, 1935, *46*, No. 210.

Reese, H. W. Verbal mediation as a function of age level. *Psychological Bulletin*, 1962, *59*, 502-9.

Reitman, W. R. *Cognition and thought: An information processing approach.* New York: Wiley, 1965.

Reitman, W. R., Grove, R. B., & Shoup, R. G. Argus: An information processing model of thinking. *Behavioral Science*, 1964, *9*, 270-81.

Restle, F. A metric and an ordering on sets. *Psychometrika*, 1959, *57*, 9-14.

Restle, F. The selection of strategies in cue learning. *Psychological Review*, 1962, *69*, 329-43.

Restle, F. Theory of serial pattern learning: Structural trees. *Psychological Review*, 1970, *77*, 481-95.

Restle, F., & Davis, J. H. Success and speed of problem solving by individuals and groups. *Psychological Review*, 1962, *69*, 520-36.

Restle, F., & Greeno, J. G. *Introduction to mathematical psychology.* Reading, Mass.: Addison-Wesley, 1970.

Revlis, R. Two models of syllogistic reasoning: Feature selection and conversion. *Journal of Verbal Learning and Verbal Behavior*, 1975, *14*, 180-95.

Rips, L. J., Shoben, E. J., & Smith, E. E. Semantic distance and the verification of semantic relations. *Journal of Verbal Learning and Verbal Behavior*, 1973, *12*, 1-20.

Rogers, C. R. *On becoming a person: A therapist's view of psychotherapy.* Boston: Houghton Mifflin, 1961.

Rosch, E. H. Natural categories. *Cognitive Psychology*, 1973, *4*, 328-50.

Rosenthal, R., & Jacobson, L. *Pygmalion in the classroom.* New York: Holt, Rinehart & Winston, 1968.

Roughead, W. G., & Scandura, J. M. What is learned in mathematical discovery. *Journal of Educational Psychology*, 1968, *59*, 283-89.

Ruger, H. The psychology of efficiency. *Archives of Psychology*, 1910, No. 15.

Rumelhart, D. E., Lindsay, P. H., & Norman, D. A. A process model for long-term memory. In E. Tulving & W. Donaldson (Eds.), *Organization of memory.* New York: Academic Press, 1972, 197-246.

Sachs, J. D. S. Recognition memory for syntactic and semantic aspects of connected discourse. *Perception and Psychophysics*, 1967, *2*, 437-42.

Safren, M. A. Associations, set, and the solution of word problems. *Journal of Experimental Psychology*, 1962, *64*, 40-45.

Samuel, A. L. Some studies in machine learning using the game of checkers. In E. A. Feigenbaum & J. Feldman (Eds.), *Computers and thought.* New York: McGraw-Hill, 1963.

Saugstad, P., & Raaheim, K. Problem solving, past experience and availability of functions. *British Journal of Psychology*, 1960, *51*, 97-104.

Sells, S. B. The atmosphere effect: An experimental study of reasoning. *Archives of Psychology*, 1936, No. 200.

Selz, O. The revision of the fundamental conceptions of intellectual processes.

In J. M. Mandler & G. Mandler (Eds.), *Thinking: From association to Gestalt.* New York: Wiley, 1964, pp. 225-34. (Originally published in German in 1913.)

Shulman, L. S. Psychological controversies in the teaching of science and mathematics. *Science Teacher,* 1968, *35,* 34-38, 89-90.

Shulman, L. S., & Keisler, E. R. (Eds.), *Learning by discovery.* Chicago: Rand McNally, 1966.

Simon, H. A., & Kotovsky, K. Human acquisition of concepts for sequential patterns. *Psychological Review,* 1963, *70,* 534-46.

Skinner, B. F. *Verbal behavior.* New York: Appleton-Century-Crofts, 1957.

Smith, E. E., Shoben, E. J., & Rips, L. J. Structure and process in semantic memory: A feature model of semantic decisions. *Psychological Review,* 1974, *81,* 214-41.

Stratton, R. P. Atmosphere and conversion errors in syllogistic reasoning with contextual material and the effect of differential training. Unpublished M. A. thesis, Michigan State University, 1967.

Suppes, P., Loftus, E. F., & Jerman, M. Problem-solving on a computer-based teletype. *Educational Studies in Mathematics,* 1969, *2,* 1-15.

Thomas, J. C., Jr. An analysis of behavior in the hobbits-orcs problem. *Cognitive Psychology,* 1974, *6,* 257-69.

Thorndike, E. L. Animal intelligence: An experimental study of the associative processes in animals. *Psychological Monographs,* 1898, *2,* No. 8.

Thorndike, E. L. *Animal intelligence.* New York: Macmillan, 1911.

Thorndike, E. L., & Lorge, I. *A teacher's word book of 30,000 words.* New York: Columbia University Press, 1944.

Trabasso, T. R. Stimulus emphasis and all-or-none learning in concept identification. *Journal of Experimental Psychology,* 1963, *65,* 398-406.

Trabasso, T. R., & Bower, G. H. Presolution reversal and dimensional shifts in concept identification. *Journal of Experimental Psychology,* 1964, *67,* 398-99.

Trabasso, T. R., & Bower, G. H. *Attention in learning.* New York: Wiley, 1968.

Trabasso, T. R., Rollins, H., & Shaughnessy, E. Storage and verification stages in processing concepts. *Cognitive Psychology,* 1971, *2,* 239-89.

Tresselt, M. E., & Mayzner, M. S. Normative solution times for a sample of 134 solution words and 378 associated anagrams. *Psychonomic Monograph Supplement No. 15,* 1966, *1,* 293-98.

Turing, A. M. Computing machinery and intelligence. *Mind,* 1950, *59,* 433-50.

Underwood, B. J. False recognition produced by implicit verbal responses. *Journal of Experimental Psychology,* 1965, *70,* 122-29.

Underwood, B. J., & Richardson, J. Some verbal materials for the study of concept formation. *Psychological Bulletin,* 1956, *53,* 84-95.

Walker, C. M., & Bourne, L. E., Jr. The identifications of concepts as a function of amount of relevant and irrelevant information. *American Journal of Psychology,* 1961, *74,* 410-17.

Wallas, G. *The art of thought.* New York: Harcourt, 1926.

Watson, J. B. *Behaviorism.* New York: Norton, 1930.

Watt, H. J. Experimental contribution to a theory of thinking. In J. M. Mandler & G. Mandler (Eds.), *Thinking: From association to Gestalt.*

New York: Wiley, 1964, 189-200. (Originally published in *Journal of Anatomical Physiology*, 1905, *40*, 257-66.)

Weiner, N. *Cybernetics*. New York: Wiley, 1948.

Weir, M. W., & Stevenson, H. W. The effect of verbalization in children's learning as a function of chronological age. *Child Development*, 1959, *30*, 143-49.

Weitzman, B. Behavior therapy and psychotherapy. *Psychological Review*, 1967, *74*, 300-317.

Weizenbaum, J. Contextual understanding by computers. In P. A. Kohlers & M. Eden (Eds.), *Recognizing patterns*. Cambridge: M.I.T. Press, 1968.

Werner, H., & Kaplan, E. The acquisition of word meanings: A developmental study. *Monographs of the Society for Research in Child Development*, 1952, *15*, No. 51, vii.

Wertheimer, M. *Productive thinking*. New York: Harper & Row, 1959.

White, S. H. Learning. In H. W. Stevenson (Ed.), *Child psychology, 62nd yearbook of the National Society of Social Studies Educators, Part 1*. Chicago: University of Chicago Press, 1963.

White, S. H. Evidence for a hierarchical arrangement of learning processes. In L. P. Lipsitt & C. C. Spiker (Eds.), *Advances in child development and behavior, Volume 2*. New York: Academic Press, 1965, 187-221.

Wickelgren, W. A. How to solve problems: *Elements of a theory of problems and problem solving*. San Francisco: Freeman, 1974.

Wickens, T. D., & Millward, R. B. Attribute elimination strategies for concept identification with practiced subjects. *Journal of Mathematical Psychology*, 1971, *8*, 453-80.

Wilkins, M. C. The effect of changed material on ability to do formal syllogistic reasoning. *Archives of Psychology*, 1928, No. 102.

Winograd, T. A program for understanding natural language. *Cognitive Psychology*, 1972, *3*, 1-192.

Wittrock, M. C. The learning by discovery hypothesis. In L. S. Shulman & E. R. Keisler (Eds.), *Learning by discovery*. Chicago: Rand McNally, 1966, 35-75.

Woodrow, H., & Lowell, F. Children's association frequency tables. *Psychological Monographs*, 1916, *22*, No. 5 (Whole No. 97).

Woodworth, R. S., & Sells, S. B. An atmosphere effect in formal syllogistic reasoning. *Journal of Experimental Psychology*, 1935, *18*, 451-60.

Zobrist, A. L., & Carlson, F. R. An advice-taking chess computer. *Scientific American*, 1973, *228*, 92-105.

Author Index

Raaheim, K., 83–85
Rabinowitz, H. S., 79, 80
Razran, G. H. S., 191
Rees, H. J., 28
Reese, H. W., 191
Reinhart, D., 51
Reitman, W. R., 5, 133
Restle, F., 39, 46, 52, 53, 70, 71, 162
Revlis, R., 164–66
Richardson, J., 41
Rips, L. J., 126, 127
Roberts, K. H., 112
Rogers, C. R., 130
Rollins, H., 48
Rosch, E. H., 54
Rosenthal, R., 173
Roughead, W. G., 97
Ruger, H., 24
Rumelhart, D. E., 103, 124, 125, 127, 167

Sachs, J. D. S., 113, 114, 116–18
Safren, M. A., 28
Samuel, A. L., 133
Saugstad, P., 83–85
Scandura, J. M., 97
Schoonover, R. A., 23, 29
Selfridge, J. A., 110, 111
Sells, S. B., 153, 154
Selz, O., 3, 4, 12, 14
Shaughnessy, E., 48
Shaw, J. C., 133
Shoben, E. J., 126
Shoup, R. G., 133
Shulman, L. S., 64
Simon, H. A., 5, 50, 51, 98, 99, 131–33, 145
Skinner, B. F., 109
Smith, E. C., 96, 97
Smith, E. E., 126
Socrates, 149, 150
Stanton, E., 23

Stevenson, H. W., 191
Stevenson, M., 48
Stone, P. I., 48, 49
Stratton, R. P., 147, 148
Suppes, P., 162

Taylor, D. W., 81
Teuber, H. L., 87
Thomas, J. C., 73, 74
Thorndike, E. L., 8, 17–20, 24, 25, 29
Trabasso, T. R., 38, 39, 42, 46, 48, 54
Tresselt, M. E., 16, 25–27, 29
Tulving, E., 44, 48
Turing, A. M., 136

Underwood, B. J., 21, 41

Walker, C. M., 48
Wallas, G., 65–67
Walter, A. A., 108
Wason, P. C., 88, 167
Watson, J. B., 22
Watt, H. J., 12
Watt, J., 130, 133
Weiner, N., 134
Weir, M. W., 191
Weiss, W., 54
Weizenbaum, J., 130, 133
Werner, H., 171
Wertheimer, M., 8, 59, 60, 88
Whipple, J. E., 64
White, S., 191
Wickelgren, W. A., 138, 145
Wickens, T. D., 47
Winograd, T. A., 133
Wittrock, M. C., 96
Woodrow, H., 170
Woodworth, R. S., 153
Wundt, W., 7, 8, 11

Yates, J., 125

Zobrist, A. L., 133

Subject Index

Accommodation, 173–76

Activity, effect on problem solving, 96–98

Adaptation, 174–76

Advance organizer, 101

Aha, 56. *See also* Insight

Algebra story problems, 98–99, 132, 141–42, 162

Algorithm, 139

All-or-none learning, 39, 52. *See also* Noncontinuity theory of rule learning

Anagram: as a task, 16–17; variables influencing difficulty, 25–29

Apes, problem solving by, 20, 56–57, 85

Approximations-to-English, 110–11

Aristotle's laws of association, 10

Arithmetic, learning of, 94–95

Artificial intelligence, 136

Assimilation: as an explanation of different learning outcomes, 92–93; as an explanation of logical errors, 152; as an explanation of order effects in oddity problems, 90; as part of Bartlett's theory, 92; as part of meaning theory, 91–92; as part of Piaget's theory, 173–76

Associationism: approach to thinking, 16–18; continuity theory of rule learning, 33–36; differences with Gestalt, 58–59; evaluation of, 29; habit family hierarchy, 18–21, 24–28; philosophy of, 9–10; problem solving set, 28–29; as a subject area, 8; thinking as covert behavior, 21–24; Wurzburg group's criticism of, 12

Atmosphere effect, 153–54, 164–65

Bartlett's theory, 104–8

Behaviorism: as an approach to thinking, 5; thinking as covert behavior, 21–24

Box problem (Duncker), 77–78

Card trick problem (Katona), 60–61

Centering, 178–85

Centralist theory, 23–24

Checkers, 133

Chess, 133

Chomsky's theory, 108–12

Circular reactions, 177–78

Classification rule. *See* Concept

Clinical method: criticism of, 172;

174; as used in cognitive development research, 172

Cognition. *See* Thinking; Cognitive processes

Cognitive consistency, 152

Cognitive development: as an area of study, 8, 9; Bruner's theory, 186–89; for concept learning, 36–37; criticism of, 193; definition of thinking, 172; for inferential reasoning, 190–91; for learning, 191–93; Piaget's theory, 172–86; for word meaning, 169–71

Cognitive process: and age differences, 176–94; distinction between lower and higher, 7–8, 11; types of, 7

Cognitive psychology: as an area of study, 7; legitimacy of, 14

Cognitive structure: and age differences, 169–72, differences due to instructional method, 92–93; distinction between propositional and algorithmic, 92; Piaget's theory of the growth of, 172–86

Cognitivism, as an approach to thinking, 5

Computer simulation: criticism of, 137, 143–45; cybernetics, 134–35; GPS, 142–43; as an information processing approach to thinking, 8, 9, 133; as a method of research, 136–37; of natural language, 130–31; and past experience, 138–39; of problem solving and thinking, 131–33; and problem space, 137–38; and the process of problem solving, 139–42; of semantic memory, 120–27. *See also* Information processing

Concept: effect of complexity on performance, 48–49; types of, 43

Concept formation, 33. *See also* Concept learning

Concept identification, 33. *See also* Concept learning

Concept learning: criticism of, 52–53; definition of terms, 33; dominance of cues, 39–42; factors influencing difficulty, 48–49; models of, 46–48; strategies in, 42–45; task,

31–33; theories of, 33–39; types of, 33
Concrete materials, effect on problem solving, 94–95, 179–85
Concrete operations, 180–85
Conservation task: alternatives to Piaget's theory of, 187–89, 192–93; of number, 180–81, 184; of quantity, 181, 184; of substance, 181, 184
Constructive memory: as part of Bartlett's theory, 108; as part of Bransford and Franks' theory, 112–13
Content error, 150, 152–53
Continuity theory of rule learning, 33–36
Counting, in nonbase 10 number systems, 51
Covert response, 20–24
Cryptarithmetic problems, 76–77, 131–32
Cue salience, 42
Cybernetics, 134–35

Decision tree, as a representation of concept learning, 48–49
Deduction: age differences in, 190–91; and algebra story problems, 162; criticism of theory of, 167; definition of, 7; and linear orderings, 155–61; and set-subset relations, 162–63, 165–67; as a subject area, 9; and syllogisms, 147–55, 163–65; as a theory, 149–50. *See also* Reasoning; Thinking
Deductive reasoning. *See* Deduction
Deep structure, 109
Determining tendency, 13
Direction in thinking: and Gestalt theory, 56, 85–87; as part of the definition, 6, 12; and Wurzburg group's theory, 12
Disc problem, 96–98, 137
Discovery method, of instruction, 64–65, 96–98
Dominance hierarchy, 40
Dominance level, 41–42
Dominance of cues in concept learning, 40–42
DONALD + GERALD problem, 76–78, 131–32

Effort after meaning, 91–92, 108
Egocentrism, 178–79
Eidetic imagery, 191–93
Einstellung, 74–77, 94–95. *See also* Rigidity in problem solving
Enactive representation, 186

End-anchoring, in reasoning, 156–57, 167
Equilibration, 174–76

Flattening, 105–6
Flow charts, 163–67, 134–35
Focusing strategy, 45
Form error, 151, 153–55
Formal operations, 184–86
Fractional goal response, 21
Free association: age differences in responses, 176; method of, 12–13, 169
Functional fixedness, 75, 77–81. *See also* Rigidity in problem solving
Functional invariants, 175–76
Functional solution, 68–70
Functional value, 70
Functionalism, 173–76

General Problem Solver, 142–43
General solution, 68–70
Generative theory of language, 108–12
Generic recall, 119
Genetic epistemology, 172. *See also* Piaget's theory
Geometry problems, 99–100, 133
Gestalt: as an area of study, 8, 9, 13; criticism of, 88; definition of thinking, 58–59; differences with associationism, 58–59; and direction, 85–87; kinds of thinking, 59–65; and past experience, 81–85; and rigidity, 75–81; and stages, 65–74; and types of problems, 56–58
GPS, 142–43
Grammar: as an explanation for deductive reasoning, 157–61; as an explanation for memory retrieval, 110–12
Guided discovery method of instruction, 96–97

Habit family hierarchy: definition of, 18–20, 22; evaluation of, 29; evidence for, 24–28; extension for continuity theory of rule learning, 33–36; and problem solving set, 27–28
HAM, 122–24
Heuristic, 139
Hierarchy of rules, 49, 51–54
Hobbits and Orcs problem, 73–74, 131, 137, 143
Human associative memory, 122–24
Hypothesis testing, models of, 46–48. *See also* Noncontinuity

theory of rule learning
Iconic representation, 186
Identity, as part of Bruner's theory, 186–89
Imageless thought, 12
Imagery: Aristotle's theory, 10; associationist theory, 10; and eidetic imagery, 191–93; in query answering, 103–4; in syllogistic reasoning, 98–99, 157; in verbal learning, 116–17
Incubation, 56, 65–66
Induction: in concept learning, 31–49, definition of, 7; in serial pattern learning, 49–54. *See also* Reasoning; Thinking
Inferential reasoning. *See* Deduction
Information processing: as an approach to deduction, 149–50; as an approach to induction, 48–49; as an area of study, 8; as a computer simulation approach to problem solving, 130–45; criticism of, 143–45; as a semantic memory approach to problem solving, 103–28; as a theory of thinking, 133
Insight: compared to trial and error, 20, 59; in Gestalt theory, 56
Instruction for problem solving: concretizing of materials, 94–95; discovery method, 64–65, 96–98; guided discovery method, 96–97; productive learning, 58–65; rule-discovery method, 97–98; sequencing of instruction, 90, 92–94, 97–98
Introspection: criticism of, 12–13; method of, 3–4; as used by Wurzburg group, 11–12
Invalid conversion, 154–55

Kernel sentence, 111–12

Language: age differences in organization of, 169–71; Chomsky's theory of, 108–12; computer simulation of, 130–31; as an explanation of cognitive development, 37–38, 186, 190; grammar as a factor in deductive reasoning, 159–60; grammar as a factor in memory retrieval, 110–12
Law of effect, 20. *See also* Associationism
Law of exercise, 20. *See also* Associationism

Learning by understanding, 59–65
Learning set, 85–86
Learning to think, 85–86
Letter transition probability, 26, 27–28
Leveling, 105–6
Lexical markings, 159–60
Linear orderings, 98, 155–61
Linguistics. *See* Language
Logical errors: content errors, 150, 152–53; form errors, 151, 153–55
Logical thinking, 153. *See also* Deduction
Long-term memory, 139–41

Matchstick problem (Katona), 61–64
Mathematical models: of concept learning, 46–48; of stages in problem solving, 70–71
Maze learning: and fractional goal response, 21; Guthrie's criticism of cognitive theories of, 6
Meaning: and activity, 96–98; age differences in abstraction of word meanings, 171; and concretizing, 94–95; criticism of, 101; and effort after meaning, 7, 92; and imagery, 98–99; and problem representation, 99–101; as a subject area, 9; as a theory of problem solving, 90–92; and two types of cognitive structure, 92–93
Means-ends analysis, 139
Mechanization of thought, 76. *See also* Rigidity in problem solving
Mediation: in concept learning, 37; in response learning, 21
Memory. *See* Memory retrieval; Past experience
Memory retrieval: for passages, 104–8, 112–17, 160–63; for past events, 103–4; for pictures, 108; for semantic knowledge, 118–27; for sentences, 109–12. *See also* Past experience
Models: of concept learning, 46–48; of information processing in problem solving, 134–35, 142–43; of linear ordering reasoning, 165–67; of semantic memory, 120–27; of serial learning, 49–53; of stages in problem solving, 70–71; of syllogistic reasoning, 163–65
Move problems, 131
Muscle activity, as a measure of thinking, 22–24